ESSAYS

IN AID OF THE

REFORM OF THE CHURCH

ESSAYS IN AID OF THE REFORM OF THE CHURCH

EDITED BY
CHARLES GORE, D.D.
Bishop of Worcester

WIPF & STOCK · Eugene, Oregon

Wipf and Stock Publishers
199 W 8th Ave, Suite 3
Eugene, OR 97401

Essays in Aid of the Reform of the Church
By Gore, Charles
ISBN 13: 978-1-60608-120-4
Publication date 01/09/2009
Previously published by John Murray, 1902

PREFACE TO CHEAP EDITION

THE widely increased interest in the subject of Church Reform has made it desirable that a cheap edition of the *Church Reform Essays*, such as would be within the reach of a larger public, should be brought out.

But it is simply the old volume in a new form. In some respects changes might have been made. Certainly, for example, I have come to recognize, more fully than when the first essay in the volume was written, that the only practicable basis for the church franchise in parishes is the Confirmation basis;—that this is the only franchise which has the least chance of securing unanimity among churchmen. But for various reasons it was decided to let the essays stand as they were written. In any case the alterations would not have been material.

C. G.

WESTMINSTER,
Ash Wednesday, 1902.

PREFACE

Boswell informs us that on one occasion in 1763 he mentioned to Dr. Johnson that very strange sayings were ascribed to him by current rumour. '*Johnson.* "What do they make me say, Sir?" *Boswell.* "Why, Sir, as an instance very strange indeed (laughing heartily as I spoke), David Hume told me, you said you would stand before a battery of cannon to restore the Convocation to its full powers." Little did I apprehend that he had actually said this; but I was soon convinced of my error; for with a determined look he thundered out, "And would not I, Sir? Shall the Presbyterian *Kirk* of Scotland have its general assembly, and the Church of England be denied its convocation?"'

After more than a hundred years we are reiterating the great and dear Doctor's question. Convocations indeed for discussion we have again since 1852, after a silence of nearly 150 years; but they exist—except on rare occasions when royal authority has given them 'letters of business'—in word only and not in power. They can debate, and resolve, but not legislate. It is this disability that the church reformers of our time are resolved to do their best to remove. We feel sure that it might be removed if the Church was fairly united and determined in the matter. But, following earlier groups of church reformers, we are convinced that before any real grant of governing powers can be given to the Convocations of the Clergy, there must be associated with them Houses of Laymen really representative of the whole body of church laity; which, again, they cannot be unless they rest upon a system of Diocesan Councils and Parish Councils, in which the laity can be exercised to take their share in managing local church affairs. In this conviction of ours we are only giving a new form to the ancient sentiment of Richard Hooker: 'Were it so that the clergy alone might give laws unto all the rest, for as much as every estate doth desire to enlarge the bounds of their own liberties, is it not easy to see how injurious this

Preface

might prove unto men of other condition? Peace and justice are maintained by preserving unto every order their rights, and by keeping all estates as it were in an even balance[1].'

These sentiment will be found to bind the writers of this volume together. The earlier essays show cause for believing that they may be carried into effect in our time. The editor's essay lays down the general principles. The second essay—Mr. Rackham's—meets the current objection to admitting the laity to a share in church government on the score of catholic authority, by exhibiting historically the position of the laity in the original constitution of the Church. The third essay—Lord Balfour's —meets another current objection, viz. that the 'established' position of a Christian body is contradictory to self-government, by showing the consistency of the two in Scotland. These two objections *in limine* being now disposed of, the reformers' idea is developed anew—by Mr. Holland's essay on the general idea of the relations of Church and State which modern politics, especially in England, seem to suggest: by Mr. Lyttelton's restatement of the reformers' demand: by Mr. Justice Phillimore's

[1] *Laws of Eccl. Polity*, bk. viii. c. 6. [8].

treatment of Parliamentary and Legal Possibilities: and by Mr. Torr's treatment of Parish Councils. After this particular reforms, which admit of detachment from the general scheme, are discussed—Church Patronage by Mr. Sturge, and the Increase of the Episcopate by Mr. De Winton; and the Dean of Norwich contributes an essay on a subject necessarily brought up by any proposals to deal, however moderately, with 'the parson's freehold'— the subject of Pensions for the Clergy. Then Dr. Fry shows the bearing of all our contemplated reforms in the Church on the general 'social question.' And the Bishop of Vermont, Mr. Watkin Williams, Mr. Speir, and Dr. Travers Smith give us information as to the government of various non-established Anglican Churches with especial reference to the rights of the laity.

I said above that certain common convictions bound the writers of this volume together. I must however explain that the essays iii and xii–xv, i. e. those whose writers belong to bodies other than the established Church of England, are purely descriptive, and their writers incur no responsibility for the general tone of the volume. The same must be said of the writers on particular detached reforms, the Dean of Norwich and Mr. Sturge. The responsibility of those gentlemen also is entirely confined to their own essays. Beyond this we are responsible for a common conviction and a common point of view, but only the editor has seen the essays of the other contributors, and the mutual responsibility of the writers must be understood, in the light of this fact, as not extending to details.

It will appear, for example, that while the editor desires the church suffrage to be given only to male and female communicants, Mr. Lyttelton and Mr. Torr prefer to allow it to all baptized and confirmed persons who declare themselves bonâ fide members of the Church of England. The Church must discuss and decide between these points of view. It will appear also that, while the writer of the essay on the Reform of Patronage would deal very gently and reverently with existing 'rights of property,' and would be satisfied with what to most of us would appear the very minimum of reform, the writer of the essay on the social question is not to be satisfied without a very far-reaching and deep-searching readjustment of social relations.

One obvious criticism on our volume is that we have not treated of judicial reform, while yet the re-organization of properly church courts in spiritual matters will naturally accompany the re-establishment of a church legislature, and is at least as peremptorily needed. The answer to this criticism is that our volume does not profess to be complete, but I have inserted as an appended note (A) a brief abstract statement by Mr. Justice Phillimore of the various forms which, in his opinion, a tolerable or possible readjustment of judicial relations between the ecclesiastical and civil powers could take.

It is the editor's profound conviction that the present is, as he has explained more at length in the first essay, the right occasion for pressing forward in the matter of self-government for the Church. It is matter for thankfulness that the Government Church Patronage Bill of this year did not lack nonconformist support in the House of Commons. This is only an indication of a general disposition in the country to give the Church fair play. And if through lack of energy or unanimity on our own part we make no serious effort to get rid of such abuses as exist—to take some examples at random—in the present traffic in cures of souls, in the apparently needless reduction of the Confirmation of Bishops to the merest farce, and in the miserable lawlessness which characterizes our Church (which only a freeing of the Church to govern herself under State superintendence can ever overcome), we must surely expect the judgement from the hand of God which we shall richly deserve.

CHARLES GORE.

Eastertide, 1898.

TABLE OF CONTENTS

		PAGE
I.	*General Lines of Church Reform.* By the EDITOR	1
II.	*The Position of the Laity in the Early Church.* By the Rev. R. B. RACKHAM, of the Community of the Resurrection	30
III.	*The Principles and Conditions of the Scottish Establishment.* By the Right Hon. Lord BALFOUR of Burleigh, Her Majesty's Secretary for Scotland	79
IV.	*Church and State.* By the Rev. HENRY SCOTT HOLLAND, Canon of St. Paul's	101
V.	*Self-government of the Church.* By the Hon. and Rev. ARTHUR LYTTELTON, Vicar of Eccles, Chaplain in Ordinary to the Queen	126
VI.	*Legal and Parliamentary Possibilities.* By the Hon. Mr. JUSTICE PHILLIMORE	150
VII.	*Parochial Church Councils.* By H. J. TORR	177
VIII.	*Reform of Patronage.* By CLEMENT Y. STURGE, Barrister at Law	198

Table of Contents

		PAGE
IX.	*Pensions for the Clergy.* By the Very Rev. the DEAN OF NORWICH	237
X.	*The Increase of the Episcopate.* By WILFRED S. DE WINTON, of the House of Laymen of the Province of Canterbury	264
XI.	*Church Reform and Social Reform.* By the Rev. T. C. FRY, D.D., Headmaster of Berkhamsted School	291
XII.	*The Position of the Laity in the American (Protestant Episcopal) Church.* By the Right Rev. the Bishop of VERMONT	320
XIII.	*Relation of the Laity to Church Government in the Province of South Africa.* By the Rev. J. WATKIN WILLIAMS, Chaplain to the Archbishop of Cape-town	332
XIV.	*Functions of the Laity in the Scottish (Episcopal) Church.* By R. T. N. SPEIR, Chairman of the Home Mission Board in that Church	343
XV.	*The Constitution of the Church of Ireland.* By the Rev. R. TRAVERS SMITH, D.D., Canon of St. Patrick's	353

APPENDED NOTES.

A.	*On Ecclesiastical Tribunals.* By the Hon. Mr. JUSTICE PHILLIMORE	371
B.	*On the Government of the Anglican Churches in Canada, New Zealand and Australia.* By the EDITOR	375

I

GENERAL LINES OF CHURCH REFORM

By the Rev. Charles Gore

I.

THE ideal of the Church as 'the body of Christ,' the representative for this world of the kingdom of God, is, it is needless to say, infinitely lofty and comprehensive. Its gradual realization for the world at large is the responsibility of the whole Church. But its realization for this country must rest especially upon the only body which can claim to be called the Church of England. In admitting at the start that this body is at present very far from being what a national branch of the Church catholic ought to be, we are only saying in other words that our Church needs reform. Such needed reform is in part, and indeed the most important part, purely moral and spiritual. It is the sort of reform which comes through clergy and laity realizing and performing their duty more worthily both towards God and towards man. Reform of this sort in the Church has—we must thankfully recognize—been continually taking place among us through the wonderful revivals of religious life and social energy which have characterized this century. But the revived spiritual activity in the body of the Church finds itself constantly impeded by features in the external structure and arrangements which a long and checkered past has handed down to us. We want, therefore, external as well as internal reforms.

These external reforms again are partly such as admit of being carried through one by one, and without any general change of machinery. The Queen's Speech in opening Parliament last February[1] made mention of a Bill for the reform of church patronage. We may hope, therefore, that the Government intends, as it is certain a Government might intend, to render altogether illegal the sale of next presentations to ecclesiastical benefices, and to render illegal also the transfer by sale of advowsons—that is of the permanent right of presentation; except, perhaps, where the transfer of the advowson is accompanied by the transfer of such an amount of landed property as would give the owner of it the predominant natural interest in the welfare of the parish to which he would henceforth hold the right of nominating the pastor; or where the transfer is made to a responsible church body. Such changes in the law could be made at once, and would remove at a single blow one of the grossest scandals in the Church as it exists—so grave a scandal, so great a cause of disgust or alienation from the Church in the minds of good men, that it is almost unintelligible how it is calmly tolerated by a generation which would view with horror the open sale of the next

[1] I let this stand as it was written. The actual Bill as introduced and amended is discussed in Essay VIII of this volume. We may welcome it thankfully as a step in the right direction, without pretending to be satisfied with the length to which it goes.

General Lines of Church Reform

presentations to professorships, or fellowships, or school masterships, or of the almost absolute right of nominating in perpetuity to those offices.

But in the main desirable church reforms, so far as they are not purely theological or moral, are connected together, and involve for their accomplishment some greater liberty of the Church, in her parishes, her dioceses, and her provinces, to manage her own properly ecclesiastical and spiritual affairs, while the State contents itself with the right to know all that is going on, and to intervene with a veto upon anything which seems to affect injuriously the civil commonwealth. That such self-government is possible in a national Church while it remains established is sufficiently shown, not only by examples from the Churches of the continent, but by one which is for practical purposes of much greater value to us, by the Established Church of Scotland. That Church, since the first establishment of its presbyterian polity in Elizabeth's reign—by the Act called 'the ratification of the liberty of the true kirk'—has afforded an example of an unimpeded liberty of self-government greater than any which is at all likely to be suggested or even desired for the Church in England. This statement will be found abundantly justified in the essay by Lord Balfour of Burleigh which stands third in this volume.

And such grant of self-government to the Church in England might seem the natural culmination of much that has been silently or noisily going on during Queen Victoria's reign in the relations of Church and State.

On the one hand there has been a most striking revival of the corporate life of the Church. It is not too much to say that at the beginning of the Queen's reign the Church was regarded, and not exclusively in hostile circles, as a department of the civil administration. There were bishoprics and deaneries and canonries, rectorships and other incumbencies, with salaries attached, larger or smaller, the holders of which were expected to perform certain more or less defined spiritual duties to the community in accordance with the requirements of custom and 'the law,' as it existed at the moment, or might from time to time be interpreted by the Courts or be modified or changed by Parliament. But there was very little idea of the corporate life of the Church as distinct from the State: very little idea that 'the Church' as by law established had either the will or the power to assert itself as a representative branch of a society much larger and wider and older than even the English nation—the Church catholic; and would be bound at the last resort to believe and worship and teach after the catholic manner, that is, after the manner in which Christians had always believed and worshipped and taught, after the manner sanctioned in the New Testament and broadly guaranteed to the Church of England in the Book of Common Prayer. Yet the revival of this corporate consciousness on the part of the Church has taken place.

It has come about fundamentally through the awakening of theological and historical study consequent upon the revival of the spiritual life and social activity of the Church. It brought with it a natural demand for proper church assemblies; and has in effect produced a revival of deliberative and consultative assemblies, in Diocesan Conferences, Church Congresses, Lambeth Conferences,

General Lines of Church Reform

and the Convocations of the clergy—in the last case not without an occasional measure of legislative authority by royal sanction; and the Church has become accustomed with more or less success to arrive at, and to express, a common mind. Meanwhile various circumstances have tended to emphasize the sense of distinction between the Church and the State, and, some of them, to produce a serious degree of antagonism. Among these circumstances may be enumerated the removal of almost all vestiges of civil authority from church officers and vestries, especially by the recent Parish Councils Act; the effects, especially the recent effects, of the Divorce Act, which in the opinion of almost all churchmen is not reconcilable with Christ's law for His society, even in its more liberal interpretation; the results of the education controversy, in which the Church has appeared more and more in the light of a powerful 'denomination'; and not least, the dealings of the Civil Courts and Parliament with the theological and ritual disputes which have been incidental to the recovering vitality of the Church. Opinions will differ as to the merits of these theological and ritual controversies, but it cannot be denied that the Courts and Parliament dealt with them singularly unsuccessfully and inconclusively on the whole. It became apparent in the course of the struggle that a very large number of churchmen were not prepared to recognize the tribunals or assemblies of a modern state as the administrators of the purely spiritual authority for legislation and discipline which Christ appeared to have entrusted to the Church[1]. It became apparent also that if churchmen

[1] No doubt Lord Penzance's court and, in a sense, the Judicial Committee

were ready to suffer the penalties of disobedience sooner than obey what they regarded as a legitimate authority misplaced, public opinion on the other hand was not prepared to tolerate their enforcement. The Public Worship Regulation Act became an admitted failure; and the courageous action of the late Archbishop of Canterbury in giving his independent Lambeth judgement, covering many of the ritual matters in dispute—a judgement which the civil authority declined to override—seemed to show that a decision of ecclesiastical controversies could be more hopefully looked for from within than from without the Church.

And more than this, coincidentally with the growing corporate life of the Church, there has been a growing disinclination in the Houses of Parliament, and in the civil authorities generally, to interfere in properly ecclesiastical or spiritual affairs. They seem instinctively conscious that such affairs are outside their natural province and commission. And this tendency which might have seemed to have its natural issue in a policy of disestablishing the Church, has in fact been accompanied by a growing perception of the value of the historical English Church, as doing a moral and social work which the State cannot do, and which no other religious agency is comprehensive or catholic enough to do in her place[1]. Thus we have three simultaneous tendencies—a growing corporate consciousness in the Church and a conspicuous revival of her corporate action ; a continually increasing

of the Privy Council claimed to be ecclesiastical courts: but it was exactly this which in any real sense they were not.

[1] See further, Essay IV.

General Lines of Church Reform

disinclination in the State to touch purely spiritual and religious affairs; a simultaneously increasing inclination to value, from the State point of view, the services of the National Church. If then we allow what none can deny, that the Church needs moderate but real government of some sort, and is in serious danger at present through lawless minorities, we can hardly fail to recognize that the tendencies of the time, in which we believe God is at work, point to a grant of self-government to the Church under due supervision, as what is at once most suitable to her spiritual antecedents and most likely to remedy some of the greatest of the evils which we all acknowledge.

Thus it is not too much to say that the demand for a limited grant of self-government to the Church—which made itself heard with such remarkable unanimity in the Diocesan Conferences of last year, and which has recently again found weighty expression in an address of the Bishop of Durham[1]—is nothing less than the natural conclusion of a whole group of religious and secular movements of the Queen's reign[2]. But as soon as even this reasonable aspiration after self-government comes into view, one practical condition of its realization immediately confronts us with peremptory urgency. It is quite certain that no English Parliament would grant self-government to the Church while the organ of this self-government is purely or almost purely the clergy.

[1] Delivered to his Diocesan Conference, Oct. 20, 1897, and reprinted by the Church Reform League.
[2] On the method of devolution which such a grant would involve see Essay VI by Mr. Justice Phillimore.

In other words a necessary preliminary to our approaching Parliament with our great request is that the Church should, with a tolerable degree of unanimity, agree upon a scheme for giving constitutional representation and authority to the laity in her parishes and dioceses, and, at least, side by side with her provincial assemblies of bishops and clergy. And that she may do this, she must agree upon a definition of the laity, or, in other words, a basis of suffrage. When the 'Church of Ireland' was disestablished in 1871 there came upon that body a peremptory requirement to prepare within a few months a scheme of constitutional government for Parliament to approve before any property could be held by the newly constituted self-governing body. Very rapidly Irish churchmen had to decide on their basis of suffrage and on the co-ordination of powers of clergy and laity. The same decision is no less really forced upon us churchmen in England—only in circumstances of less peremptory urgency—if we would make the first step towards giving effect to our desire for self-government. And to co-ordinate the laity with the clergy (and, let it be said, presbyters with bishops) in regulating the affairs of the Church, is only deliberately to return to the primitive ideal of the New Testament and the purest Christian centuries.

II.

Nothing can be more important than to establish this proposition—that the proposal to co-ordinate laity with clergy in the government of parishes, dioceses, and

General Lines of Church Reform

provinces is not a revolutionary measure, but demonstrably a return to the original Christian ideal, a 'reversion to type' of the sort at which the Anglican Church at least is always in all things bound to be aiming.

The original institution by our Lord of a Ministry in the Church in the persons of the apostles, and its perpetuation by apostolic authority down the centuries is, I believe and have elsewhere endeavoured to prove, a fact apparent in the earliest Christian documents. It appears in these documents as the necessary organ of the corporate worship; as specially responsible for handing on the tradition of doctrine and morals; and as maintaining the principle of unity and order because it acts as a necessary centre for all Christian life and Christian action in the local church or in the Church catholic. If this statement is regarded by any, or in any points, as disputable, at least let it be said that our church reformers are not prepared to challenge it.

But if this for our present purpose be taken for granted, it does not follow that the Church is a simple hierarchy. On the contrary, if hierarchy it can be called, it is hierarchy largely tempered by spiritual democracy. It was to be the very principle of the new covenant as prefigured in prophecy that in it the gift of the Holy Spirit should be given to 'all flesh,' i.e. to the elect people as a whole: so that in a sense never realized among the Jews, they could be as a body a royal priesthood, or kings and priests every one; so that they should not have to depend simply on a few outward teachers of truth, but 'all should know God from the least to the greatest.' This was the ideal in prophecy of the new covenant[1]. It is the realization of this ideal which is recognized in the Church by St. Peter, particularly at the moment of Pentecost. 'This is that which was spoken by the prophet Joel. I will pour out of my Spirit upon all flesh;' and later in his epistle, 'Ye (altogether) are a royal priesthood, to offer up spiritual sacrifices[2].' It is recognized again by St. Paul, who emphasizes, as one aspect of his catholic gospel, that there is no inner circle of spiritual life or knowledge within the Church of the believers, but that 'every man' is to be 'perfect' or a 'spiritual man,' and can be made so[3]. It is recognized again by St. John when he emphasizes that 'all Christians have an unction from the Holy One and know all things, and need not that any one should teach them[4].' This doctrine of the priesthood of all Christians survived and was maintained as a doctrine in the Church, in interpretation of the 'unction' which from very early days accompanied the rite of confirmation with laying on of hands. That was regarded, it is not too much to say, as each man's or woman's ordination to a proper share in the kingship and priesthood of Christ. The holy oil, say the early mediaeval writers on liturgical matters, is stamped upon the forehead to remind each Christian child that he must wear 'the diadem of kingship and the dignity of priesthood[5].'

And this was not a bare ideal. In the apostolic writings the whole of each local church acts together. The rich apostolic ministry of varied gifts supplies truly

---

[1] Jer. xxxi. 34, Joel ii. 28.
[2] Acts ii. 16, 1 Peter ii. 5.
[3] Col. i. 28.
[4] 1 John ii. 27, Rev. i. 6.
[5] Cf. quotations in my *The Church and the Ministry*, p. 89 n. 4.

the organs of a united body, constituted in its rich organization by the divine act to be one and undivided. The Pastoral Epistles are indeed letters to the clergy, and St. Paul's speech at Ephesus is an address to the clergy. But the rest of the epistles are written to churches at large. The discipline of grave moral offenders which St. Paul insists upon ('Have not ye to judge those that are within?') is matter of administration by the Church as a whole acting with the Apostles; the whole Church is at least concerned in the 'retaining' and the 'absolving' of the great sin of which the First and Second Epistles to the Corinthians make mention[1]. So in all the epistles the churches are addressed as concerned all together in the maintenance of truth and worship and of moral discipline. It is of a piece with this that there should be recognition of the function of the laity in the election of those who are to be consecrated to the sacred ministry, especially in the case of the first deacons: more particularly because, when men are once set apart for the sacred offices, it is the business of the Church as a whole to provide them with the necessaries of life. General church management; moral discipline; election and approbation of officers; financial provision:—these from the beginning are affairs of the Church in which the Christian laity are to have a large share.

The same impression is given in the next age[2]. The

---

[1] The punishment or penance is inflicted by 'the many' i.e. the majority of the Church (2 Cor. ii. 6), and the Church in bulk is encouraged to forgive the offender (2 Cor. ii. 10).

[2] See the following essay for detailed proof of what follows, with quotations.

earliest remaining documents are not, with one exception, letters from one bishop to another or from bishops to presbyters. There are letters from a great teacher, Ignatius or Polycarp, to whole churches. There is a letter from one church, voiced by its bishop, to another—the epistle (miscalled) of Clement to the Corinthians. There is a manual of ecclesiastical directions and moral teaching addressed to the whole of some unknown community. In these documents generally the laity are recognized as having the right to elect, or at least to approve, the men who are to serve as presbyters or deacons. Again they have a recognized power of control over these officers when they are elected. This comes out most plainly in the Epistle of Clement, which is written to reprove the Corinthians for the lawless exercise of such power. And in the earliest local disciplinary councils the presence and influence of laymen is manifest. Nowhere again are these principles more self-evident than in the writings of the great and typical maintainer of episcopal authority, Cyprian. He insists continually on their maintenance. 'He resolved,' he says, 'from the beginning of his episcopate, that he would do nothing privately by his own voice, without the counsel of the presbyters and the consent of his laity.' This principle he carried through as consistently as circumstances admitted in his early struggles on matters of discipline. And throughout he gives most explicit recognition to the right of the laity to elect or approve their ecclesiastical rulers, and to keep a hold on them in the way of discipline after they are elected.

The share of the laity properly so called in the great

General Lines of Church Reform 13

councils of the fourth and following centuries is very slight. It is no doubt difficult to exaggerate the share of the emperors in them. The idea in fact of the general council appears to have originated from the emperor, and the emperor or imperial representative was most frequently the effective president. The emperor wanted to govern the world in peace. The peace of the Church, now recognized as God's ordinance, was an important element in the peace of the empire. Therefore he would summon the representatives of the Church all over the world, and so aim at a basis of agreement in vexed theological and other matters. But the imperial function in all this is rather that of the State or of the police, than that of the laity. The summoned representatives of the Church were, of course, mainly bishops. This belonged to them in their representative office, as guardians of the traditions and the creed. They were, besides this, sometimes themselves theologians, or if they needed theologians to assist them, found them naturally almost always among ecclesiastics. The local laity at the place of assembly were rightly excluded.

Meanwhile the elements of democracy in the Church were being slowly overthrown by the imperialized tendencies of the now established Church; and in part their overthrow was justified by the turbulence of the church mobs. But certain principles receive continual enunciation. It is hardly too much to say that the fathers and ordinals lay a stress on popular election or approbation of clergy hardly less marked than that which they lay on sacramental ordination. It is the greatest Pope of the fifth century who says to the

African clergy, 'No reason can tolerate that persons should be held to be bishops who were neither chosen by the clergy, nor demanded by the laity, nor ordained by the provincial bishops with the consent of the metropolitan.' Again, 'He who is to preside over all must be elected by all.' It is a Spanish bishop who writes, 'As to consecrate a bishop belongs to a bishop, so to choose a bishop belongs to the laity[1].' The Church was in fact the very nursery and home of the principle of representative government. Again, all through the Nicene troubles the informal influence of the faithful laity who would not accept bishops or teachers who represented alien doctrine, was so great a counterpoise to imperial pressure that it is the opinion of well-informed contemporaries that in that great crisis the laity saved the Church.

There were however in the fourth and many following centuries four influences steadily at work, tending to dislodge the laity from their original share in church government. The first was the spiritual apathy and moral unfitness of the great bulk of nominal Christians; an apathy and unfitness owing, in the earlier part of this period, to the crowds who flocked into the Church after it was freed from the peril of persecution and began to bask in imperial favour; in the early mediaeval period owing to the fact that half-savage races were, like the Franks, brought untamed and unconverted into the Church in a mass, and could be the subjects of nothing except discipline, and were not in fact subject to very

[1] Priscillian, *Tract*, ii. p. 40; cf. *Church and Ministry*, pp. 102-3, for other quotations, and the following Essay, p. 73.

General Lines of Church Reform 15

much of that. A lax and unconverted laity are not in place, and do not feel themselves in place, at the council boards of the Church.

The second cause, already alluded to, lies in the fundamental tendencies of the successive ages, first imperial, then feudal. When emperors and courts, or kings and chieftains, governed secular society, and when the Church was closely allied to the State, it could hardly be otherwise than that imperialized and feudal methods should prevail in the Church. Thus the original representative episcopacy became papal or prelatical.

Thirdly, the high level of general education which often prevailed in the Christianity of the empire—so that, for example, Chrysostom at Antioch can assume and insist that even the workmen of his congregation should have a family Bible to study in their homes—gave way in the early Middle Ages, especially in the West, to a state of things when all learning was confined to 'clerks,' and with learning also all capacity for spiritual rule.

Lastly, among the forces tending to depress lay influence in the Church has been the love of power on the part of the clergy. The love of domination and of having their own way on the part of the clergy is a patent fact in history, and, I may add, in personal experience. There is no age or place without its Diotrephes who loveth to have the pre-eminence. But a laity at all like the primitive laity, and circumstances at all like those surrounding the early Church, could have kept them in check. As it was, the spiritual apathy of the laity, and the dominance of imperialist or feudal ideas, and the lack of lay education gave what is most ambitious in the clerical mind and nature its prolonged opportunity. And it took advantage of it.

But in our age education, and religious education too, is, so far at least as its opportunities go, very widely diffused; and social influences are democratic rather than monarchical or aristocratic. The two permanent obstacles to the restoration to the laity of their original position in the Church are the clerical love of exclusive control, and the widely diffused and deeply ingrained lay apathy. And of these two undoubtedly the latter is the more powerful. An uprising of the laity that was on the one hand tolerably intelligent and moderate, and on the other fairly widespread and influential, could beyond all question effectively claim, I do not say its right, but rather its responsibility: it could obtain what it legitimately claimed. It would have the best, and probably the majority, of the clergy on its side.

As it is, a layman is commonly, in our day and Church, understood to be a man who, whatever his religious opinions, goes to Church on Sunday: a man perhaps who has been confirmed and gone occasionally to Communion: who subscribes some pence, or shillings, or guineas, according to his class, to church objects; and who votes for the real or supposed interests of the Established Church; but otherwise leaves it to the clergy to carry on the business of religion while he sits in the pew and exercises his cheap privilege of criticizing 'the parson.' What a contrast such a state of things presents to the apostolic conception of the royal and priestly people worshipping and acting as one body:

General Lines of Church Reform

a conception which was the actually formative ideal—even though the imperfectly realized ideal—of original Christianity.

Now the continual appeal of Anglicanism is to the early Church. How can it be denied that we in particular ought to be endeavouring to realize its ideal of church government, by formally recognizing the rights and responsibilities of the laity? There is one answer to the question which it is important to notice, for it is true but not adequate. The rights of the laity, it is said, were not *formally* recognized in the early Church. They were part of the accepted atmosphere of early church life, and were voluntarily made the basis of his method of government by such a man as Cyprian, but they never became subject matter of church legislation. They were guaranteed by no canons, and they ought not to be so now. The clergy of the Church, bishops and presbyters, are wrong-headed indeed if they do not pay regard, as Dr. Pusey, for example, so insisted that they ought to do, to the feelings of their parishioners and communicants. But there is danger in going beyond precedent, and there is no precedent for *formulating* the rights of the laity by canonical legislation.

To this the answer appears to me to be clear. The reason why the rights of the laity were not safeguarded in canonical legislation is that canonical legislation only then began when imperialist influences in an established Church were steadily setting in to give an aristocratic or monarchical direction to all her institutions. But in the New Testament and earliest centuries the principles are continually asserted. And, to give an example, the principle of lay election or confirmation of church officers, admits of being formulated in canonical legislation precisely as well as the principle of episcopal ordination. If we believe in our appeal to the original Christianity, our new canonical legislation, which must form itself, must be not a mere culling of old canons, but a real application of original catholic *principles* to present-day needs. The appeal must be not only to precedent—is there any such canon?—but to principles. Is there not such and such a maxim or understanding of original Christianity which justifies or requires such legislation?

Let those, therefore, who propose reform, give every guarantee that what is proposed is not out of harmony with original Christian principles.

III.

Without going into more detail than is desirable at so early a stage of discussion, let us answer the question, What functions do we of the Church Reform League propose to assign to the laity (when it has been settled—for that question is still to come—who are rightly called church laymen), and what is it we do not propose to assign to them?

To take the latter part of the question first, let it be asserted that our whole proposed reform is conservative and constitutional, and there is therefore no suggestion of interference with the functions of the clergy in the administering of sacraments—with such principles as that only bishops shall ordain or confirm and only presbyters offer the eucharist. We welcome the present recognition of lay teaching and lay preaching, under proper safeguards, but desire to introduce nothing in this department not already accepted in principle. We recognize the principle that the bishops are the appointed guardians of the doctrines and traditions of discipline and worship in the Church, and do not desire that laymen should have any share in ecclesiastical deliberations which have for their end the determination of doctrinal questions for the purposes of church government. Of course the region of theology as a science is and remains as open to a layman like Mr. Gladstone as to a bishop like Dr. Westcott. Of course also in the legal aspects of doctrine laymen have their legitimate sphere. And when a proper ecclesiastical legislature is established with houses of bishops, presbyters, and laity, the laymen should, in the judgement of the present writer, have a veto on any proposed change in the accepted ecclesiastical standards, i.e. on the Book of Common Prayer. No *change* in ecclesiastical formulas or rubrics should be possible against the consent of the body of the laity.

But in passing from what we do not propose to assign to the laity to what we do, it is important to begin at the lower end of the administrative ladder—the parish. It is certain that it is in the parish administration first of all that the healthful revival of corporate responsibility must take place. Here then the parish church [1] council would become a recognized and regularly constituted body, with assigned rights. Of these I mention four.

(1) It should have a restraint upon unfit appointments. The patron should be bound to report his proposed

[1] See further, Essay VII.

nomination first of all to the parish council of the vacant parish; they should have a right to protest on assigned grounds to the bishop, and the bishop, if he thinks the grounds of protest reasonable, should have the power to require the patron to make a fresh nomination. If a second nomination is equally objectionable, the patronage might lapse to a Diocesan Board. But in the opinion of the present writer it is desirable to limit the rights of private patrons, not to abolish them. He believes on the whole that individuals, or small groups of individuals, make better appointments in many cases than mixed boards. Of course the rights of all patrons might also be limited, as those of cathedral chapters are at present, by some general legislation as to the standing of those who are eligible.

(2) The parish council should in the case of the immorality or incompetence of the clergyman be qualified to make a representation to the bishop, and the bishop should have increased power to bring about the removal of those who are no longer pastors but stumbling-blocks[1].

(3) The parish council should, under such restrictions as diocesan or general legislation might impose, determine the destination of a large part of the collections of alms made in church.

(4) It should have some recognized power to restrain alterations in the accustomed ritual or mode of worship, supposing it to be not illegal. The best way would probably be that a proposed change, unless it were prescribed by the rubrics or expressly allowed in all churches by proper authority, should be mentioned to the council,

[1] On the possibilities of a retiring Pension Fund, see Essay X.

General Lines of Church Reform

and, if the majority of the council should object to it persistently, the matter should be referred to the judgement of the bishop, or the proposal should be dropped. Of course a great many of the most earnest advocates for ritual advance will object to any such restriction. But the point they should take into consideration is that in all matters there must be 'give and take'; that it is better to give qualified authority to an organized and recognized council than to allow a vague, irresponsible power to unauthorized individuals, as too often is done at present; and that this principle, once accepted, affords the best security for the maintenance of whatever steady advance is made in the methods of worship.

Naturally the parish councils would elect lay representatives to the diocesan council, and some committee of the diocesan council must deal with the financial problems involved in the compulsory retirement of incompetent incumbents and in other subjects. Another committee would constitute a diocesan board of patronage, to which gradually a good deal of patronage would probably accrue by voluntary gift. The whole council would have certain legislative powers intermediate between the parish council and the house of laymen. But probably when the two extremes were fixed, it would be easy to determine the rights of the diocesan body. We make no proposal to modify the present system of appointment to bishoprics. But the present writer cannot fail to emphasize that the *congé d'élire* affords, as things are, an effectual power of protest at the last resort to the cathedral chapters, if they are not afraid to suffer for their convictions: and the confirmation of bishops might, probably without any legislative change, be also made a reality, effective in extreme cases.

The diocesan councils would of course elect representatives to the House of Laymen, which would sit at least side by side with the Houses of Convocation, having a right of veto on proposed changes in the Prayer Book, and, on matters other than those which concern doctrine and worship, legislative rights co-ordinated with those of the clergy.

I have been speaking of the power we would assign to the laity, and I have indicated, I trust, that what is proposed would merely be giving constitutional effect to the ideal of the early Church. But the object of all this restoration of administrative functions to the laity is the restoration, in due measure, of self-government to the Church as a whole. In the parishes that will no doubt mean chiefly an admission of the laity to share a government already exercised by vicars or rectors and bishops. But in the dioceses it should mean also a restoration to the presbyters of their true synodical position as advisers and counsellors of the bishops. In the provinces it would mean a reform of the Lower Houses of Convocation, so as to make them more truly representative of the second order. Further it would involve a co-ordination of the powers of the three houses in each province and of the provinces to one another. Only when some practical proposal on all these subjects has been prepared, should we be ready to present a scheme to Parliament and to make our reasonable request, that as we had provided ourselves with an adequate machinery for self-government, we should be allowed, saving the legitimate rights of the

IV.

It now remains to approach the important question, Who are to be considered 'the laity[1]'? And in approaching it, it is very important to remember that we are only considering who are to be allowed to exercise the church suffrage and take their share in church government. These rights of Christian citizenship have been almost unrecognized in our Church for many generations, and proper safeguards must be provided in promoting their revival. But it is not proposed to *deprive* any inhabitant of the country of any right which he already exercises. Those who are not prepared to give any account of themselves ecclesiastically—and they are very many—would still be at liberty to use our churches, join in our services, enjoy our music, and listen to our sermons, as much as they do at present. Let them continue to be most welcome to make all the use of the Church they can. For the Church has become a great tree, and the birds of the air come and lodge in the branches of it.

But we need some further security for those who want to exercise an ecclesiastical franchise. No self-respecting society, civil or religious, from a great nation or church down to a debating society, can be asked to allow a right

---

[1] It will appear in Essay III, p. 90, that Parliament in 1874, for the first time, defined 'a congregation' in the Scottish Establishment, and declared it to consist of communicants and such other 'adherents' as should be accepted by the Kirk Session under the rules of the General Assembly. What Parliament did in Scotland, it may surely do in England.

of controlling its affairs to those who are not showing allegiance to its principles by the performance of certain elementary duties of members. In other words, Mazzini's principle applies to churches, as well as to states—'political rights are only the correlative of political duties done.' Or as it is excellently expressed in a recent number of *The Baptist*—'It is not only anti-scriptural, but against common sense, to take into partnership in the management of any spiritual concern those who either do not agree to the fundamental principles of the corporation, or, if admitting such to be accurate, are too negligent to carry them into execution.'

Who then are to be considered to be in performance of the minimum of church duties? Who are to be recognized as laymen qualified to exercise a church suffrage, or (what is a different matter) to serve in church offices? I think the best answer, or the only answer in accordance with really Christian principles, is that all should be in this sense accepted as laymen, with the right of laymen, who being baptized and confirmed are also communicants in the Church, thus continuing in 'the fellowship and the breaking of the bread'; and who have not been publicly convicted of some scandalous offence.

But this, it will be said, is to revive the old scandal of the communicant test. To this I should reply, it was indeed a scandal to religion when to receive the communion was a necessary qualification for civil office. Such an arrangement drove men to communion who had no religious motive for going, because they were otherwise debarred from public honour or emolument. But the church suffrage, or the lay offices of the Church, would have no sufficient emolument or social honour attached to act as a bribe; there would be no pressure put upon any one's conscience. It would, however, be exceedingly undesirable that any one should be able hastily to obtain the suffrage in view of any particular question, or hastily to lose it by omission to communicate. Let us have a communicant roll in each parish or quasi-parish church. Upon this roll the name of each confirmed person would be entered, and from it would be transferred on change of residence[1]. Any one would lapse off the roll if he had failed to make his communion, say for the period covered by two successive Easters: and could not be restored to it again till the following Easter. Those on these rolls would be allowed to exercise their suffrage, after the age of twenty-one, unless, indeed, they had been convicted in the civil courts of certain scandalous offences against the moral law. Persons so convicted should lapse off the roll, and should only be restored by the bishop with consent of the diocesan council.

Considering that women constitute in England to-day, as in most other ages and countries, the religious heart of the nation, I do most confidently think that they should be allowed to exercise their suffrage as lay people, and probably to fill a certain proportion of seats on the parish council.

It will be observed that such an arrangement as has now been proposed does not suggest any doctrinal test being applied to the laity; and this is thoroughly in accordance with the ordinary custom of the Church. It is only church *teachers* who should be required to

[1] Essay VII will suggest the recognition of congregational, as well as territorially parochial churches.

give guarantee of their agreement with the Church's positive creed. Of course when laymen come forward as church teachers, they may expect to be asked to give the necessary guarantee. Otherwise they should be left to approach the altar without having to answer any questions. Moreover if what is here suggested involves a certain discipline of the laity, it is a self-acting discipline, and not one which subjects a parishioner to any possibly arbitrary jurisdiction of his vicar or bishop or council.

There is however an objection felt to such an arrangement as this, which may be expressed thus:—From a variety of causes, not all equally discreditable—amongst them the inherited effect of a serious mistranslation of Scripture in our Bible and Prayer Book, which led to the belief that any one unworthy communion might be an eating of eternal damnation—it has come about, that there are in very many places very few male communicants, especially of the working classes. Thus the church suffrage would hardly to any real extent be representative of labour; and consequently the social advantage of such an institution would be greatly reduced. It is therefore proposed by not a few of our most energetic church reformers, that, while all those elected to serve on church councils should be required to be communicants, the right to vote should be extended to all who, being baptized—or baptized and confirmed—profess themselves *bona fide* members of the Church of England[1].

Now I fully recognize the lamentable drawback referred to above to the communicant suffrage. I recog-

[1] See Essays V and VII.

General Lines of Church Reform 27

nize also that the requirement of baptism excludes those who are Jews or members of some other religion than the Christian: and that confirmation would be a guarantee that the voter had not been brought up in traditional hostility to the Church or separation from it. But it would still remain true that we were giving a church vote, and therefore a share in controlling the Church, to a great multitude of people who are giving no real guarantee that they are identified with our aims and principles. For in any anxious situation for the Church, when the result of a vote would be specially important, the cry might obtain vogue that the Church was a national Church, and all Englishmen were members of it who had not specially separated themselves from it; the declaration of *bona fide* membership would then count for nothing, and the real adherents of the Church might be swamped in numbers. Besides, it is contrary to all analogy or precedent in other departments to allow a right to vote to be determined by an individual's unsifted statement about himself. It would be a different matter if there could be a free sifting by a church court of those who offered themselves as 'adherents,' such as exists in Scotland[1]. But a proposal to introduce such a sifting in our day in England would excite more opposition than a qualification by communion. That qualification follows also the ordinary method of making a right of suffrage depend not upon a disputable question, but, as far as possible, upon one of fact.

It is for this reason that I prefer, in spite of its disadvantages, the test of communion, and even believe

[1] See p. 91.

that the revival of the lay right on this basis might stimulate a wholesome interest in the Church, and cause a growth of communicants from the right motive.

V.

The exact qualification for the church suffrage is, of course, a matter for the Church to determine. It is enough for an individual to express his opinion. But before I conclude I would summarize my contention. It is, in fact, threefold: that the time has come for the Church to apply for greater control over her own affairs; that for the purpose of such control the laity should, in primitive fashion, be associated with the clergy: that the laity must mean faithful members of the body of Christ, however defined.

That there is serious need to let this contention be heard is evident. The apostolic ideal of the Church is written for ever. All the members are 'fellow-citizens with the saints,' that is, citizens, with the responsibilities of citizenship, in the city of God. All together make up the royal and priestly people for worship and for discipline. All together constitute the kingdom of righteousness and light, which is to make unceasing aggressions upon the kingdom of darkness and sin. And what have we as things are? Clergymen, so identified with the work of the Church that to enter into that order is still called 'going into the Church'—clergymen, I say, actually teaching and ruling, well or badly; and flocks ministered to, mostly passively. But where is the Church disciplining itself, worshipping, believing, conferring and acting, as one body? The apostolic ideal we churchmen must revolve and ponder, and we must walk in the

General Lines of Church Reform 29

steps of disestablished or non-established churches of our own communion in reviving its reality. The very beauty of the ideal will fascinate our dull imaginations and stimulate our flagging wills. It must be added that the experiments of the churches in communion with our own in the direction of its realization are certainly encouraging[1].

There is another reason for bestirring ourselves which appeals with special force. It is the duty of removing stumbling-blocks from the path of men of honest conscience. Multitudes of good men have been driven from the Church by scandals; many are still so driven out. For real scandals still remain. It is a scandal that the cures of souls should be bought, like common merchandise, in the open market—souls for whom Christ died. It is a scandal that the Church being what she is should be so tied in fetters of the State as to have no freedom to manage the affairs committed to her by Christ. It is a scandal that the faithful laity should have no power to prevent an improper appointment to the pastoral office or to cause the removal of what is no pastor but an incubus. It is a scandal that the worshipping laity should be utterly at the mercy of an arbitrary incumbent who simply chooses to cause a revolution in the customary worship. It is a scandal that a pastor should be subjected to the unregulated tyranny or even insults of some wealthy or violent individual among the inhabitants of his parish. These are serious black blots on the Church's system. These are scandals and what is worse, or better, removable scandals—scandals which it lies with us to remove. When will churchmen wake up from their apathy?

[1] See Essays XII–XV.

II

THE POSITION OF THE LAITY IN THE EARLY CHURCH

By the Rev. R. B. Rackham

IF we turn back to a time in the history of the Church when there begins to be sufficient literature to present us with a fairly adequate picture of her life, that is to the fourth and fifth centuries, we shall find it exactly described by the earlier saying of St. Cyprian[1], that 'the constitution of the Church rests upon bishops, and by these rulers all her action is directed.' In a word, the bishops are the rulers of the Church. They are supreme in their own dioceses, and meeting in synods they legislate for the Church, their canons becoming the Church's law.

The records of the Councils, however, reveal a development in process. In the fourth century, for instance, we can trace a growth in the power of the bishops, and especially the development of the power of the metropolitan over his fellow-bishops. But this was not the beginning of development. There are but scanty remains of the canonical literature of the earlier centuries,

[1] Ep. 33. 1 (Hartel).

but there is sufficient to show that there had been a development in the position of the clergy as against the laity. From St. Cyprian's letters we gather that the presence of the laity was an accepted feature of the councils of the third century. Their presence is also mentioned at Elvira in 305, but after that there is but seldom an allusion to it; the formula 'with the presence of the people' disappears or is replaced by 'the presence of the deacons.' In the earlier literature we find great demands made on the convert to Christianity, there are conditions to be complied with, professions and occupations to be given up. The later canons are also full of similar restrictions and prohibitions, but in this case they apply to the clergy alone. The laity have as it were dropped out of sight, and to be reduced to lay communion has become the common penalty for bishops and presbyters. At the same time there is a significant change in the meaning of the word *Fratres* or *Brethren*. To St. Cyprian it meant the whole body of his fellow-christians: now it generally denotes fellow-bishops. Thus it is obvious that a development has taken place and that a large element of the Church, that is the laity, has as a body been sinking more and more into the background[1]; and to try and restore the picture of their original position in the church life of the earliest centuries is the task of this essay.

The task is not an easy one. The remains of the Christian literature of those centuries are scanty, and we have to depend largely upon writers of a later date,

[1] A similar process can be detected in the ordinals, see below, pp. 74-5.

writing at a time when the episcopal government of the Church and the professional distinction between clergy and laity had attained their full development, and naturally their writings reflect the conditions of the age in which they lived. Again, most of our authorities were themselves ecclesiastics, a fact which must have exercised some influence, if an unconscious one, on the colouring of the picture they draw for us. We can to some extent estimate this influence by comparing the two great church historians, Eusebius and Socrates, our chief authorities for the first three and the fourth centuries respectively. Now Eusebius was a bishop, and a courtly bishop. In his invaluable history he is very careful to preserve the successions of bishops in the great sees, but in describing the succession of any individual bishop he uses the simple words *succeeds* or *is appointed*, and it is only from the record of some unique circumstances which led to the election of Fabian as bishop of Rome that we learn that the people had any voice in the succession at all. On the other hand Socrates was a layman, and to him we are indebted for many important notices of the laity, and among others for detailed accounts of the episcopal elections in his own city in which the people play a very prominent part, as we shall see later on.

Another difficulty lies in the absence of any direct information, discussion, or legislation as to the position of the laity in the early Church. Our only resource is to study carefully the early writings, the principles of their theology, and the background of church life which they imply. But this very want is itself most significant.

the Early Church

It shows that the distinction between clergy and laity had not yet become a matter of practical difficulty in the administration of the Church. The sharp line of cleavage as between two different 'kinds' of men which marked the Middle Ages is as yet unknown. There are indeed differences of function: there are those set apart for the work of the ministry; there are 'apostles, prophets, evangelists, pastors and teachers.' But all these are organs of one body, to which body belong all the members of the Church. This doctrine of the unity of the Church is most clearly laid down by St. Paul in his epistles, especially under the simile of the body and its members. The Church is a body, and this the body of Christ, so that all individual churchmen are members of Christ; all share in one life, the life of Christ; all are animated by one spirit, the Spirit of Christ. And it is this doctrine which we find realized in actual fact in the history of the Church. Externally it was the insistence on this unity which was the safeguard against the manifold forms of error and the bond of communion between the distant local churches. But the truth had also its inward aspect, and that no less important. If the Church was one body, it must act as one body. There might be special organs or instruments by which, and by which alone, the Church could speak or manifest its varied activities, but the action of the Church was the action of one body, one organism, in which every member had its share.

The unity of the Church carried with it a revival of the true idea of 'the laity.' A 'layman' was a member of the *Laos* or *People*, that is, the people of God. But already by the time of the Incarnation the common use of the word among the Jews was to denote the body of those who were not priests. Christianity then came to revive the true meaning of the word. The Church was the true people of God (1 Pet. ii. 10), of which all alike were members, whether clergymen or laymen. And if now again the word 'laity' has shrunk back to its narrower sense, it shows that a great division has been developed in Christianity, contrary to the spirit of its original ideal. How far we have fallen from that is shown by the very fact that the word 'layman' simply bears a negative meaning, standing for one who is not a clergyman. For in the early days to become a layman was to be called to a position of great spiritual dignity and privilege: by baptism one was made a member of the people of God. It was also a call to obligation and responsibility. For to become a Christian was to become a marked man, it was to adopt a life of great contrast and opposition to the life of the world, it was to become a member of a society which, with principles and laws of its own, stood over against the hostile world as a rival organization. For the citizenship of this world was substituted the citizenship of the Church: and accordingly the newly-baptized entered into a new sphere of duty and responsibility; that is, to the Church. As St. Clement expressed it, 'the layman is bound by the layman's ordinances.'

The preceding essay has already shown how this ideal of the unity of the body was the guide of the action and government of the Church of the New Testament,

the Early Church

and we will only notice now that already at the very outset we find the conditions of the problem of church government, that is, the existence of two sets of authority in the Church side by side—on the one hand the apostles and other officers, with their commission received from above; on the other the whole body of the Church, with the authority of the indwelling Spirit. At first, through the brotherly love and enthusiasm of the new-born Christianity, no friction will be felt; but sooner or later the two authorities will come into conflict, and to preserve the balance between them will be the problem for the Church.

Passing out of the New Testament, we find ourselves in the same atmosphere as we read the earliest Christian writings—the *Didache* or *Teaching of the Twelve Apostles*, and the Epistles of St. Clement, St. Barnabas, St. Ignatius, and St. Polycarp. Like the apostolic epistles, they too are addressed not to the officials of the Church, but to the Church itself, to 'the brethren,' and it is 'the brethren' who are to make response. The *Didache* can hardly be considered as representing the normal and full life of the Church[1], but its evidence is unmistakable. Its injunctions, both moral and liturgical, are addressed to the community: 'thus baptize ye,' 'let not your fasts be with the hypocrites,' 'thus pray ye,' 'thus give ye thanks,' 'on each Lord's day be ye gathered together

---

[1] The *Didache* is a very early Christian writing, dating probably from the first century. Most scholars, however, are of opinion that it emanates from some community of Jewish Christians lying outside of the line of the fuller church life, perhaps in Syria, and having a very inadequate grasp on the meaning of Christianity,—such Christians in fact as would be the ancestors of the later developed Judaizing heresies, the Nazarene and Ebionite Christians.

and break bread and give thanks.' The community elects its own officers: 'elect therefore unto yourselves bishops and deacons worthy of the Lord[1].' There are indeed apostles and prophets possessing an independent authority. But even these, or at least the prophets, are to a certain extent under the control of the community: for they are to be tested whether they be true or false[2]. There are also signs of a corporate exercise of discipline, in provisions against idleness on the part of a Christian[3], and in the reconciliation of discordant brethren before coming to the holy eucharist[4].

A far more important witness than the *Didache* is the Epistle of St. Clement, being a letter written in the last ten years of the first century, and so possibly within the lifetime of St. John, and the work of Clement, bishop of Rome as he would now be styled[5]. The name of Clement, however, does not occur. It is 'the church of God which sojourneth at Rome' that writes to 'the church of God which sojourneth at Corinth,' and this letter is conveyed by three messengers 'sent from us.' There had been grievous disorder at Corinth; an outburst of party spirit, arising out of personal ambitions and jealousies, had resulted in the removal from their office of certain presbyters who had 'blamelessly served the flock of Christ' and 'in blamelessness and holiness offered the gifts.' And Clement, or rather the church of Rome through Clement, intervenes in an attempt to restore

---

[1] Ch. 15. [2] For other instances of control, see cc. 10, 11.
[3] Ch. 12. [4] Ch. 14.
[5] Such is the conclusion of Bishop Lightfoot, who discusses the question of Clement's episcopate in his *Apostolic Fathers*, I. i. pp. 63–72.

the Early Church

peace and vindicate justice. His appeal, however, is made not to the clergy but rather to the laity, for he writes 'We see that you have removed certain of good conversation from their blameless and honoured service[1].' St. Clement does not imply that they had exceeded their powers, but that they had exercised them unjustly, in removing ministers who were holy and blameless: and he exhorts them all to repent, to do everything in order, and to submit to one another and to the proper authorities in the interests of peace. There had been one or two ringleaders who had intruded into the room of the deposed, and to these he makes an appeal to withdraw voluntarily. His language is striking: by their nobleness of character, by compassion and love, he appeals to each to say 'If I am the cause of faction I withdraw; I will retire whither you will; I will obey the injunction *of the whole body*[2].' It is evident, then, that in matters of public importance the exercise of discipline rests with the whole body, while its enforcement largely depends upon voluntary submission.

In this body, however, there must be variety of function. The unhappy state of affairs at Corinth was in fact a state of disorder, and Clement has to vindicate the good order of the Church. The Church is like a body or an army, and in these as a condition of order there must be some to direct and to govern. Accordingly we read of 'rulers,' of '(presbyter) bishops and deacons' expressly appointed for the ministry of the flock, and their position was one which attracted to itself 'honour' and 'a name,' and so had become an object of ambition.

[1] Ch. 44.   [2] Ch. 54.

These officers were appointed either by the apostles or since their time by 'other notable men,' but not without '*the consent of the whole Church*[1]'; and the duty owed to them by the rest of the body was not the obedience of subjects but the voluntary submission of 'less honourable members' for the sake of the welfare of the whole. 'Submit yourselves'—that is the constant exhortation, and it also denotes the duty of wives to their husbands, and indeed of all Christians to one another: 'submit yourselves each one to his neighbour[2].' It was in the sphere of divine worship that the difference of function was most marked, and Clement's chief illustration of good order is taken from the ritual worship of the Old Testament, where the different ranks of ministers were of divine appointment. Similarly in the Christian Church the chief 'service' of the presbyter or bishop was that of 'offering the gifts' in the holy eucharist, and into that service none might intrude without the divine commission[3]. Yet even here the laity were not without a definite place and duty or 'ordinance'; every one was to 'give thanks in his own order[4]'; for on every one had there been an outpouring of the Spirit, and all together 'were wont to stretch out their hands' in earnest and constant prayer for the brotherhood[5].

Thus in St. Clement as in the New Testament we find a double authority at work, the authority of the officials or rulers and the authority of the body of the Church; and at Corinth, for a time at least, the power of the people seems to have obtained an unduly predominant position.

[1] Ch. 44.   [2] Ch. 38.   [3] Ch. 40–42.
[4] Ch. 41.   [5] Ch. 2.

the Early Church

Such a co-ordination of authority was not unknown at the time. Classical antiquity had been characterized by the extensive prevalence of *collegia* or guilds of men associated together for purposes of mutual benefit or enjoyment in connexion with some religious worship. These guilds, though jealously watched and restricted by the centralizing Roman authority, were still flourishing at the time of the origin of Christianity, which to the eye of the Roman Government would have itself appeared as a new 'guild.' And certainly there was this resemblance between the institutions—we find in the guilds a similar balance of authority. On the one hand the priests in charge of the religious rites, guided alone by their sacred books and traditional 'law,' were entirely independent in the exercise of their duties: on the other hand, the constitution of the societies was entirely democratic: 'in the administration of business all the power belonged to the assembly (consisting of all the members); its control was incessant, its authority absolute [1].' This assembly also elected the priests, who at the end of their term of office were accountable to it for the discharge of their functions.

If in the church of Corinth the laity were enjoying an excessive influence, the balance was soon to be restored by St. Ignatius. In the year 115 or 116 Ignatius, bishop of Antioch, but now a prisoner, was passing through the province of Asia on his way to martyrdom in Rome, and in the chief Asiatic cities he found the churches in a state of disunion. Not only were there false teachers and

[1] Foucart, *Associations religieuses*, p. 13 (the chief authority on the subject).

heresies, but churchmen themselves were doing what was right in their own eyes and acting in such independence of their bishops and clergy as even to hold separate meetings for worship. To heal these divisions and restore unity to the Church was one of the desires which lay deepest in the martyr's heart and moved him to write his ardent and moving letters to the churches. And the remedy he had to urge was simply this—return to the bishop, submit to the bishop, do nothing without the bishop. For the bishop is the centre of unity in the Church: 'Wheresoever the bishop appear, there let the people be also, as wheresoever Jesus may be, there is the catholic Church[1];' 'as many as are of God and Jesus Christ, these are with the bishop[2].' It is his authority which ensures validity: 'let that be held a valid eucharist, which is under the bishop or his delegate. . . . it is not lawful apart from the bishop either to baptize or to hold a love feast, but whatsoever he shall approve, that is also well pleasing to God, so that all that is done may be valid and secure[3];' 'without' the bishop with his presbyters and deacons, for these offices are inseparable, 'there is not even the name of a church[4].' Hence 'he that is within the sanctuary is pure, that is, he that doeth aught apart from the bishop and presbytery and deacons, such a one is impure in his conscience[5];' nay, 'he that doeth aught in secret from the bishop is serving the devil[6].'

Nothing could be stronger than utterances like these, and yet we observe that they do not convey the idea of an autocrat or absolute ruler, but rather of a member

[1] Smyrn. 8. [2] Phil. 3. [3] Smyrn. 8. [4] Trall. 3.
[5] Trall. 7. [6] Smyrn. 9.

the Early Church

of the body whose consent and co-operation—in most cases the co-operation of a spokesman or head—is indispensable in any action of the body. From St. Clement we learnt that the greatest necessity for this authority lies in the sphere of public worship, for it is on the worship of God that the unity of the Church depends. So in the passages where Ignatius is most vehement on the need of union with the bishop, we generally find an immediate reference to divine service, whether it be to eucharist or baptism or love feast or other meetings for worship. And again as in St. Clement the power of the rulers seems to depend upon voluntary submission, for the same appeal constantly recurs—'Submit yourselves to the bishop and to one another[1].' This reminds us of the other source of authority—the Church as a whole, and this is likewise recognized by St. Ignatius. With one exception his letters, so episcopal in tone and doctrine, are written not to the bishop but to the church in each several city. He speaks of the Ephesians as his 'schoolfellows,' as 'fellows of St. Paul in the mysteries of God,' as being all 'God-bearers and Christ-bearers[2].' The reiterated charge to do nothing apart from the bishop implies a power of action in union with the bishop, and accordingly he gives directions to the churches to avoid false teaching, to meet together for worship more frequently, and to pray for himself and the widowed church of Syria[3]. In particular he bids the churches of Smyrna

---

[1] Magn. 13. [2] Eph. 3, 9, 12.
[3] Cf. Eph. 7, 13, 21; Magn. 14; Trall. 6, 7, 11, 13; Phil. 2, 4; Smyrn. 4, 10.

and Philadelphia to elect and send delegates to congratulate that church on its recovery of peace[1]. In a similar way Ephesus, Magnesia, and Tralles had already sent delegates to meet and escort Ignatius himself, and in these delegates, their bishops with presbyters and deacons, he had seen and welcomed their whole multitude[2].

The preservation of a letter to a fellow-bishop, Polycarp of Smyrna, affords a happy illustration of the unity of the Church. In the midst of pastoral advice to Polycarp, Ignatius suddenly includes the whole Church: 'do ye labour together, wrestle, run, suffer, sleep, rise up together as God's stewards and assessors and ministers[3].' Some of the directions he had previously given to the churches he now repeats to the bishop individually, urging him for instance to hold more frequent services[4]. This is most striking in the case of the delegates to Syria, for now he writes to Polycarp to summon an assembly and elect the messengers who are spoken of as sent by him, whereas Ignatius had at the same time written most definitely both to Polycarp's flock that 'their church should elect an ambassador,' and to the Philadelphians that they should do the same 'as a church of God[5].' This in fact reveals to us Ignatius' ideal of church life. The Church acts as one body: of this body the bishop is the head or chief member, so that without him there can be no action on the part of the body; but with his co-operation action

---

[1] Phil. 10; Smyrn. 11.   [2] Eph. 1; Magn. 2; Trall. 1.
[3] Polyc. 6.   [4] Cf. Polyc. 4 and Eph. 13.
[5] Cf. Polyc. 7, 8 and Smyrn. 11, Phil. 10.

the Early Church

is so much the action of the whole Church that it can be ascribed indifferently now to the bishop and now to the Church.

There is still remaining a letter of this same Polycarp to the church of Philippi. It is very short, but in harmony with the conclusions already drawn. For he writes about a presbyter Valens and his wife, who had sinned, and asks the Philippians not to treat such as enemies but to 'recall them as frail and erring members that ye may save the body of you all,' as if they were amenable to the body of the church.

Our authorities for the church history of the remaining years of the second century are scanty, but they afford interesting illustrations of the development of synodical action and of the correspondence between churches. This correspondence is still addressed to the brethren, as is the case with the famous letters which describe the martyrdoms of St. Polycarp (A. D. 156) and of the martyrs of Lyons and Vienne (A. D. 177), and are inscribed respectively—'The Church of God which sojourneth at Smyrna to the Church of God which sojourneth in Philomelium, and to all the dwelling-places of the holy and catholic Church in every place;' 'The servants of Christ sojourning in Vienne and Lyons to the brethren in Asia and Phrygia.' Dionysius, a bishop of Corinth at this time and a great letter writer, writes 'to the Athenians,' 'to the Lacedaemonians,' 'to the Church which sojourneth at Gortyna,' and so forth: while a century later (about 250 A. D.) the letters of his greater namesake Dionysius, bishop of Alexandria, are generally addressed to bishops or individuals.

The history of Montanism shows us how the Church could act as a brotherhood in dealing with grave matters of faith and discipline. In Phrygia about the middle of the second century Montanus, who claimed to be himself the Paraclete, began to preach a new age of the Spirit, and the Church was much exercised as to what she should make of this 'new prophecy.' The 'brethren in Gaul,' who had written the account of the martyrs' deaths, now wrote 'their own judgement' on the matter, at the same time forwarding copies of letters written by the martyrs themselves on behalf of peace not only to the brethren in Phrygia and Asia but also to Eleutherus, bishop of Rome. In Phrygia itself there were public disputations in church, and certain bishops attempted to exorcise the 'prophets,' but were prevented by their followers. Ultimately, as a contemporary informs us in the pages of Eusebius, when 'the faithful in Asia had at many times and many places met together and examined the recent utterances, and finding them profane rejected the heresy, the Montanists were driven out of the Church'; and very soon the new prophecy was 'rejected with loathing by the whole brotherhood throughout the world [1].'

Almost in the next chapter Eusebius passes on to the great Paschal controversy as to the observance of Easter which raged at the end of the century during the pontificate of Pope Victor (190–202), and we can discern an advance in methods. Eusebius tells us of numerous 'synods of bishops' and of synodical and episcopal letters, while Victor had recourse to the plan of excom-

[1] In Euseb. *Eccl. Hist.* v. 16 and 19.

the Early Church

municating those who did not agree with him. There is other evidence that about this time there were regular meetings every year of the bishops in certain provinces for disciplinary purposes. At the beginning of the next century, the third, two important councils met at Iconium and Carthage to discuss the re-baptism of heretics, and they are referred to by Cyprian and Firmilian as if they had been composed of bishops only; but Cyprian's contemporary, Dionysius of Alexandria, uses an older phraseology in calling them 'synods of the brethren.' It is certain, however, that presbyters and deacons were present at and took part in such synods; for at the celebrated Council of Antioch in 270, which condemned the heresy of its bishop, Paul of Samosata, it was the ability of a presbyter, Malchion, which laid bare the heresy; and the synodical letter runs from the bishops and presbyters and deacons and the churches of God in those parts 'to their fellow-ministers throughout the world, bishops and presbyters and deacons, and to the whole catholic Church under heaven[1].' However, we are anticipating, for the best information as to contemporary councils is to be found in the pages of St. Cyprian, whose letters give us a most vivid picture of church life in the West, and especially at Carthage where he was bishop or 'pope'[2] from the year 248 until his martyrdom in 256.

Through the force of circumstances St. Cyprian, like St. Ignatius, became a great exponent and defender of the episcopate. Difficulties with an insubordinate clergy,

---

[1] Euseb. vii. 30.   [2] As he is styled by the Roman clergy, Ep. 31.

with extraordinary pretensions on the part of confessors, with schismatical bishops, with a bishop of Rome, compelled him to think out and formulate not only the position and rights of the individual bishop but also his relation to his fellow-bishops and the Church at large. If Ignatius discerned that the bishop was the centre of unity in each church, Cyprian perceived the necessary corollary that there must be unity in the whole episcopate: 'as from Christ there is one Church throughout the world divided into many members, so the many bishops in their harmonious multiplicity make but one episcopate[1].' 'There is one God, one Christ, one Church and one Chair founded by the voice of the Lord upon Peter,' and therefore 'no altar can be set up, no new priesthood established other than that one altar and one priesthood[2].' Nor with his strong character was Cyprian likely to yield aught of episcopal prerogative: divisions arise, he says, 'when men do not obey the priest of God or reflect that there is in the Church at one time but one priest and one judge in the place of Christ[3].' Hence any concessions which he makes to the laity we can make use of to the full: and bearing in mind these doctrinal presuppositions we shall be surprised to find the comparatively large sphere assigned to them in church administration.

St. Cyprian's was a popular election; 'with ardour and affection,' he writes to the people, 'ye made me bishop[4].' He was 'peacefully chosen by the suffrage of the whole people,' which was itself a sign of divine guidance; and

[1] Ep. 55. 24.
[2] 43. 5.
[3] 59. 5. In Cyprian *priest* usually stands for *bishop*.
[4] 43. 4.

so he enumerates the factors in the appointment—'the judgement of God, the vote of the people, the consent of the fellow-bishops [1].' If we add the clergy we shall have a full account of the proper election of a bishop; as was that of Cornelius at Rome who in 251 was 'made bishop by the judgement of God and His Christ, the testimony of nearly all the clergy, the vote of the people then present, and the college of bishops [2].' In 236 there had been a distinctly popular appointment at Rome, which is described for us by Eusebius [3]. 'The whole brotherhood was gathered together in church for the election, and many illustrious names were in the minds of the multitude,' when the interposition of what Cyprian would have called a divine judgement occurred: a dove flew on to the head of Fabian. At once 'the whole people as if under the impulse of one divine Spirit, with one soul cried out "he is worthy," and without delay they took and placed him on the bishop's throne [3].' The constitutional share of the laity in an episcopal election is carefully considered by St. Cyprian in answer to two churches of Spain who were in trouble through the claims of rival bishops [4]. He rests their right on the need of blamelessness of life and character in the candidate for a bishopric, for of this the people of the city are the best witnesses and judges. Accordingly 'God has appointed that no episcopal ordination should take place without the knowledge and presence of the people, so that the lay folk there present can make known the misdeeds of the evil or the deserts of the good; and that

---

[1] Ep. 59. 5, 6.   [2] 55. 8; cf. Cornelius' own account in Eus. vi. 43.
[3] *Eccl. Hist.* vi. 29.   [4] Ep. 67, especially sections 4, 5.

ordination is to be held just and lawful which shall have been subject to the judgement and suffrage of all.' And such he declares is 'the custom handed down by divine and apostolic tradition and observed in nearly all the provinces,' for it requires that 'for the due ordination of a bishop the nearest bishops of the same province should together visit the flock in need of a pastor and then, in presence of the people who have the fullest knowledge of the life of each candidate, one should be chosen bishop.'

This picture is in entire accord with the evidence of the earliest canonical remains. Thus the *Canons of Hippolytus*, which probably date from the end of the second century, prescribe that 'the bishop shall be chosen by all the people ... and in the week in which he is to be ordained, let the people say "we choose him."' They then go on to describe the ordination, of which a fuller account is contained in the eighth book of the *Apostolical Constitutions*. This work received its present form probably in the fourth century, but a much earlier document is here incorporated, which enacts that 'for bishop one shall be appointed who is in every way blameless and has been chosen by all the people; and when his nomination has given satisfaction, the people shall meet on the Lord's day together with the presbytery and the bishops then present, and the chief bishop shall ask the presbyters and the people if this is he whom they demand for their ruler, and when they have consented he shall next ask if he has the testimony of all to his fitness for this great office ... and when all have borne witness that he is worthy ... they shall be

the Early Church

asked again for the third time, " Is he indeed worthy?"' One of the oldest canons is that which requires the assistance of at least two or three bishops at an ordination of a bishop, and an illustration of its origin is to be found in a very early and curious document called the *Apostolical Church Order*, which contains this order : ' If there be a scarcity of men, and the number of those able to vote for a bishop be within twelve men, they shall write to the neighbouring churches, that three chosen men may come from them and try him that is worthy,' &c. That this public testimony was not a mere form is proved by the notoriety it obtained and the impression it made on the pagan world. Even an emperor was influenced by it. For his biographer[1] informs us that Alexander Severus, who was emperor from 222 to 235 (before Cyprian's time), adopted the practice of posting the names of his nominees for the sake of public testimony to their character, ' deeming it monstrous that such a precaution should be observed by the Christians and Jews in ordaining their priests and should be omitted in the case of provincial governors to whom were committed the lives and fortunes of men.'

Owing his own election in some marked way to the people, it was natural that Cyprian should make it his rule to do nothing on his own judgement without 'the counsel of the clergy and the consent of the laity[2].' And as there is nothing to mark this rule as an innovation, so it was faithfully acted upon. In ordaining clergy, for instance, it was his habit ' first to consult them, i. e. the

[1] Lampridius in the *Augustan History*, i. p. 957.
[2] Ep. 14. 4.

clergy and laity, and in common counsel to weigh the character and merits of each[1].' And when the exigencies of his exile constrained him to ordain on his own responsibility, he was careful to announce what he had done 'to the clergy and all the people[2].' His letters on points of discipline are generally addressed 'to the clergy and people' of such a place, while to his own laity he sometimes wrote independently of the clergy[3]. Similarly he asks the Roman bishop, Stephen, to write to the people of Arles bidding them to substitute another in the room of their present bishop Marcian, who was to be deposed by his Gallic colleagues[4]. In any case letters to bishops and clergy are also to be read to the people, so he asks Pope Cornelius to read his letters to the brethren that 'both at Rome and here the fraternity may be instructed by us in all matters.' But the request was unnecessary, for it was Cornelius' custom 'always to read Cyprian's letters to the most eminent clergy who presided with him and to the most holy and honourable people[5].' In fact it was the ordinary rule for all important matters to be submitted to the whole church. Thus when there was a contest over the bishopric of Rome between Cornelius and Novatian, Cyprian read the letter announcing Cornelius' ordination to 'all the brethren' then sitting in council, so that the brethren in Africa 'with sincerity and firmness approved the priesthood' of Cornelius[6]. Similarly at Rome when

---

[1] Ep. 38. 1. See also 64. 1.   [2] Epp. 38, 39, 40.
[3] See the titles of Epp. 1, 38–40, 58, 65, 67; 17, 43.
[4] 68. 3.   [5] 45. 4 and 59. 19.
[6] 45. 2, 3. Cyprian, however, rather stretched the privilege of a chairman in deciding on his own responsibility *whose letters* were to be read

the repentance of some malcontent confessors had been accepted by the bishop and presbytery, 'as of necessity followed, all their action had to be made known to the people,' and accordingly 'a great concourse of the brethren met together,' and the confessors were publicly received back into the Church [1]. Again discussions on matters of the faith were still frequently held in church, as had been the case in the Montanist controversy. This we learn from Cyprian's contemporary, Dionysius of Alexandria, who in order to combat the millenarian errors of a bishop, Nepos of Arsinoe, publicly disputed in his church at Arsinoe for three days from morn till eve in the presence not only of the 'presbyters and teachers' but of all the laity who cared to attend [2]. In fact the approbation of the whole Church was recognized as the indispensable seal of any action, and St. Cyprian in defending his own episcopate pleads the 'four years' approval of the people [3].' This principle he carries to its extreme point when in writing to the Spanish churches he practically makes the people the judges of their bishop, for 'they must not flatter themselves that they are free from sharing his guilt if they communicate with a sinful priest or give their assent to an unlawful episcopate': they are bound 'to separate themselves from a sinful president and abstain from the sacrifices of a wicked priest, seeing that with them above rests all the power both of choosing worthy priests and rejecting the unworthy [4].' Following holy scripture and St.

---

to the council, and in not permitting Novatian's legates to be heard (44. 2). See also 59. 2.

[1] Ep. 49. 2.   [2] Eus. vii. 24.   [3] Ep. 59. 6.   [4] 67. 3.

Ignatius Cyprian finds his theological basis in the unity of the Church, and 'the Church is constituted of bishop and clergy and all who are standing upright[1].' Upon the believer 'the Holy Spirit is shed in His fulness,' and this gift is poured out 'on the whole people of God without respect to differences of sex, of age, or of rank[2].' In public prayer there should be 'one consent, one simple and united harmony of the brethren[3].' His laity he addresses, not as his flock or his children or his subjects, but as his 'brothers': and he associates them in his pastoral work when, on the connivance of the presbyters at the disorders consequent upon the pretensions of the confessors, from his exile he writes to his 'brethren in the laity,' exhorting them to guide the individual penitents and 'by their counsel and restraint to moderate the presumption of the lapsed[4].'

What we want, however, is some definite information as to the recognized position of the laity in the ordinary machinery of church government. And for this the episcopate of St. Cyprian is of especial value. The councils which he held annually had to deal with disciplinary questions of great importance—the readmission to the Church of the lapsed, and the rebaptism of heretics—and his correspondence is full of information as to their working, especially in the case of the first council about the lapsed. No doubt the bishops took the leading part; only their votes[5] were recorded and the decision would go out in their name, and so the

---

[1] Ep. 33. 1. *The standing* are those who had not lapsed in the persecution.
[2] 69. 14.   [3] 11. 3.   [4] 17. 3: cf. 65. 4.
[5] *Sententiae* or *opinions* were equivalent to our votes.

council might briefly be spoken of as a synod of bishops. So does Cyprian write in one or two places of his first council[1]: but it is just in the case of this council that he lays such great stress on the presence and co-operation of the laity. This co-operation is naturally emphasized chiefly in letters to the laity: when, he writes to them, 'our fellow-bishops are assembled, we shall be able to examine the action of the martyrs in accordance with the discipline of the Lord, the presence of the confessors and also your vote[2],' or as elsewhere, 'in accordance with your wish and the common counsel of us all[3].' In writing to the clergy he includes their assistance[4]: and thus we have the normal composition of a council— 'bishops, presbyters, deacons, confessors, together with the faithful laity'—recognized as such by the Roman clergy and serving as the type of a council to be held at Rome as soon as a successor to the martyred bishop Sixtus is appointed[5]. In the correspondence about the later councils on rebaptism, there is little or no allusion to the laity, but that the former precedent was still maintained is shown by the formal record of the most important council when eighty-three bishops met at Carthage on September 1, 256, 'together with the presbyters and deacons, a great majority of the people also being present[6].' The *raison d'être* of this assistance of

---

[1] Ep. 20. 3; 55. 4.   [2] *sententia*, 17. 3.   [3] 43. 7.

[4] 19. 2; cf. 43. 3.

[5] 30. 5, 8. In 45. 2 is a picture of the brethren standing in a reverent crowd, the bishops sitting on their 'thrones' and the altar set in the midst.

[6] Archbishop Benson ascribes the error into which the council fell to the silence on the part of the laity. But there is no evidence to show that

the laity is given by the Roman clergy, when they maintain that it would be intolerable for a matter, like the case of the lapsed, in which many had been concerned, to be settled except after discussion and a public decision by the many, 'for a decree cannot stand unless it has evidently been accepted by a great majority[1].' In the same way St. Cyprian reserved the case of the clergy who had deserted their posts in the persecution for discussion with his colleagues and also the whole people—for 'the fullest deliberation was necessary in coming to a decision which would constitute a precedent for the future treatment of the ministry of the Church[2].'

This instance brings us to the other side of church life, the judicial exercise of discipline, and this seems to rest entirely in the hands of the bishop. If councils laid down the lines of discipline, the bishop administered it in individual cases. Cyprian speaks of him as 'judge in the stead of Christ.' And yet here again there is evidence that the bishop's judgements were not uttered 'without the cognizance of the people.' As before, it is in his letters to the laity that this emerges: certain insubordinate presbyters are, he writes, to plead their cause 'before us and the confessors and also the whole people,' and 'everything shall be examined in your presence and with the aid of your judgement[3].'

---

they held a different position or were more silent than at the earlier councils. We hear more of the laity in connexion with the treatment of the lapsed because that was a matter which affected them more closely, and on which they had strong feelings. To judge from the subsequent history the laity would most probably have been on the bishops' side, and in any case we can be sure that Cyprian's flock would have faithfully followed their beloved bishop. [1] Ep. 30. 5. [2] 34. 4. [3] 16. 4 and 17. 1.

the Early Church

A passage in the fifty-ninth letter gives a graphic picture of such exercise of discipline. Cyprian as bishop was sitting in church and carefully examining the cases of the lapsed or schismatics who were petitioning to be received again into the Church: 'the brethren' were present in numbers and frequently 'opposed their reception with firmness and obstinacy.' 'Would that you could be present, most dear brother,' Cyprian writes to Pope Cornelius, 'at the return of these misguided perverts: you would see what a task it is to teach the brethren patience, to soothe their indignation, and win their consent to the recovery of the wicked. At the return of the submissive they are filled with joy, but great is the outcry and resistance at the reception of the incorrigible. Persuasion is almost impossible. I have to extort from them their consent to the admission of such: and their just indignation has found some vindication in the lapse of some whom for very pity I admitted in opposition to their protests[1].' Similar scenes were taking place at Rome, and the letters of Cornelius contain several allusions to the laity: it was 'in accordance with their overwhelming suffrage' that he forgave certain repentant confessors: 'at the intercession of all the laity present' one of those who had ordained the rival bishop Novatian was received into lay communion: the previous ordination of Novatian to the presbyterate had been resisted 'not only by the clergy but by many of the laity[2].'

---

[1] Ep. 59. 15.
[2] 49. 2 and Eusebius vi. 43. For a similar incident fifty years earlier see Eus. v. 28.

In the writings of St. Cyprian then we still see in practical working the idea of the Church as one body, and at the same time the two co-ordinate authorities—the authority of the whole body and the authority of its chief member the bishop with his commission from God. There is indeed a third seat of authority, the 'bench' of clergy, and it was among them that Cyprian met with most opposition. But with the faithful loyalty of his *plebs* his position was so secure that practically the power of the clergy was merged in that of the bishop. The constitutional position was clear. The bishop and clergy had a unique position in divine worship, it was they who 'offered the gifts and sacrifices': in matters of faith they held the office of teachers: and in the spiritual sphere they had the direct responsibility to God of tending the flock as its shepherds. Besides this in judgement and council the bishops acted as the administrators or stewards of the Church: but here all their action was referred to and ratified by the people, and if the people readily accepted their government it was because they were regarded as the representatives of the Church, a position which was to some extent secured by the method of their appointment. The preservation of such a constitutional balance was however not an easy matter. As a church grew in numbers and importance, the position and eminence of its bishop would receive a proportionate development; administration would tend to become government; convenience would lead external authorities to deal with the bishop as *de facto* ruler of his church; the bishop himself would frequently have owed his position to his personal

the Early Church

abilities; and lastly not to speak of personal ambition and love of authority, there would be the inveterate tendency to magnify one's office. And thus we find that a great bishop like Cyprian becomes in fact the ruler of his church, and is followed implicitly by his people; while fifty years later, on the eve of the last great persecution (A.D. 303), Eusebius draws a melancholy picture of the rivalries and ambitions of the prelates of the Church, who being courted and honoured with excessive respect by the civil rulers, 'were eager to transform the office they coveted into a despotism [1].'

The greatest impetus to this development was given by the conversion of the emperor. By his conversion a new factor was introduced into church life and government, viz. imperialism, which while it gave an emphatic confirmation to the authority of the bishops, began secretly to undermine the constitutional position of the laity. Naturally imperialism was not favourable to democracy. The whole tendency of the imperial system was to destroy all independent civil or popular life and to substitute for it a great bureaucracy centering in the person of the emperor. But in the gradual extinction of liberty, there was one body which made an obstinate resistance and so became the stronghold of democratic feeling. That body was the Church: and accordingly on the Church the emperors had instinctively waged an almost unceasing war—as we know, in vain. But what force cannot extort, friendship can win. By his conversion the emperor became a member of the Church

[1] *Eccl. Hist.* viii. 1.

and sat among the laity. But in that body independence and despotism could not for long sit side by side: one must sooner or later oust the other; and thus as Aaron's rod swallowed the rods of the magicians, the emperor absorbed into his own person most of the prerogatives of the laity.

To speak more accurately, the effect of the emperor's conversion was to introduce a third order or estate into the Church—that of kings and rulers. Long before the conversion of Constantine the person of the emperor had assumed proportions more than human. He was considered a god; and his worship, enthusiastically accepted by the provinces, was one of the chief ties which gave unity to the empire. The Christians of course would die rather than offer a grain of incense to his 'majesty,' but they were not insensible to the glamour of his position. In fact, as we can see from the *Apologies*, their reverence for his office was the greater as they recognized in it a dispensation of God Himself. Hence, when the emperor himself becomes a Christian, we shall not be surprised to see him step into a position in the new religion similar to his place in the old. He is indeed a 'minister of God'; he is consecrated to his office with holy oil; and his person, his edicts, his commands are 'sacred' and 'divine' to the Christians as well as to the pagans. This process began from the very first, for the gratitude of the Christians to their deliverer knew no bounds, as is evident from the almost impious adulation paid to Constantine by the most learned bishop of the time, Eusebius. In the pages of his *Divine Life of the Blessed Constantine*, that emperor, though he remained unbaptized until his last illness, and some of his actions grossly belied his Christian profession, figures as hardly less than an inspired saint. Eusebius looks upon him as a universal bishop or 'overseer' of the Church. It was certainly a position which he claimed. 'You are bishops,' he said to some, 'of matters within the Church; I also am the bishop, ordained by God, of matters without the Church[1].' And his actions corresponded to his words, for 'especial attention did he pay to the Church of God, and when any were at variance in the different provinces, as a kind of general bishop appointed by God he assembled synods of His ministers ... thus he exercised a care over the Church that was never weary[2].' This care indeed was not only episcopal but pastoral, for 'he exhorted his subjects as far as in him lay to follow a godly life'; he wrote 'innumerable letters, some to bishops ordaining measures advantageous to the Church, in others he even addressed the laity, calling them—saint that he was—his brothers and fellow-servants'; and the composition and public delivery of sermons or orations on religious subjects was one of his favourite employments[3].

A great deal of this oversight was inevitable. The recognition of the Church by the State gave birth to a new department of legislation, i.e. that on matters ecclesiastical, and all legislation emanated from the emperor. Thus Constantine issued edicts to guarantee the free exercise of the Christian religion. This was absolutely necessary, but he went further. He granted civil immunities to the clergy, and to the decisions of episcopal synods the force of law. Again, not content with

[1] *V. C.* iv. 24.   [2] i. 44, 46.   [3] iv. 24, iii. 24, iv. 29, 55.

measures against paganism, he 'thought it incumbent on him to extirpate another race of godless men as being pernicious to the human race,' and enacted the first law against heretics. It was also inevitable that he should intervene to restore order when the dissensions within the Church threatened the public peace. Thus he attempted to settle the strife of the Donatists in Africa and to compose the storms which beset the origin of Arianism, and this by writing to the bishops, by sending episcopal delegates and summoning synods. Once more, as possessing the power of the sword, he inevitably became the ultimate court of appeal. For this, without going so far back as St. Paul's appeal to Caesar, a precedent had been set in the preceding century. For when Paul of Samosata, after his condemnation by the synod of Antioch already mentioned, declined to vacate his episcopal dwelling, the synod had appealed to the emperor Aurelian, although a pagan. Aurelian referred the matter to the bishops of Italy, and then in accordance with their verdict Paul was 'with the greatest ignominy expelled from the Church by the civil power[1].' And now Constantine set the example of banishing and recalling bishops and clergy for their ecclesiastical views, a custom which was faithfully and fatally maintained by his successors. Accordingly he became the recipient of appeals. Thus when the synod of Tyre had deposed St. Athanasius, he made his way to Constantinople, and there, coming upon the emperor in the public streets so suddenly as to cause a panic, demanded to be reheard, whereupon Constantine ordered

[1] Eus. vii. 30.

the Early Church

the synod to come at once to Constantinople and in his presence prove the purity and impartiality of their judgement[1].

How far was this 'general oversight' which was consequent upon the possession of supreme power recognized in principle by the Church? There was no definite utterance on the subject, and the mind of the Church can only be gathered from careful study of the actual course of events, and in this it must be borne in mind that Constantine himself was not even a layman of the Church, for he did not receive baptism until the end of his life. In the first place, then, the emperor summoned synods, and his summons was unhesitatingly obeyed. For indeed the command of an emperor was not to be trifled with, as we can see from his letter to the Council of Tyre: 'I have sent to the bishops whom ye desired to come and take part in your deliberations, I have also sent the consular Dionysius both to admonish those who are bound to attend the synod and to maintain order. For if a bishop, which I hardly expect, shall venture to disobey our command and refuse his attendance, we shall send a messenger to expel him by an imperial edict, and teach him how unseemly it is to resist the emperor's decrees when issued in defence of the truth[2].' The holding of synods was Constantine's chief method of exercising control over the Church. Thus, to settle the Donatist controversy, he first 'commanded' a number of bishops selected by himself to meet at Rome, and then, the Donatists being still dissatisfied, a larger number to meet at Arles in 314; Arianism occasioned

[1] Constantine's letter in Socrates i. 34.   [2] Eus. *V. C.* iv. 42.

more councils; but the great glory and crown of his reign, 'the garland which he wove for Christ with the bond of peace and presented as a thank-offering to his Saviour,' was the great Council of Nicaea of 325, the first General Council. And, like this, all the subsequent general councils were summoned at the imperial command.

For, indeed, it was the unity of the empire and the power (and very often the purse) of the emperor which made a really general or universal council possible. And in all probability it was the imperial and statesmanlike mind of Constantine which first conceived the idea of a single council to represent the whole Church. In fact, to consult a sufficiently numerous body of its chief representatives was the most obvious method the emperor had of ascertaining the mind of the Church and so settling ecclesiastical causes. It was the course adopted as we have seen by Aurelian, when he left the decision as to the rightful occupant of the see of Antioch to the Italian bishops. And as soon as the emperors become Christian, and the affairs and faith of the Church begin to exercise a vital influence on their government, we find ourselves in the age of councils; and for about two centuries the history of the Church is the history of her synods. This conciliar development, then, was not so directly an outcome of the essential life of the Church as of the new position she was called upon to hold in relation to the State. Naturally in these synods the share of the laity grew less and less. We do indeed hear of laymen present at Nicaea. The fathers were accompanied, as Eusebius tells us, by a train of 'presbyters, deacons, and innumerable other attendants'; and among these attendants, Socrates does not omit to add, were 'many of the laity skilled in dialectic and full of zeal for argument on either side [1].' It does not seem likely that they took an active part in the council itself, but we know that one of the most prominent debaters was a young deacon, Athanasius. Obviously, however, it was unfair for the local laity to have any predominant influence in matters of general importance. The bishops were regarded as representatives of their churches, of their clergy and laity alike, and to their churches they reported their transactions in synod: we still have Eusebius' letter to his church of Caesarea, with his account and explanation of his proceedings at Nicaea [2]. And lastly the presence of the emperor and his secular magnates was probably deemed a sufficient compensation for the absence, and representation of the mind, of the laity.

In the actual proceedings of the councils a distinction was drawn between spiritual and secular matters: it was accepted as an axiom on both sides that matters of faith should be decided only by bishops and clergy; and there are no lack of definite assertions by the emperors that such matters lay without their province. That province was to maintain order and act as chairman, to regulate the proceedings and carry into effect the decisions of the synods. But it is not always easy to draw the line between the spiritual and the secular, between presiding over the formalities and exercising an active influence over a debate, between enforcing synodical mandates and deciding what mandates shall be enforced. Constantine's assistance at synods is thus

[1] Eus. *V. C.* iii. 8. Soc. i. 8.   [2] Soc. i. 8.

described by Eusebius: 'He did not disdain to attend at these synods, and take his share in their episcopal oversight. Yes, he would even sit in the midst as one of the many, without his bodyguard and surrounded only by his most trusted friends. In debate he gave his support to those who were more inclined to the sounder measures and peace and stability, while those who were obstinate he opposed[1].' If such was Constantine's ordinary practice, it is in the general councils that we shall find the best illustrations of imperial action.

There has been much controversy as to what bishop presided at Nicaea. But in fact Constantine presided. He entered the council chamber with a body of attendants, and after a show of humility in waiting for the bishops' permission took his seat on a chair of gold. Where however the emperor sat, he could occupy none but the first place; and so after the delivery of an oration in his honour, he opened the session with a speech and then gave the bishops leave to debate: he was the recipient of a number of petitions which he burnt with a rebuke to the bishops: and then 'he gave a patient hearing to all, listening to their speeches with steadfast attention, and in part by helping the arguments of each party in turn he reconciled the most contentious opponents, and so by persuasion or rebuke brought them all to one mind[2].' This is no doubt the version of a flatterer, but of a flatterer who was an eye-witness. The conclusions arrived at were the work of the bishops, and they communicated them to the churches affected. But

[1] *V. C.* i. 44.   [2] Ib. iii. 13.

in their letter they state that they had been assembled 'by the grace of God and the most religious emperor Constantine,' and that the heresy of Arius had been discussed 'in his presence.' And Constantine added his own confirmation to the synod by banishing Arius and his followers and writing letters 'to the catholic church of the Alexandrians,' 'to the bishops and peoples (i.e. laity),' 'to the churches,' in which he laid stress on his own presence 'as though I were one of you' (for he was still unbaptized). Henceforward imperial confirmation or ratification becomes the invariable adjunct of the acts of general councils.

The Acts of the great Council of Chalcedon in 451 are very voluminous and detailed. From them we learn that it had been summoned 'at the command of the most divine and pious lord Marcian, eternal Augustus.' His representatives, seventeen 'most magnificent and most glorious magistrates,' sat before the altar rails in the midst; and this 'most excellent senate' acted as chairman. It was at their command in compliance with the demand of the papal legates that Dioscorus, the haughty patriarch of Alexandria, took his seat in the midst for trial: by their permission Eusebius of Dorylaeum, who had been condemned by Dioscorus, read his petition to the emperor that his case might be reopened. They controlled the order of procedure, and at the end of the first session gave judgement that Dioscorus with his fellow-presidents at the robber council of Ephesus should 'be liable to the sentence of the sacred synod: to be canonically deprived of their episcopal dignity, with a reference of what should follow (i.e. their banishment) to the sacred Head (i.e. the emperor).' Next day they demanded from the bishops a statement of the faith, allowing an interval of five days for its preparation. Meanwhile the sentence on Dioscorus, which had been repeated by the synod at another session apart from the magistrates, was sent 'to the most sacred and pious lord' for his ratification. At the fifth session the statement of the faith was read: difficulties arising, the matter was referred to 'the sacred Head,' who ordered a committee of bishops to draw up another formula, the magistrates insisting on the insertion of St. Leo's phrase about the two natures in Christ. At the sixth session Marcian was himself present and addressed the synod; the 'definition of faith' was read, subscribed, and ratified by the emperor; and then he submitted to the council some disciplinary rules to be made into canons and confirmed by his edict.

The next step in the extension of his control over the Church was for the emperor to issue on his own responsibility formularies to be accepted by the Church as her rule of faith. Such were Zeno's *Henoticon*, Heraclius' *Ecthesis*, and Constantine's *Type*. But at last they had outstepped their limits. The spirit of liberty, which never dies in the Church, rose up in opposition: and the despotic power of the emperors was baffled by the obstinate resistance of clergy, monks, and laity; but the fierceness of the struggle has left its mark in the existing religious divisions of the East.

In the West the history of the lay element in councils ran very much the same course. At the Council of Elvira in 305 we meet for the last time with the phrase, *the deacons standing by and all the people.* But three centuries later the laity reappear in the form of secular princes. In the interval indeed there had been a canon (of Tarragona in 516) directing bishops to bring with them to synods 'some of the secular sons of the Church,' and lay judges were to hold their assizes contemporaneously with the annual synods according to a French canon of 439 and the third council of Toledo in 589. This council inaugurated a new *régime*. At it Recared, king of the Goths, his queen and chief barons signed the catholic confession of faith on their conversion from Arianism, and henceforth the Gothic kings or their princes are generally present at the Spanish councils[1]. In France the western emperor, Charles the Great, revived the example of his Byzantine brethren in exercising an active and paternal control over the affairs of the Church, in particular by summoning and presiding at the important Council of Frankfort in 794; and there have been no lack of sovereigns since to follow in his footsteps. There is one very important document which shows that even in the early Middle Ages the distinction between spiritual and secular was not always sharply drawn. At a meeting of some bishops to dedicate a church at Orange in 529, Caesarius, archbishop of Arles, drew up some theological definitions against semi-pelagianism, and to give these the greater effect Liberius the governor and seven other 'illustrious' officials who were present at the

[1] As at the councils of 618, 633, 636, 653. The canons of 633 contain a description of a synod, and 'the laity who have merited the right to be present' enter after the clergy. The canons of 653 are also signed by sixteen lords of 'illustrious' rank.

synod appended their signatures, using the same formula as the bishops—*I . . . consent and subscribe.*

We have traced the disappearance of the laity from synods, but in another department, the appointment of bishops, their influence was longer maintained. The testimony and consent of the people had been required from the first, but as the people increased in numbers and the bishoprics in importance, the appointment of a bishop tended more and more to become, at least in the great centres of population, a matter of popular election. To resist this influence we find the Council of Laodicea forbidding episcopal elections to be left 'to the multitude,' and other canons made the consent of the metropolitan indispensable. But besides bishops, the emperors were naturally jealous of this popular prerogative. For by this time the bishops of the great sees such as Rome and Milan, Alexandria and Antioch and Constantinople, had attained a position among the most prominent personages of the empire: civil war or peace depended on their theological opinions: and their election was frequently the occasion of riot and even bloodshed, especially among the turbulent populace of the eastern capitals. Even at Rome itself the bloody strife between the partisans of Damasus and Ursinus is notorious, and the aid of troops had often to be invoked to secure the succession of a new patriarch. Nevertheless, in spite of emperors or bishops, in the great capitals election by the people held its ground. St. Ambrose of Milan owed his ordination to popular acclamation; St. Athanasius was elected by 'the whole multitude and people of the catholic church' in

the Early Church

Alexandria. Even when the choice of the people was by some means anticipated, a very decided veto still lay in their power. They could refuse to accept the bishop appointed for them; and such refusals were so common in history that the position, rank, and duty of such rejected and 'vacant' bishops, or bishops without a see, was the subject of constant legislation.

How the imperial intervention began, and in many cases was imperatively called for, is seen in the case of Antioch about the year 330, which also presents us with the first *congé d'élire*. Eustathius, the bishop of Antioch, had been deposed by a synod of Arianizing bishops, who nominated as his successor Eusebius of Caesarea and submitted his name to the emperor as being acceptable to 'the mind and wishes of bishops and people.' The laity, however, took another view of the proceedings and the consequence was 'a terrible sedition, and the outburst of a flame which threatened to destroy the city.' The Church was split into two factions, and 'the magistrates and the rest of the populace joined in the quarrel, which would have been settled by the sword but for fear of the emperor.' Constantine, however, 'like a saviour and physician of souls applied healing remedies.' He wrote to the citizens, rebuking them for their disorder and exhorting them to lay aside faction in seeking for the fitting candidate; to Eusebius, congratulating him on his reluctance to be translated; and to the bishops, intimating that Euphronius of Cappadocia and George of Arethusa were 'men approved in the faith,' and that to select either would be acting in accordance with the apostolic traditions. It is hardly necessary to add that one of them, Euphronius, obtained the bishopric[1].

A profitable lesson in the methods of episcopal election would be to trace the fortunes of a single see, and fortunately the historian Socrates, a citizen of Constantinople, has left us in his history some very full notices of the episcopal successions in his native city. When bishop Alexander died in 340 he left in writing the names of two of his clergy who became the candidates of the orthodox and Arian parties respectively. The 'battle of the people' was for a long time indecisive, but at last victory inclined to the side of the Nicene candidate, Paul, who was accordingly ordained. This, however, filled the emperor Constantius, an Arian, with fury: he banished Paul and translated Eusebius from Nicomedea to Constantinople. On his death 'the people again introduce Paul,' but in vain: this time he is expelled by force, and Macedonius 'is seated on the throne by the prefect rather than by the Church's law.' On the accession of an orthodox emperor, Theodosius, in 379, 'by the common vote of many bishops,' Gregory was summoned from Nazianzus to the oversight of the catholic party, but when the Council of Constantinople met in 381, he returned home again, and 'Nectarius was seized by the people and advanced to the episcopate, being ordained by the hundred and fifty bishops of the council.' When Nectarius died in 397, 'a contest immediately arose about the appointment of his successor, various names being put forward.' At last, after much counsel, one of the eunuchs at court made mention of the

[1] Euseb. *V. C.* iii. 59-62. Socrates i. 24.

eloquence of John, a presbyter of Antioch, the celebrated Chrysostom: and at once 'by the common vote of all together,' that is of both clergy and laity, he was sent for by the emperor Arcadius, and to make his ordination more imposing a synod of several prelates was summoned by the imperial command. Seven years later John was banished, and on the death of his successor, 'in consequence of the number of aspirants to the vacant see,' a considerable interval elapsed before the ordination of Atticus. 'After the decease of Atticus a violent contest arose about the appointment of a bishop; various persons were proposed—a presbyter, Philip, was put forward by one party, Proclus by another: but the unanimous desire of the people was for Sisinnius. All the laity longed for his appointment because he had a great reputation for piety and especially for care of the poor. So the zeal of the laity won the day, and Sisinnius was ordained.' This so chagrined Philip, that in his history of Christianity, he wrote 'some very sharp criticisms on the appointment, reflecting on the bishop, his consecrators, and above all on the laity,'—remarks which Socrates is unwilling to transcribe. We are now within the period of our historian's personal recollections, and the fuller information reveals more clearly the growing influence of the government. In 428 so great was the rivalry among the clergy that 'the authorities determined that no ecclesiastic of Constantinople should fill the vacant see.' But their own choice of 'a stranger from Antioch' was disastrous, for he was none other than Nestorius, the originator of Nestorianism and the terrible controversy to which it gave rise. After his deposition 'there was again a dispute.' This time Proclus, now a bishop, 'was the favourite of the majority, and their votes would have carried the day, had not some influential persons interfered, alleging that the Church's law forbad the translation of bishops: this assertion gained credence among the people, they relaxed their efforts,' and after four months Maximian was ordained. Maximian died in his third year, 434: and 'the emperor Theodosius had recourse to a clever stratagem in order to prevent the customary strife and tumult which attended the election of the bishop. For while Maximian's body was yet unburied, without delay he caused the bishops present in the city to seat Proclus in the episcopal chair, having fortified himself with the consent of the bishop of Rome, in view of the canonical difficulty about translation [1].

These transactions at Constantinople were but a type of what was happening elsewhere. Only at Alexandria, removed from proximity to the court, the people held their own, and their obstinate resistance to imperial pressure in elections and matters of faith resulted in the final severance of the Coptic Church from the 'royal' Church of Constantinople.

In the West the balance of power was better maintained, for the share of the laity in elections and ordinations was receiving renewed confirmation, at least in theory. It was probably the encroachments of the imperial and secular powers that caused the popes to reassert the privileges of the laity in their letters and rescripts. Thus we have the maxim of Celestine, quoted

[1] See Socrates ii. 6, 7, 12, 13, 16; v. 6, 8; vi. 2, 20; vii. 26, 29, 35, 40.

the Early Church

by the councils of Orleans in 549 and Paris in 557, that 'no bishop is to be imposed upon a people against their will.' Leo the Great enumerates, in language somewhat indefinite, the ingredients of a due election—the 'wishes of the citizens, testimony of the people, decision of the notables, and election of the clergy,' and he pronounces that 'he who is to preside over all must be chosen by all[1].' These ancient principles, however, had never been lost sight of in the canons of the western councils. In the fourth century indeed there was a great development of the metropolitan's authority in the election of a bishop, and as in the East there were enactments against popular elections[2]. But in the sixth and seventh centuries there was a great revival of legislation on the subject, based upon primitive principles, due no doubt to the arbitrary and violent interference of the great. A metropolitan was to be chosen by the bishops with consent of the clergy and people, but in the case of an ordinary bishop the canons speak most distinctly of election by clergy and people with consent of the bishops of the province. If it is sometimes put the other way—election by bishops, consent of clergy and people—a council at Rheims in 625 most definitely ordered that 'none is to be ordained bishop except a native of the place who has been chosen by the general vote of the whole people and accepted by the provincial bishops[3].'

The witness of the canons is fully corroborated by that

---

[1] Ep. x. 4; cf. x. 6, xiii. 3, xiv. 5, clxvii. 1.

[2] As at Carthage in 390, and Braga in 572.

[3] The councils are: in France—Orleans, 533, 538, 549; Clermont, 535; Paris, 557, 615; Rheims, 625; Chalons, 649; in Spain—Barcelona, 599; Toledo, 633. See also the councils of Valence, 374, and Arles, 443.

of the liturgies. The forms of ordination of the early Middle Ages most clearly provide that a new bishop should be elected by the clergy and people of his city. After the election they were to send to the metropolitan a 'decree' or petition for consecration, which declared that 'by common vote and consent they had elected such a presbyter to be their bishop'; and before he consented to ordain, the metropolitan must publicly examine the petitioners as to the regularity of the election and the fitness of their candidate [1]. This election by clergy and people is distinctly specified in all the documents connected with the ceremony, e.g. the public announcement of election [2]. At the ordination itself the consent

---

[1] The Roman Order given by Mabillon (*Mus. Ital.* ii. p. 85), probably the oldest of all, begins thus: 'When the bishop of a city is dead, another is chosen by the people of the city, and a decree is to be made by the priests, clergy, and people, and they come to the apostolic lord (the pope) bringing with them a petition for the consecration of the bishop-elect who accompanies them.' On a Saturday a chaplain 'introduces the people of the city,' the pope examines them, the decree is read, and the pope ends by saying to the elect: 'Since the wishes (*vota*) of all agree on thee, thou shalt fast to-day and be ordained to-morrow.' The ceremony itself began with the announcement: 'The clergy and consentient people of ... have chosen ... to be ordained their bishop; let us therefore pray, &c.'

In all other forms and mss., except in one ms. found by Morin (*de Ordin.*, p. 265), instead of the chaplain introducing *the people of the city*, we read that the archpresbyter shall introduce the elect *with the clergy of his church.*

At the ordination there was, and still is, another examination of the elect, but in only one ms. (Morin. *de Ordin.*, p. 224) is found at the end the interrogation of the congregation by the consecrator: '*Dearly beloved brethren, have you chosen this presbyter to be your bishop?*' '*We have chosen him, all of us.*' '*Is he just? Is he worthy?*' '*He is just and worthy.*' '*By the help of the Lord ... we will ordain him, if you all consent.*' '*We all consent.*'

[2] And also the metropolitan's commendatory letter and 'edict' or instruction to the ordained.

the Early Church

of the people was secured by an appeal to them to give their testimony by acclamation[1]. The same testimony was required in the case of presbyters and deacons, for, as the address still runs in the present Roman ordinal, 'of necessity the people will give the readier obedience to that presbyter to whose ordination they have first given their assent[2]:' and to give all opportunity for making objection, the service began with the public challenge known as the *Si quis*. However, it is unnecessary to dwell on these details, for the forms, if not the substance, still survive in great measure in the modern ordinals.

In conclusion it remains to point out the most serious effect of the influence of the empire upon the Church, which is to be looked for not so much in her external organization as in her inward spirit. In the fourth and fifth centuries, through a variety of causes, the growing distinction between clergy and laity became complete and unalterably rigid. Clerical life was transformed into a profession, and Christians were sharply divided into two classes of men. Of course from the beginning there had been a ministry, and none but ordained ministers could perform ministerial functions—only bishops

[1] That is in the early Gallican form known as the *Missale Francorum* of the sixth or seventh century (Muratori, *Lit. Rom. Vet.* ii. p. 669). But it disappeared in the Gregorian form which came into general use later on.

[2] This *allocution to the people* which occurs in the *Missale Francorum* is still read in the modern Roman office, but the actual acclamation of the people has been omitted together with the old conclusion: 'If ye keep silence we cannot learn your devout response, which we await. But what will be most acceptable to God we know, that is for the Holy Spirit to give to the hearts of all one consenting voice. It is your duty therefore by public utterance to express your choice.'

could ordain, only bishops and presbyters celebrate the eucharist, only clergy lead the public worship. But outside the walls of the church and the celebration of divine worship the distinction between Christians was not so evident. The clergy wore no special dress: frequently, like St. Paul, they had to work for their living: and in converting the heathen, in the defence of the gospel, in wielding the pen, in suffering for the faith, they had no special advantage over the laity. In the earlier time also the Christian body had been conspicuous for its variety. The lines of the hierarchy of office, or differentiation of function for the purposes of worship, were crossed by other divisions. There was a hierarchy of 'spiritual gifts,' of exorcists, of workers of miracles, of healings, of tongues, and above all of prophets. The order of prophets held a most prominent position in the Church, and yet 'prophecy' was not confined to a class; 'ye can all prophesy,' St. Paul wrote to the Corinthians. The various orders of spiritual gifts will always maintain their position in the Church, even though no longer under the exceptional forms in which they were manifested at first. When these miraculous gifts were passing away, their place was taken by a hierarchy of merit, won by suffering for Christ—of martyrs and confessors. If the 'witness' for Christ in a persecution escaped actual death, he received the title of *confessor*, which carried with it the dignity of *presbyter* and a seat among the clergy, but, as there was no laying on of hands, without the power 'to offer.' These confessors were regarded with an unbounded admiration by their fellow-churchmen. Such confidence was felt in the power of their intercessions that they were spoken of as forgiving sins; and at last their irregular influence caused such confusion in the regular working and discipline of church life as to provoke a serious controversy. Once more there was the hierarchy of intellectual gifts. 'Teachers,' like schoolmasters now, formed a regular class, and this class was not limited to the clergy. The famous catechetical school of Alexandria, the Christian university of the first centuries, was often presided over by a layman, as, for instance, by the great Origen. Origen indeed was permitted by the bishops of Palestine to preach in church in their presence while yet a layman; and when a protest was made, precedents were forthcoming. In literature, among the earliest apologists and defenders of the faith laymen are to be found. Even as late as the fifth century it was a layman, Eusebius, who rising up in the great church at Constantinople, first denounced the heresy of its bishop Nestorius. And to laymen, to Socrates, Sozomen, and Evagrius, we are indebted for most valuable church histories. But in the epoch we have been describing, under the pressure of officialism and professionalism, all these varied manifestations and ministrations of the Spirit were lost sight of or absorbed in the one great division of the Church into clergy and laity, officials and non-officials.

The rigidity of this division however inevitably provoked reaction. On the one hand, the spirit of religious independence, liberty, and elasticity found a new vent in the outburst of monasticism, which in its original forms was emphatically a lay institution, and formed a rallying-point for the democratic feeling of the Church. On the other hand, there was the production of what may be called 'the lay mind.' Of this the lawyer and historian Socrates is a great type. He is indeed a genuine catholic, full of zeal for the faith, and author of a church history; and yet it is easy to notice in his great work signs of impatience with the technicalities of theological controversy and irritation at the arrogance of bishops, a sarcastic humour which enjoys venting itself at their expense, a dislike of persecution and a delight in broadmindedness or any special recognition of the laity. Instances of such recognition he does not fail to commend as in the case of Silvanus, bishop of Troas, who 'acquired a widespread reputation' because contrary to custom he appointed laymen instead of ecclesiastics as judges in his court[1]. And we cannot do better than conclude with a picture he gives us of church life in the fifth century, still keeping to the old paths. At Synnada in Phrygia there was a large congregation of Macedonian heretics under a bishop of their own, Agapetus. The orthodox bishop Theodosius, in his zeal for the faith, went to Constantinople to obtain fuller coercive powers. But during his absence Agapetus 'formed a wise and prudent resolution': 'after communicating with his clergy, he called together all the laity under him and persuaded them to adopt the orthodox creed. They consented to his proposal, and then he proceeded immediately to the church, attended not merely by his own adherents, but by the whole body of the people.' There he occupied the bishop's seat, and by preaching the catholic doctrine reunited the whole people[2].

[1] Soc. vii. 37. [2] vii. 3.

III

THE PRINCIPLES AND CONDITIONS OF THE SCOTTISH ESTABLISHMENT

By Lord Balfour of Burleigh

THE request made to me is that I should write a short statement of the principles on which the Church of Scotland is governed. With this request I am glad to comply, and, as the space which can be allowed to me is very limited, I shall proceed to do so without preface or explanation, save this, that I am most anxious not to be supposed to believe that what is found suitable in Scotland must necessarily be capable of transplantation to the south of the Tweed. I shall be satisfied if anything I write can give a clear idea to those who are interested in such matters, how they are arranged in Scotland, and, as the settlement has stood the test of time and experience, it may not be going too far to claim that it is at least worthy of careful attention and consideration.

It would scarcely be possible better to summarize the principles upon which the alliance between Church and State in Scotland is founded than by quoting a saying attributed to the Emperor Constantine who, soon after he declared himself a Christian, is represented as having addressed an assembly of churchmen in these words—

'You are appointed by God overseers of those things which are within the Church, and I of those which are without [1].'

It is not too much to say that this states the principle which will be found to run through all the Acts of the Scottish Parliament which deal with the subject, and that no attempt to depart from it will be found in any of them. The two most important of these statutes became law respectively in 1592 and 1690. The Act of 1592 is usually known as the Charter of the Church in respect that by it, after a long struggle, the Church first secured recognition of her jurisdiction. It is too long to quote as a whole, but it is easily accessible to those who are anxious to study the subject. For our present purpose the important point to notice is that it does not profess on the part of the State to create a church jurisdiction as a new thing, but expressly recognizes it as already existing. Its title is, 'Ratification of the libertie of the Trew Kirk.' It specifies the 'materis to be intreatit [2]' in the several courts of the Church, and recognizes the supremacy of the General Assembly, as to which court it declares—

'That it sall be lauchfull to the Kirk and ministrie everick zeir [3] at the leist, and ofter, *pro re nata*, as occasioun and necessitie sall require, to hald and keepe Generall Assemblies.'

---

[1] Eusebius, *de Vita Constantini*, lib. 4, c. 4.
[2] That is, 'matters to be treated.'   [3] That is, 'every year.'

the Scottish Establishment

It contains this important sentence:—

'And decernis and declaris the saides assemblies, presbiteries, and sessiounes, jurisdictioun and discipline thereof foresaid, to be in all tymes cuming maist just, gude, and godlie *in the selff.*'

Then certain Acts are repealed which it is declared—

'Sall na wise be prejudiciall nor dirogat oniething to the privilege that God has given to the spirituall office-bearers in the Kirk, concerning heads of religion, matters of heresie, excommunication, collation, or deprivation of ministers, or ony sic-like essential censouris, speciall grounded and having warrand of the word of God.'

The Act of 1592 has remained in force continuously except during the two periods of episcopacy, and was embodied in the Act of Settlement of 1690. In that Act the Act of 1592 is referred to as the 'Ratification of the Liberty of the True Kirk,' and, except with regard to some matters affecting patronage, was expressly re-enacted.

The Act of 1690 was in turn embodied in a very special manner in the Act of Union between England and Scotland, and all this legislation is declared to be an essential and fundamental part of the Articles of Union.

In his *Digest of the Laws* of the Church, the Rev. William Mair, D.D., of Earlston, Moderator of the General Assembly in 1897, defines 'jurisdiction' as 'authority to administer or apply law,' and proceeds:—

'Judgement in a case by the highest court possessing jurisdiction (or by a lower not appealed from) is as if the law itself had expressly stated the case and judgement.

Such authority emanates only from the legislative power and royal prerogative. Christian churches claim to possess it from the royal prerogative of their divine Head to the extent of their needs, over their members. But as the word "jurisdiction" in the legal phraseology of the country means only that which is derived from the human head of the State, let us for clearness designate the divine jurisdiction of the churches as power of church government. It is evident that, besides possessing this power, a church may in addition possess jurisdiction if the State pleases and the church accepts. This is the position of the Church of Scotland, and this is the position presented in the Statutes. While, therefore, it is correct to say that the "jurisdiction" of the Church, in the accepted legal sense of the word, proceeds wholly from the State, it is incorrect and inexcusable to omit or conceal that this which is from the State is *in addition to*, and carries with it *acknowledgement of*, the power of church government, which belongs to the Church itself.'

These then are the principles upon which the alliance between Church and State in Scotland is founded; and though controversies, bitter and prolonged, have arisen as to the respective limits of the spheres of the civil and the ecclesiastical authorities, controversies which have left deep marks on the history of Scotland, the principles themselves are now admitted on all sides to be beyond challenge. In recent years especially the jurisdiction of the Church has been admitted by eminent judges of the Court of Session, with a frank distinctness which leaves nothing to be desired. In 1861 a case occurred in which a minister having been charged with intoxication lodged defences, and was cited to appear personally

the Scottish Establishment

at a certain meeting of presbytery; on this occasion he was represented by counsel and agent, who pleaded intervening insanity, but the presbytery, in respect of his having lodged defences, refused to stop proceedings. A note of suspension and interdict was then presented against the presbytery in the Court of Session, and the First Division, affirming a judgement of Lord Jerviswood, refused the note without answers. Lord Ivory, in the course of his judgement, used these words:—

'If we arrived at any other result it would be going contrary to the whole principles of independent jurisdiction, which separate the ecclesiastical from the civil courts. Each is independent of the other, and each has its own exclusive field of jurisdiction, and within that field is paramount. No more can we interfere with an ecclesiastical jurisdiction, keeping within its competency, than the ecclesiastical jurisdiction could interfere with us, keeping within our competency, or with the Court of Exchequer or Court of Justiciary in matters proper for these courts.'

In the Auchtergaven case in 1870, Lord Moncreiff, then Lord Justice Clerk, said:—

'If, therefore, this were a case in which we were called upon to review the proceedings of an inferior court, I should have thought a strong case had been made out for our interference. But whatever inconsiderate dicta to that effect may have been thrown out, that is not the law of Scotland. The jurisdiction of the church courts as recognized judicatories of this realm, rests on a similar statutory foundation to that under which we administer justice within these walls. It is easy to suggest extravagant instances of excess of power, but quite as easy to do so in regard to the one jurisdiction as the other. Within their spiritual province the church courts are as supreme as we are within the civil ; and as this is a matter relating to the discipline of the Church, and solely within the cognizance of the church courts, I think we have no power whatever to interfere.'

And the Lord President Inglis is equally distinct in the case of the Presbytery of Lewis *v.* Fraser in 1874, when he said that—

'The Presbytery is an established judicature of the country as much recognized by law as the Court of Session itself.'

One other important point remains to be noticed, viz. that an Act of Parliament of 1693, after ratifying, approving, and confirming the Act of 1690 'in the whole heads, articles, and clauses thereof,' ordains—

'That the Lords of their Majesties' Privy Council, and all other Magistrates, Judges, and Officers, give all due assistance for making the sentences and censures of the Church and judicatures thereof to be obeyed or otherways effectual as accords.'

In a case which involved the question of the Civil Court granting a warrant to compel the attendance of a witness before a presbytery, Lord President Inglis having quoted these words then went on to say—

'I want nothing stronger or more comprehensive than that. Whenever the church courts are unable of themselves to carry out their own orders made to explicate their own jurisdiction the civil courts are bound to step in and give all due assistance.'

The Act of 1693 also contains a provision to the effect

the Scottish Establishment 85

that after that date no person shall be admitted as a minister of the Church unless he subscribes the Westminster Confession of Faith, and declares it to be the confession of his faith; and ministers are required by the same Act to own the presbyterian government of the Church and to promise that they 'will never directly or indirectly endeavour the prejudice or subversion thereof.' It is therefore beyond the power of the Church during the continuance of the alliance with the State to depart by any decree of its own either from the Confession of Faith or from presbyterian church government.

The government of the Church of Scotland, then, is—under the General Assembly—by Synods, Presbyteries, and Kirk Sessions, and I shall endeavour to indicate in outline the powers and functions of these courts, and their relation respectively to each other, as well as to consider the manner in which each of them is constituted. In some respects the questions with which we are concerned have been made the subject of actual legislation by the Assembly. In others the practice depends not upon Acts of Assembly but upon its judgements as the superior court, or on judgements of the inferior courts not appealed against, or on practice long continued, which has thus obtained the force of settled law.

In the first place it may be well to consider some points which, speaking generally, are common to all the courts of the Church. For example, the functions of each court can only be discharged within its own bounds, and its meetings must be held subject to the same limitation, except with the consent of a superior court. With the exception of meetings for certain special purposes (which are well established, but which cannot be specified here without risk of going too much into detail), each Synod and Presbytery before rising determines when and where it will hold its next meeting, and its place of meeting is publicly announced. The General Assembly adheres to the same form in passing from one session to another, but, as Dr. Mair points out, this form would not be appropriate at the close of its sitting, because the time and place which it then fixes are not for itself but for another Assembly, so that it cannot, in strict phraseology, be said to adjourn. Its form is—'the next General Assembly of this National Church is appointed to be held,' &c. It is therefore the case that every court of the Church, except the Kirk Session, always has on its records a resolution to meet at a fixed time and place, understood to be publicly known, within its bounds. The quorum of all church courts below the Assembly is generally regarded as three, but this depends on custom, as it has not been fixed by Act of Assembly. In the case of Synods and Presbyteries only one of these three may be an elder. Every court is presided over by a Moderator, who is now always a minister. It must be so by law in the case of a Kirk Session, and it has so long been the universal practice in the case of all other courts that custom has now practically acquired the force of law, though Dr. Mair quotes a case as having occurred in 1600, in the Presbytery of Glasgow, in which a minister and elder were proposed, and the elder was elected. Every court, however, above the Kirk Session, possesses

the Scottish Establishment

the privilege of electing its Moderator, and though in some cases various routine methods are followed, it is probably not competent for a court to come to any resolution which would interfere with freedom of election. The Moderator during his tenure of office is responsible for calling or declining to call a meeting in any emergency which may arise, and while the court is sitting he is the judge of order, and calls upon members who desire to speak, but he is in no sense master of the court, and probably his ruling depends in the last resort upon the concurrence of the court over which he presides. Every church court must also have a Clerk, and makes its own terms of engagement with him. The Clerk is the keeper of the records of the court. The minutes of each meeting of a court must bear the place and date, and (except in the case of the General Assembly) the names of all the members who were present, and that the court was constituted and closed with prayer, and must be attested by the signatures both of the Moderator and the Clerk. The minutes must be written without interlineations or deletions, and no court can of its own authority order the deletion of any of its records when once they have been attested. If any alteration becomes necessary it must obtain the consent of the Court of Judicature immediately superior to it.

The Kirk Session is the lowest of the courts of the Church. Every ecclesiastical parish has its Kirk Session, which consists of the minister and the elders. There is no limit to the number of elders of which a Kirk Session may be constituted, but it cannot act if by death or resignation or other accidental cause the members are reduced below two besides the minister. As we have seen, the minister presides in virtue of his office at every meeting, and it is settled law of the Church that a Kirk Session cannot meet without a minister present and presiding. If there should be a vacancy in any parish the Presbytery will appoint one of its number to act as Moderator during the continuance of the vacancy. The functions of the Kirk Session are thus defined by Dr. Mair:—

'It belongs to the Kirk Session to maintain good order, to cause the Acts of the Assembly to be put in execution, to administer discipline, to judge and determine cases, and to superintend the religious and moral condition of the parish. They judge of the fitness of those who desire to receive the sacraments, and have charge of everything affecting the Communion Roll. Theirs is the responsibility of receiving and giving certificates of transference. They make up the roll of the congregation on the occasion of a vacancy. They determine the hours of public worship, the times of dispensing the Lord's Supper, and days of special public thanksgiving or humiliation. They appoint a ruling elder of their number yearly to attend the Presbytery and Synod. They add to their number, receive resignations of their members, put them on trial if necessary, and censure, suspend, or depose them. They are responsible for the discharge of such duties as the Acts or resolutions of the Assembly may lay upon them—for example, the making of the collections that are ordered.'

The minister is accountable for his conduct to the Presbytery and not to the Kirk Session, and it will be borne in mind that a decision in regard to most of the

the Scottish Establishment

matters just specified as coming under the jurisdiction of a Kirk Session is subject to review by the Presbytery, and so on through the higher courts by means either of complaint or appeal. The Kirk Session are also responsible for the fitness of those whom they resolve to add to their number as elders. If they desire to know whom the congregation would select it is not inconsistent with law that they should take such means to find out as in their discretion they see fit, but this is not obligatory upon them, and whatever course they may take the whole responsibility remains with them, subject to the supervision of the superior courts of the Church. An Act of Assembly, passed in 1889, regulates the questions to be put to those selected for the eldership before their ordination[1], and the formula to be subscribed by them at the time. The questions involve approval of the administration, worship, discipline, and government of the Church, and approbation of the Confession of Faith as approved by the Church, and ratified by law in 1690, and all the newly appointed elders promise to submit themselves to the discipline and presbyterian government of the Church as established by law, and that they will never directly or indirectly attempt the prejudice or subversion thereof.

In its Kirk Session every parish possesses a governing court, which is responsible for keeping up to date a roll of the members of the Church. There is no necessity for a franchise, in the sense of determining who are and who

---

[1] I use the word 'ordination' because it is the usual expression, but those set apart as elders remain and are regarded by the Church as 'laymen.'

are not members of the Church, for any of its judicial or administrative purposes, but it is instructive to notice the course taken by Parliament in 1874, when the Act for regulating the patronage of the Church was passing through its various stages. The object of the Act was to repeal the Statute of Queen Anne which had been imposed upon the Church in 1712, and to take the patronage of churches out of the hands of the Crown, the Universities, and the lay patrons, where it had remained since that year, and to place it in the hands of the congregation. The operative section of the Act of 1874 is in the following terms :—

'From and after the commencement of this Act, the said Acts of the tenth year of the reign of Her Majesty Queen Anne, chapter twelve, and the sixth and seventh years of the reign of Her present Majesty, chapter sixty-one, shall be repealed, and the right of electing and appointing Ministers to vacant churches and parishes in Scotland is hereby declared to be vested in the congregations of such vacant churches and parishes respectively, subject to such regulations in regard to the mode of naming and proposing such Ministers by means of a committee chosen by the congregation, and of conducting the election and of making the appointment by the congregation as may from time to time be framed by the General Assembly of the Church of Scotland, or which after the passing of this Act, but before the next meeting of the said General Assembly, may be framed by the Commission of the last General Assembly, duly convened for the purpose of making interim regulations thereanent.'

In the definition clause the word 'congregation' is declared to mean and include—

the Scottish Establishment

'Communicants and such other adherents of the Church as the Kirk Session under regulations to be framed by the General Assembly or Commission thereof, as provided in the third section hereof, may determine to be members of the congregation for the purposes of this Act.'

It will thus be seen that the definition of 'adherent' and consequently of 'congregation' is avowedly left entirely in the hands of the courts of the Church. It may be interesting to state for facility of reference the actual definition which has been settled, and which has now been in operation with general approval for a considerable number of years. The roll of the congregation contains:—

'(1) As communicants all persons, not being under Church discipline, whose names are upon the Communion Roll at the date of the occurrence of the vacancy [1] after it has been revised by the Kirk Session as at that date; as also those who are, and at that date were, parishioners in communion with the Church of Scotland, and have given in certificates within the time intimated in terms of Schedule A 2, provided such certificates are sustained; (2) as adherents, such other persons, being parishioners or seat-holders not under twenty-one years of age, as have claimed in writing within the time intimated as aforesaid, and in the form of Schedule B, to be placed on the Electoral Roll, and in regard to whom the Kirk Session are satisfied that they desire to be permanently connected with the congregation, or are associated with it in its interests and work, and that no reason exists for refusing to admit them to the Communion if they should apply. As regards adherents, the decision of the Kirk Session shall be final.'

[1] i.e. vacancy in the office of parish minister.

The next of the courts of the Church is the Presbytery, which consists of the minister of every fully constituted ecclesiastical parish within its bounds, and one elder from each, the elder sitting for a year by election of his own Kirk Session, and being eligible for re-election after the rising of the General Assembly in each year. The number of parishes which may be included in a Presbytery is quite indefinite. The General Assembly cannot of itself create a new parish, but it has the power of altering the boundaries of Presbyteries at will, and of either adding existing parishes to or taking them from any Presbytery, and of establishing new Presbyteries, without reference to any civil authority. There are at present eighty-four Presbyteries of the Church. The Presbytery regulates its own times and dates of meeting. Its Moderator, who is always a minister, is usually chosen to hold office for six months at a time. The Presbytery has many important duties to perform. Upon it is laid the duty of maintaining and enforcing the existing laws and usages of the Church in such matters as the performance of public worship and the administration of ordinances. With it lies the duty of oversight of ministers in discharge of their duties and in their conduct, and with power to try, sentence, and depose them. The Presbytery is the court which licenses men to preach and ordains them to the office of the ministry, and admits or rejects those appointed to charges. It is the guardian of the interests of the Church in all matters within its bounds, and is really the pivot upon which most of the administrative work of the Church depends.

It is worthy of notice that in some matters connected

the Scottish Establishment

with glebes, and with the repair of churches and manses, the Presbytery exercises an important civil jurisdiction; but in these matters an appeal from its decision would not go to the superior church courts, but to the civil courts.

Until the year 1868 review of a decision of the Presbytery in these matters was obtained in the Court of Session, and the procedure was substantially the same as in appeals from any inferior civil court. In that year an Act of Parliament was passed which changed the procedure, and gave certain jurisdiction to the sheriff of the county, with a restricted right of appeal to the Lord Ordinary of the Teind Court.

Three or more Presbyteries, as the Assembly may regulate, compose a Provincial Synod. There are at present sixteen such Synods, and, speaking generally, they correspond more or less exactly to the ancient dioceses of pre-reformation times. All the ministers included in any of the Presbyteries within the bound of the Synod are members of that court, and the same elder who represents his Kirk Session in the Presbytery is its representative in the Synod, so that the actual number of ministers and elders actually entitled to attend the Synod may be equal. Neighbouring Synods 'correspond' with one another by sending one minister and one elder, who are entitled to sit, to deliberate, and to vote with the members of the Synod to which they are sent.

The highest ecclesiastical court is the General Assembly. While all ministers attend Presbyteries and Synods, the Assembly is a representative body, and is constituted afresh by election each year; the representation of the several Presbyteries in the General Assembly is settled in proportion to the number of parishes in each Presbytery.

As last settled by an Act of Assembly in 1893, every Presbytery now sends one minister for every four ministers on the complete roll of the Presbytery, and for part of four, and one elder for every six ministers, and for part of six. And in addition, the Royal Burghs of Scotland and the Universities are each entitled to send a representative, who, in the case of the Universities, may be either a minister or an elder, but in that of the Burghs can only be an elder. The result is a possible Assembly of 704, of whom 371 are ministers, and 333 sit as elders.

A Presbytery cannot send as one of its ministerial representatives any one who is not on its own roll. The Burgh election is by the Town Council, and the abstention or opposition of any number of the Council does not affect the right of the rest to elect, this being a public trust which they are not entitled to abandon. The lay representatives, both of Presbyteries and Burghs, must be bonâ fide acting elders, and each must have a certificate from the Kirk Session of which he is a member attesting the fact. The General Assembly claims the right to meet when it chooses, but by long custom the meetings are held annually, and commence on the third Thursday of May, lasting until the Monday week following. The procedure cannot be better described than in the following terms, which are taken from an article published in the Year Book of the Church of Scotland.

the Scottish Establishment

'A General Assembly is annually convened in Edinburgh in May, and transacts business on ten lawful days. The time and place of meeting are decided by an Act passed at the last diet of the previous Assembly, and authoritatively intimated by the Moderator. After this the Lord High Commissioner, on the part of the Sovereign, makes a similar intimation. On the day and at the place thus determined, a sermon is preached " in the High Kirk" by the Moderator of the last Assembly, who announces, at the conclusion of public worship, that the supreme ecclesiastical court is about to meet, and afterwards opens the meeting with prayer. The clerks having previously made up a roll of members from commissions which have been lodged with them in due form, one of the ministers on that roll is then chosen Moderator. Thereafter, the Lord High Commissioner, appointed to represent the royal person in the General Assembly, presents his commission, and subsequently a letter from the Sovereign, which documents, with the Assembly's sanction, are read by the first clerk and ordered to be recorded. The Commissioner next addresses the Assembly from the throne which he occupies; and the Moderator, in their name, replies to the speech of His Grace. Several committees are then named, through one or other of which all the business to be transacted by the Assembly must be transmitted. That business may be briefly described as consisting of (1) Complaints, or appeals, or petitions against decisions of Presbyteries or Synods; (2) Overtures (i.e. proposals) or petitions that certain things should be done by the Assembly, either to effect changes in the law or practice of the Church, or to protect her from danger, or to increase her usefulness, or to promote the cause of Christ at home or abroad; (3) Reports from Standing Committees appointed by the last Assembly to prosecute missions, and for other purposes ; (4) Reports from committees nominated by the Assembly itself to deal with matters remitted to them. When its business has been transacted, the Assembly is dissolved first by the Moderator, in the name of the Lord Jesus Christ, the Head of the Church, and then by the Lord High Commissioner in the name of the Sovereign.'

Under the first of the headings mentioned in this account of the Assembly are included all the judicial business which has to be brought before it. That is, such cases (if any) as affect the character and status of ordained ministers, licentiates, elders, or it might be church members, though these last rarely reach the Assembly. There are also included under the heading of judicial business any disputes about the filling up of charges in vacant parishes or congregations. All these matters must come up after having been the subject of process in the inferior courts, and they must come up in one or other of the following ways:—(1) Complaint; (2) Appeal; (3) Reference; (4) Inspection of the Records of the inferior courts ; and (5) Petition, but this only in cases where the petitioner could not competently have taken any other course, or was obstructed in attempting to do so.

Complaint and Appeal differ only in name, Dissent and Complaint being the technical name given to the appeal of a minority of members of an inferior court who ask the superior court to review a decision arrived at by a majority of their colleagues ; an appeal being what its name implies, an appeal by any one at the bar of an inferior court against any decision in his case at

the Scottish Establishment

which that court may have arrived. If an inferior court entertains doubt or apprehends difficulty or inconvenience in giving a decision, it may refer the matter in question to a superior court; but Principal Hill says of the practice, 'that it is more conducive to the public good that every court should fulfil its duty by exercising its judgement,' and the practice is not now followed, except in very special cases or from a desire to obtain an authoritative settlement of some important question which has arisen in an inferior court shortly before the annual meeting of the Assembly, but which could not be taken there with sufficient rapidity by the usual process of complaint or appeal.

Most of the administrative work of the Assembly comes before it by means of reports of committees appointed by one Assembly to report to the next, or by the Assembly itself to report to a meeting on a later day of the same session. And it is scarcely too much to say that it is in this administrative work its chief functions are now to be found. It is perhaps not strictly within the scope of this essay, but in order to give an accurate idea of the importance of the General Assembly this point must be emphasized. Reports on Foreign and Colonial Missions, and on each of the various forms of Home Mission Work, come up for consideration and for discussion every year. Technically the committees only hold office for one year, but they are usually reappointed with only slight changes in their membership.

In this way the General Assembly not only regulates the procedure, but organizes the Christian efforts and stimulates the Christian life and work of the members of the Church in every parish in Scotland.

There only remains to be mentioned the process by which the legislative authority of the Assembly is exercised.

All proposals for legislation must be instituted by what is called an overture to the Assembly; an overture may be transmitted by a Synod or Presbytery, or may be proposed to the Assembly by any number of its own members. Should the Assembly approve of any overture which would either rescind any standing Act of Assembly, or would involve an essential alteration of the existing law or practice of the Church, it must, under an Act of Assembly passed in 1697, which is known as the Barrier Act, be remitted for consideration to the Presbyteries of the Church. Their opinion on it must be reported to the next Assembly; each Presbytery deliberates and votes separately on the proposal, and if the majority of them approve, the next Assembly may, if it remains of the same opinion as its predecessor, convert the proposal into a standing law of the Church. If less than half of the Presbyteries have reported approval of the proposed legislation, the Assembly may either abandon it or send it down again to the Presbyteries in the same or an amended form.

The Assembly claims and exercises the power of converting any proposed legislation into an interim Act when 'this is necessary in any emergency or for more effectually carrying out existing laws of the Church,' and if this is done it becomes binding upon the Church till next General Assembly.

the Scottish Establishment

The Barrier Act is not part of the constitution of the Church, but it could not be altered without the consent of a majority of Presbyteries, a consent which is never likely either to be asked or to be given; and it will at once be seen what an important safeguard is thus supplied against any rash or hasty legislation.

In all the courts of the Church all those who are members, whether ministers or elders, have equal rights of speaking and voting. The votes are counted together and the majority prevails. Should it be impossible for the Assembly to conclude all its business, or should an emergency arise which calls for a meeting of its members before the time for another Assembly to be convened, the constitution of the Church allows the Assembly, before it separates, to appoint a Commission, which is now made to include the Moderator and all the members and one other minister. The instructions given to the Commission are 'to advert to the interests of the Church on every occasion, that the Church, or the present establishment thereof, do not suffer or sustain any prejudice which they can prevent.'

Four specific days are mentioned when, if there is business, the Commission should meet, but it can meet oftener if it thinks fit.

The Commission is not, however, a court of the Church, and beyond what is specially committed to it must not interfere with judicial business.

In conclusion, I should like to say that I am only too painfully impressed with the meagre and insufficient description I have been able to give of the constitution and practice of the Church of Scotland within the space permitted to me. The two points to which it seems to me important to direct notice are that the State recognizes a jurisdiction as inherent in the Church, and while adding to it and providing means whereby it can be carried into effect, does not profess to confer it *ab initio*; and further, that within her sphere the Church of Scotland possesses legislative power to regulate her own affairs as may from time to time be necessary without reference to any external authority whatsoever. If I have suggested anything which seems worth further study to those who take an interest in the subject, I shall feel that I have not written altogether in vain.

IV

CHURCH AND STATE

By the Rev. Henry Scott Holland

'The system of an antique religion was part of the social order under which its adherents lived... A man did not choose his religion or frame it for himself. It came to him as part of the general scheme of social obligations or ordinances laid upon him, as a matter of course, by his position in the family and in the nation... This account of the position of religion in the social system holds good, I believe, for all parts and races of the ancient world in the earlier stages of their history. The causes of so remarkable a uniformity ... must plainly have been of a general kind, operating on all parts of mankind without distinction of race and local environment: for in every region of the world, as soon as we find a nation or tribe emerging from prehistoric darkness into the light of authentic history, we find also that its religion conforms to the type which has been indicated [1].'

ALL religion has one continuous story. Its inherent and elemental unity of purpose is never lost through the process of its growth. It advances to new fields; it reveals new possibilities: but it retains, in the fuller

[1] Robertson Smith, *Religion of Semites*, Lect. II, pp. 29, 31.

development, the essential qualities that characterized the germ from which it sprang. Revelation enters to lift it on to higher levels of activity, to transfigure it by infused energies that purge, and kindle, and enlarge, and enrich: but the note of transfiguration is that it retains the old type and the old material in the act by which it transforms them. Religion, in becoming far more than it was before, does not lose what it has been.

And, here, in this universal form of ancient religion, we recognize something that belongs to its elemental nature. Here is the germinal type which it may transcend, but never drop. Qualifications, intricacies, complications—these there must be, now that the primitive limitations and simplifications have been left so far behind. But, still, religion should show itself to be to man what it was at the beginning. Still it must include these rudimentary functions which it originally undertook, and through which it exhibited its primary character and significance.

Are we not, therefore, right in asking to-day of Christianity, in which all man's religions are summed up into completion, that it should manifest the power to fulfil the part which these antique religions undertook—that in some way or another, according to its proper measure, allowing for all the growth of individual responsibility to which it appeals, and for the wider spiritual horizons of the world beyond death which it has lain open, it should satisfy the original social needs for which religions existed?

We see what those needs were. Man, born into an organized society, should find himself encompassed about with a religious system. Without this he is incomplete,

Church and State

he is not equipped to play his part. This religious environment will not be of his own choosing or framing, any more than his family, or his nationality. It will be there, 'as part of the general scheme of social obligations and ordinances laid upon him, as a matter of course.' Within it, nourished, disciplined, evoked, he will, of sheer necessity, discover his capacities, put out his growth, arrive at his full stature. That was the primitive need. Is it a need that can ever cease? In the answer to that question lies the solution of the problem of Church and State.

Church *and* State. The two were once united: they are now distinct. That is the vital difference between the ancient Pagan and the modern Christian world. And the story of the severance is given us in the tragedy of Israel. The religion of Israel was, under one aspect, the crowning achievement of that ancient system in which a 'religion was part of the social order under which its adherents lived.' To a Jew, in a more exact and imperative degree than to any other man on the face of the earth, his religion was identified with 'those social obligations and ordinances laid upon him, as a matter of course, by his position in the family and in the nation.' Every detail of his home, of his food, of his household, of his business, of his taxation, land-tenure, sanitation, recreation, was done under the direct sanction of his God. It was, itself, included in his religious loyalty: it was his mode of serving God. He could not hire a servant, buy a house, pay a debt, reap a field, without declaring, by the act, that this God of Israel was his God. The civil order, which marked Israel out among the nations as a distinct polity, defined its spiritual position, as a separate religion. State and Church were one thing. But within this fusion lurked the seed of disruption. The identification of the true worship of God with a definite social order involves the limitation of God to the peculiar people to whom that social system was their national embodiment. The worship of such a God must carry with it the polity of a distinct and marked nationality. But the spiritual discipline of Israel brings out into ever increasing distinctness that this God, who is the God of Israel, is Himself the God of the whole earth. He may wear the aspect of a tribal God. He may be perpetually misinterpreted in that sense by His own adherents. It was no easy matter to disentangle their own conception from the swarm of tribal deities to whom, by identification of Himself with one tribe, He wore so emphatic a resemblance. Only by the pains of prophetic travail did Israel lay hold of its secret—that this peculiar identification represented an act of favouring choice by which the Lord of Lords, the High and the Holy, who inhabiteth eternity, having set Himself to embrace all the nations of the earth within a single and universal purpose, had, for this end, selected Israel His servant, and had said of Zion, 'Here will I dwell, for I have a delight therein.'

Now—how was this catholicity of purpose to be reconciled with the limitation of God's favour to the civil order of a separate nationality? It might be justified as a preparation, a method by which the universal end should be reached. But when the end was touched, when the moment for the widening of the hope beyond the borders of Israel to the multitude of the peoples arrived, what was to happen to the State within the lines of which the hope had been hitherto withdrawn? When the seven nations took hold of the skirts of the Jew, saying, 'Tell us! for God is with you'—were they bound also to accept from the Jew the one and only form of society which God could recognize? Could they only pass in within the favoured sanctuary at the cost of abandoning all that made them national? Must they adopt a law of meats and drinks, and household arrangements, and civic regulations, which, however wise and kind and fair, was not theirs, nor could ever be the natural expression of their varied experiences and characters? Is there only one way of holding property which God can sanction, and only one rule for buying and selling, and only one fashion of government? That was the dilemma which was bound to face the Jew whenever his Messianic promise rose to its larger hope. His triumph would be the ruin of his ancient privileges. As soon as his God was revealed to the nations as the one God of all the earth, He must cease to show Himself under tribal limitations, through a special and local social law. That was the challenge that thundered at the door of the Church of Christ from the first hour in which it laid open the catholicity of that salvation which came to the whole world through the Jews.

It was the first question which they had to determine for themselves under the Holy Ghost, without the visible presence or tangible guidance of Jesus Christ. He had lived as a Jew, under the obligations of Jewish ordinances, which He fulfilled, as coincident with the true service of God. He had left the further problem for them to solve. And, at a tremendous risk, they dared the solution, driven to the one and only conclusion which the full Catholic Faith admitted by the vehement impulse of the great Apostle who made it his mission to assert the complete value of the good news that, in Christ, there could be no national distinctions or separations—no Jew and Greek, no Barbarian and Scythian. Henceforward, the absolute identification of the cause of Christ with any one state-system is an offence against its catholicity. For any such identification would tie it down within the limitations of some particular national development or of some particular moment in the growth of human society.

Church and State are now inevitably separable. Christianity has made them so. It is bound, by its inherent life, by its primary claim to universality, to sit loose to the social conditions amid which it finds itself at work. It must be independent of all, if it is to be free to do its business at all times and in all places.

This is the first position. Christianity starts with the severance of Church and State which it has itself created.

But is that its final word? Has it parted for ever with the human story? Has it divided the secular from the spiritual, and left each free to go its separate way? Has it cut human nature in half, and called the spirit away from its earthly city to a heavenly country? Does it propose to ignore the varieties of human experience, and to abolish the racial distinctions which make men what they are?

To ask these questions is to answer them. If Christianity did any one of these things, it would have falsified itself. For what is it but the news of an Incarnation, of the Spirit entering more fully than ever into the flesh

Church and State

and possessing it; of God's manifestation being here on earth; of God making good all that is human; of the entire unity of the whole man, body, soul, and spirit; of the impossibility of dividing any natural element in man from God?

Christianity is the proclamation of the Divine entry into History; of the Divine submission to the historical conditions of human experience; of the Divine sanction given to the things of time and the affairs of earth, to the body, the home, the city, the nation. A kingdom of God come down here, visibly, audibly, tangibly, evidently, manifested on earth—this is its first and last message.

How, then, are we to reconcile this offer of peace on earth, good will to man, with the severance that it itself has forced between the city of God and the city of men—between Church and State?

We all know. The severance is essential in order that the fusion may be attained. (1) The power to effect the Incarnation enters from without. The resources by which God brings in the new kingdom upon earth spring from beyond earth. Sin has corrupted the ancient founts; and the start must now be made afresh, if the human story is to retrieve itself, if the human development is to be brought out of degradation into victory. The Church of Christ is to be the storehouse of these untainted powers on which man may for ever draw for his own peace. In her are to abide, lodged and secured, the eternal sinless succours which shall be free to all, down all time, throughout all the spaces of history, fresh and pure and sweet, that again and yet again, after all his sinning, man may turn, and take, and recover, and revive. For this end, the Church must be, for ever, separate—a thing apart from all states and systems; indifferent to temporary and accidental collapses; able to shake herself loose from all degradation; plainly asserting, by her very existence, the distant spiritual Home from which she draws all her life. She is nothing if she is not unearthly, heavenly, supernatural. Her promise of peace on earth depends on her pledge that it comes from out of Heaven. The Church is, therefore, separate and elect, an Assembly of the Saints, a Household of God. (2) But, issuing from this vantage-ground, her one office is to retrieve, recover, revive, release the full stature of humanity, which, without her infused vitalities, it cannot attain. All the varieties and distinctions that fill up the measure of human experience find themselves realized in Christ, the integral man. In Him the Jew becomes a Jew, and the Greek a Greek. Christ had gone behind and beyond these racial divisions, only that, issuing thence, He might recreate them into their original significance. Each separate nationality discovers its place, its function, its development, its ripe achievement, in the one Body. Their contrasted types are not overswept and blotted out in the unity of the Spirit; but are fertilized, emphasized, utilized, so that the very contrasts of character serve to explain and enrich each other. The distinct individuality of nations, as of persons, is heightened by being taken up into the manhood of the Son of God. To each nation Christianity, then, enters with the offer that it can and will give the special interpretation of its peculiar type. It will appreciate

Church and State

its congenial institutions. It will lay itself alongside of that social organization by which its characteristic temper has historically found expression. So far as that organization is true to the natural instincts and is the proper product of a peculiar temperament, and of a special experience, and of a distinct environment, so that a nation's heart beats in it, Christianity will sanction it, fuse with it, co-operate with it, help, if it may be, to purge it of elements that disturb and disfigure it. It can afford to do this, because its creed impels it to believe that, only through the varieties of race, carried forward to their highest power, can the manifest richness of the Christ be revealed. The historical mission of the Church is to draw nation after nation into the process of redemption, so that each may contribute its quota to the manifestation.

Here then is the theology that lies behind and determines the relation of Church and State in any given country.

That relationship is bound to bear witness to a double-sided fact.

1. The Church is catholic; and it is therefore separable from the State. It can never consent to sink its self-identity. It can never afford to lose its spiritual and world-wide and age-long independence. It must sit loose to all local accidents, all natural distinctions, all temporal organizations, all evolving conditions of civilization, all forms and fashions of government. It can never identify itself with any nation, as if the nation and the Church were the same body under different aspects. All such language is reactionary. It carries

us back to the Pagan, or at least to the Jewish, ideal. Even in taking up the Old Testament language, which attributes such divine sanctity to social institutions, it has to use it with a difference, remembering that the complete identification of the religion with the State was only to be purchased at the cost of limiting God's Church to one nationality. That was true then. It is not true now.

The Church of Christ must therefore retain her own independent organization, by which she can verify her identity amid every variety of social condition, and can transmit it, unbroken and unhampered, down all the shifting chances of the centuries. She must have her own officers, her own 'plebs,' her own institutions, her own feasts and rites and memorials and ordinances, her own ethical habits and obligations, her own organs of self-government and self-interpretation. ' This is what constitutes her catholicity. Her animating principle, her authoritative life, cannot lie within any national limits. If she admits the nation's mind to be her soul, controlling and directing her from within, fixing her worship, defining her creed, she has surrendered her birthright for a mess of pottage. She may gain the local allegiance, but she has forfeited her prerogative. If she ever takes a form which is English and English only, she has betrayed the central truth of St. Paul's gospel, that in Christ there is no distinction of races.

2. But even as the very Apostle who made it his mission to assert that in Christ there was neither Jew nor Greek, was also the very man who could to the Jew become a Jew, and to the Greek make himself a Greek,

Church and State

so this Church of Christ, secure of its independent origin, has, for the very reason that it starts from behind and beyond all race-divisions, the secret of pliability by which it is free to pass into the heart of every race in turn. Each nation has to receive its special interpretation from the one Gospel; and the Church has the task set it to make that interpretation intelligible in a language that is understood, through forms that are congenial. It must bring the good news into the native scenery of each state, so that it belong to the atmosphere, the colour, the tone of the place. To the English it must make itself English, to the French it must become French, so that, by all means, it win some. It does not propose to cancel national differences, but to embrace and exalt them. And it is here that it still offers to fulfil that ideal of all antique religions with which we started. It recognizes, as they did, that nationality is a sacred thing, which culminates in religious acts of corporate life. A nation cannot terminate abruptly at a secular frontier, within which it can rigidly confine its operations. Human life is far too continuous to permit of any such isolation of one department from another. Body touches spirit ; reason touches faith ; trade touches conscience ; social bonds knit themselves up into the obligations of spiritual brotherhood ; civic fraternity runs up into the Divine Fatherhood. You cannot finally stop anywhere between the lowest and the highest. You may make abstractions which are good enough for limited practical expediencies, between secular and spiritual, between legal and moral, between civil and religious ; but such abstractions are never ultimate. There is a unity which transcends the distinction; and this unity is always making itself felt all down the graded levels on which life has been sorted. Whenever and wherever life at any point becomes intense, there the spiritual shows itself through the secular; there the temporal incident takes on the aspect of eternity. It is this fusion, this mingling of heaven with earth, of the divine with the human, which ancient religions crudely symbolized, in their dread lest any social act should take place without the note of divine sanction upon it. Nervously, feverishly, they pressed in with their scrupulous ritual; so that a man moved about timidly anxious lest he should, in the tiniest detail of household or husbandry, have forfeited the divine companionship. Now we have learned the freedom of children in a Father's house. We are not afraid lest we should have omitted the ceremony which secures the benediction. Yet still our freedom does not, surely, mean that our temporal actions are less deserving of divine notice than we once fancied them, when we were savages. Still we need, at least as much as ever, to walk and talk, and eat and drink, and buy and sell, and sing and play, as in the eye of God. And this, not merely as individuals, but as a people, with a common type of civic life which we and our forefathers before us have together nursed and fed and raised into active growth, and which embodies our instinctive judgements and our native tendencies and our corporate emotions. This nationality of ours is the peculiar contribution that we are to bring to the wholeness of human nature. This is our treasured heritage, to be handed

Church and State

on for better uses. Tears and blood have gone to its making; its joys have been dearly bought: but they are well worth all the cost. As we feel the deep sway of its story, as we mix our own little efforts with its historic movement, as the pulse of a great national hope beats through our blood, we cannot but become aware of the solemn issues that are at work upon us. The common actions of life win dignity and awe. 'The light that never was on sea or land' lays its touch on daily things. Nothing is secular; all is sacred. And religion should appear as the realization of this recognition of the mystery in life. It should not stand apart in spiritual isolation; but should carry out, over the surface of society, in every variety of detail, this blending of two worlds in one. It should be a public and corporate embodiment of the sanctity that underlies all human brotherhood. Not for ourselves alone do we live or die; we are owed already to others; we are agents in the national existence; we count for others' welfare; and they are all concerned with ours. Birth and youth and marriage and sickness and death, these are no solitary experiences of our own; the entire State takes part in them, notes them, provides for them, registers them, secures them about with care and forethought. They have a dignity, a purpose, a seriousness, which, as our own they would never possess. And we require that religion should recognize this their social as well as their individual worth. We require that it should be able to lay a hallowing hand on this public and national significance of our personal experiences. It should be there, in some form that carries with it social and public value.

This is what the universal common-sense of man demanded of its ancient religions. That common-sense would make the same demand still, if it were not hampered by theological perplexities. Our most unhappy divisions have had this disastrous result— that, not only have they splintered into fragments the force with which a united Christianity should have told upon the world, but also they have distracted the normal and natural craving of the spirit in man. That craving, wherever it instinctively asserts itself, looks to find in religion the natural completion of its social acts. It expects it to be present at every point at which the life of the community realizes its own solemnity, its inspiration, its significance, its burden, its sorrow or its joy. There should be forms and methods, traditions and habits, which should be the sacred heritage of the whole body, whenever its heart is stirred by great events, so that its members could draw together under the pressure of a common emotion, to marry, to bury, to crown, to fast, to give thanks, to ratify a decision, to close an old year, to open a new. These religious acts of national remembrance should 'be part of the general scheme of social obligations and ordinances laid upon a citizen, as a matter of course, by his position in the family and in the nation.'

Who can doubt that this must be the natural form of a community's existence? And it is this which is denied us by the present complicated situation. The divisions of Christians have rendered it impossible. The attempt to express it through one Church, which half the Christians in the country had repu-

Church and State

diated and forsworn, involved an obvious injustice: and as against this injustice, the cry for Religious Equality carried the general conscience with it. It was inevitable. No ideal can be asserted in defiance of the conditions which alone can justify its existence. It cannot attain its end, however excellent, by means which outrage equity and strike at the rights of personal conscience. It is no good for the Church of England to persist in acting as if she was the spiritual representative of the nation, if, as a fact, she is not. 'Religious Equality' is a demand which corresponds with the actual facts. And, at this moment, the spiritual expression of the State has to be made, not through the Church of the State; for to do this would be to offend religious equality; but through a curious form of Christianity which has been improvised for the occasion and is called 'Undenominationalism.'

This is the paradox. The State has a Church established as its organ on the spiritual side of life: yet whenever momentous social needs require the State to act on its spiritual side, it is forbidden to use its special organ. It can only appear on its religious side in a form which defies its official religion.

There are, for instance, no social needs more momentous and more near to the spiritual life, than education in all its forms, and marriage. Yet the State may initiate nothing in School, or College, or University, that is not 'undenominational'; and, in marriage, it has flagrantly parted from the Church's principle and tradition.

So again, the State, recognizing, with a firmer hold, the range of its peculiar obligations towards the broken, the weak, the damaged, gathers the multitudes of neglected children into vast Industrial Schools; searches out the blind and the dumb, and undertakes their fathering; raises immense institutions to house the weak-witted and the poor. Hospitals must surely follow soon. Now in all this, it is bound to bring forward its spiritual responsibility. It has of necessity to initiate, for such as these, the religious situation. This is just where you would expect it to take action through its proper and official organization for spiritual progress. Yet this is exactly what it is barred from doing, as things stand. 'Yes! because equitable considerations forbid it to give its national weight to what the nation refuses to support.' Quite true. That is a statement of justice which is unanswerable. Only it still remains true that, under the dismal necessities which justice recognizes, the loss to the national life is tremendous. That life is curtailed of its normal completion. By native instinct, it should find itself passing up, at certain points, through social, economic, moral pressure, into the spiritual domain. It should see its own work fuse with the activities of religion, with the responsibilities of a Church. And anything, however necessary and just, which forbids this intermingling at the points where it should spontaneously occur, leaves the life thwarted and maimed.

This is what we are all becoming miserably aware of. We have been working hard for fifty years under the impulse of religious equality, to discover a way of peace between warring sects: and lo! now that we have entered into our new empire, we find it a solitude and a waste.

Church and State

Every day the blank is felt more acutely. For every day we are learning more and more the vital unity of the human brotherhood: and, with that, comes inevitably the sense of awe, of solemnity, of dignity, which belongs to this deep social communion. Every day we feel the burden of its responsibilities to be heavier, the demands for sacrificial surrender of individual to corporate interests to be more urgent. The will has to nerve itself to a harder task: the passion of love is summoned to a nobler exercise. As the tension sharpens, the cry for the underlying strength of religious sanctions and religious succours grows more intense. The heart of the nation pulses to a more mystic music. Secularism, with its narrowness, its hardness, its rigidities, is dying fast out of the land. The people desire to come together under the breath of a larger inspiration. They would, if they might, clasp hands together and swear the great oath which binds them to live and die in·the might of a companionship which is deep as life and stronger than death. And, while the secular movement is thus straining to touch the spiritual, the same impulse, working in a counter-direction, has drawn the spiritual down towards the secular. Religion, which had once persuaded itself that it sat apart and could live for itself and to itself alone, has felt the stirring of a wider mission. Its heart has been turned to the old weary kindly earth, to 'men with their wives, and women with their babes.' It was to these that it was sent to bring news of good will. It was upon this earth that the kingdom of God was to come. Here and now God was to justify Himself, in visible work done for those who toil and suffer.

The Church of Christ exists to give health and dignity and peace to flesh and blood. There is no form of social or material life which does not cry out for its benediction. It must be found with its healing grace in the very thick of human concerns.

So, as the State feels after a Church which its needs necessitate, the Church opens out towards the State on behalf of which it holds its resources. Everything conspires to draw the two together. Everything works against intensifying their separation. Yet the entire movement is in arrest, because, under existent conditions, it cannot fulfil itself except at the cost of gross injustice. The fusion that is desired is only possible, if it can rest upon a public rational agreement which is spontaneous, natural, traditional, hereditary, free from all suspicion of favouritism, and independent of theological dispute. The moment that the civil State takes sides in a theological discussion, it has travelled outside its sphere and its capacities. This is the modern conclusion: and on this we can never go back. The civil power, the civil sword, shall never again, while we remain what we are, attempt this illegal and impossible task. The State has learned, through many a bitter experience, to keep its fingers out of the fire. In this it is rightly secular. Not that things secular are not sacred: but that the State is an organization which exists for certain definite ends which belong to men's temporal well-being. The judgement, the authority, the experiences which qualify it for this its true purpose, are not those which necessarily endow it with spiritual insight. It will make just such a mess of religious matters, if it attempts to handle them, as

Church and State

would a Church, if it tried its hand at governing a State. Each has gained this much wisdom that neither will try any more to do the other's work. Certainly the Church, if it is capable of learning anything from experience, must have learned the folly of attempting to manipulate human affairs: and correlatively one would imagine that 'Erastianism,' in the old sense, was dead and buried. The civil power will never set itself to the task of defining its own religion.

This is the conviction that rules modern society; and it is this absolute conviction which is bound, when once it understands itself, to rule out of court our friend 'Undenominationalism.' 'Undenominationalism' is, as a phenomenon, so interesting, because it is an expression of the very movement of which we have been speaking. It is the reaction of Nonconformity from the earlier ideal which pronounced for the total separation of the State from Religion. Any contact between the two confused (it was supposed) and corrupted both. Better that the secular should show itself decisively secular, and the spiritual keep itself untainted. But that is the ideal that has somehow ceased to work. And now it has become evident that the functions of State and Church must overlap. So far we are all agreed. But, since we can agree about nothing beyond this, the Nonconformist supposes that the State can, itself, prescribe the grounds on which we might agree. It can take the common and essential elements underlying all Christianity, and adopt them as its own. But this is for the State to undertake the task that, according to all modern conviction, she is bound to decline. She is undertaking to define what are the essential elements underlying our common Christianity. She is entering on a work of extreme theological delicacy: just the work for which an elected board or an educational office is the least fitted in the world. The move is utterly reactionary. It is dead against the modern conception of what are, and of what are not, the functions of civil government. It sweeps the secular State back into the hopeless turmoil of theological controversy, to deliver it from which had been the supreme virtue of all political advance since Locke.

No! The problem set us, the problem which Undenominationalism so naïvely recognizes, can only be solved by exactly the opposite method to Undenominationalism. The problem is that the State's work refuses to isolate itself from religious demands. As the State follows up its proper task it arrives at points where it needs a religion to go on with what it has begun—to undertake for it what it needs for its own civil purposes. But the growth of the modern mind has made it inconceivable that the State should involve itself in theology. Never again will the civil power set about defining or erecting a religion of its own. What, then, is open to it? How can it obtain that which it is bound to require with ever-rising urgency, as fast as it learns to appreciate its larger responsibilities?

There is one way left: and the way is perfectly practicable. It can, while holding itself utterly free from all theological disputes, invoke the aid of the existent and organized religious bodies wherever its own work passes beyond its own area of action. It can lend them civil

Church and State

sanction wherever they are required to do civil work. It can bring all the Denominations into authorized action, so that each can verify, within the sphere of its own adherents, the primal necessity that religion should appear as implicated 'in their social and habitual environment.' It can utilize, for civil purposes, the entire force of existent Denominationalism.

This, at least, the State might accomplish with complete impartiality. It would, by so doing, follow on the lines of human nature, which absolutely refuses to divide itself sharply into secular or religious. It would bear witness to the worth of religion for purposes which are purely civil. It would allow the secular life to be touched by that solemnity, that consecration, which is instinctively essential to it, and without which it is starved of its proper honour and grace and warmth and joy.

But though this impartial use of the religious Denominations would cover a large section of the State's demand, it nevertheless fails it, as an expedient, just where the civic demand intensifies its urgency. For the State, as we have already said, is more and more recognizing that it exists for the sake of the weak rather than of the strong. Its great effort is to close the ranks, to keep the nation compact, to prevent the march from degenerating into a loose straggling disarray, in which those who fall out are ever dragging further to the rear. Its eyes are set upon the broken and the disordered, who cannot keep the pace. How are they to be held together, to be kept up to the mark? Outcast children, robbed of their birthright by their parents' helplessness—how are they to be redeemed from the damage? And how are the infirm, the diseased, the deranged to be saved from ruining themselves, or disorganizing the market through their inadequacy to respond to its conditions? The State provides for these contingencies. Here is its peculiar responsibility. And these melancholy multitudes, more especially put in its charge, are exactly those for whom a religious environment is most needed; and yet they are precisely those who do not know their own need, and can claim the good offices of no particular religious organization. What can the State do here but, out of its own initiative, call in the aid of some such organization? It wants to possess the acknowledged right to do this; so that there be no doubt about it, no hideous squabbling, no suspicion, no dodging.

Besides these cases there are, again, the great moments when a nation's heart is stirred by some emotion that is bound to take a religious form. Is it the marriage of a king? Is it the burial of a statesman? Is it an agony of war? Is it a thanksgiving for a hard-won peace? It may be necessary for us, through our wretched divisions, to scatter, at such hours, to our separate dens, and each do what is right in his own eyes. But what a pitiful loss! What an irony! The greatness of the emotion lies in its power to draw men together, to make all hearts beat as one, to cancel all sense of separation. And we use it only as an occasion on which to emphasize our separations, and to distribute ourselves into compartments. Under such treatment the spiritual force of the opportunity evaporates.

We need some form to which the vast majority can afford to rally—some historical body to which the State

Church and State

can appeal to give its national feeling some sort of national expression.

Old thoughts, these; old pleas. Yes! But they were once only associated with old lost causes, with impossible ideals, with fossilized Toryism, with mediaeval ecclesiasticism, with high and dry Anglicanism. Their present significance lies in this—that they are coming back to us from the opposite quarter. Democracy, as it ceases to be merely a section of the working community, and becomes the spirit of the entire body, exhibits its natural craving to emphasize the national unity, to emphasize the deeper issues of national life, to emphasize the spiritual solemnity of the national task. But its upward movement must find itself uncomfortably arrested, if, just when it most desires to embody this higher unity, it is thwarted by a mob of battling sects, with whose theological differences it has not the slightest concern. It will either sink back in sheer disgust into the secularism from which it seemed to be making good its escape, or it must discover some one organization that can satisfy its aspirations.

For this national need there is only one such organization conceivable. If it cannot do it, nothing can. And if nothing can, the democratic movement sours down into an angry and ugly failure to achieve its own proper intention. It will be conscious of having missed its aim, and it will bitterly resent it; it will express that resentment in a fierce recoil from all religion whatever. That is the immediate situation.

The nation is growing ever more sensitive of the place that religion ought to take in its civil life. It is intensely opposed to the Erastianism which would make a religion of its own. It looks for a Church that could be called in to do for it what it wants done, but what it cannot do for itself. Such a situation reduces the entire problem to one question—Can the Church of England fulfil the part required? And as the question is simple, so the answer reduces itself to the simplest possible terms. Only if she can reform herself.

Church reform has, hitherto, been hardly worth considering, because it involved, as things stood, unmitigated Erastianism. Parliament was bound to come in, and Parliament would insist on manipulating the reforms itself: and this would mean the disruption of the Church there and then. The Church would not ever obtain any scrap of reform from the Lords, and she would rather die than accept the type of reform which the Commons would inflict upon her. Church reform was, therefore, inconceivable, except through the way of Disestablishment. And that was the preliminary stage, which, therefore, postponed reform until it had been first faced.

But now the tendencies work against Disestablishment, and are likely to work more and more against it. And, again, now for the first time, the State seems prepared to abandon the Erastianism which blocked the way. It is inclined to say, 'We will never again attempt to handle theological matters in Parliament. The House of Commons is the very last body in the world that should attempt to exercise spiritual authority. It is wholly unqualified, by the conditions essential to its representative and democratic character, for any claim whatever to embody the mind of the laity of the Church. It is practically incapable of arriving at any ecclesi-

Church and State

astical decision; and it is positively determined to make the introduction of theological questions impossible. All this has become inevitable by the necessities of political development. But we sorely want a religious organization which can do something to embody and to hallow the national responsibilities. Cannot this Church, which alone offers any prospect of this, do something to make itself adequate, effective? It is clogged by abuses, by clumsy absurdities, by legal scandals. You all know them; you all confess them. Why cannot you give them a clean sweep? We will no longer obstruct you; we will allow you free play to put yourselves in the best possible condition. Widen your area of action; broaden your methods; cast out your rubbish; free your agencies; trust your own capacities; liberate your laity; have faith in your own suffrage; prove your spiritual fitness for the task that you alone can fulfil. If only you can make it evident that you are national in fact as well as in theory, that is all we desire.'

Are we not drawing nearer to the day when the nation might so appeal to us? Such an appeal would allow to the Church its own right to its own existence. It has an organization of its own which can never be merely national: for it is catholic; it is universal; it links it to all times and all peoples. This organization is inherent to it; it is its own vital and supreme necessity. The State need not touch it. It only asks of it to prove, by solid facts, that it can adapt itself to national needs.

That is the appeal. It is an appeal that is absolutely justifiable. Can we meet it?

V

SELF-GOVERNMENT OF THE CHURCH

By the Hon. and Rev. Arthur Lyttelton

THE various topics which are summed up in the term church reform centre in that which is the subject of this paper. Unless the Church has a certain freedom to legislate for herself, there can be no satisfactory church reform. It is true that during the two centuries in which the Church of England has been practically devoid of the power of self-government, many ecclesiastical measures have been passed, some, if not most, of which may legitimately be called reforms. But it is impossible that churchmen should be satisfied with such a method of government as this. In the first place, though some of the church legislation since 1700 has been good and beneficial, some of it has not, while other measures equally or even more desirable for the efficiency of the Church have been repeatedly demanded in vain. The Church has had a good deal of legislation that she did not want, and has failed to obtain much that she does want. And though the positive side of this grievance has undoubtedly diminished of late years, the negative side has become more and more accentuated. It is poor comfort to be told that at all events Parliament has left off injuring us, when we complain that it will not reform us. Nor is it likely that a purely external and unrepresentative system of government can ever produce satisfactory church legislation. Parliament, when it deals with church affairs, is compelled to proceed in the dark. There is no method of ascertaining the real wishes of the majority of churchmen, no certainty that Parliament does not represent the minority, or even that its action will not be dictated by those hostile or external to the Church. The spasmodic, ill-considered, partial legislation of this century is a standing proof of the incompetence of Parliament, under the present constitution, to deal satisfactorily with the affairs of the Church. But, in the second place, even assuming that parliamentary government of the Church was in detail all that could be desired, that it responded to all the particular needs of the Church without delay and without defect, still, from a more general point of view, it would be hopelessly inadequate. For the Church, as for the individual, a certain degree of freedom is essential to true life. To be governed from outside cannot satisfy the corporate aspirations of the Church. We are becoming more and more alive to the truth that the Church is more than an aggregate of individuals, of parishes, even of dioceses, that she has a corporate existence and great corporate responsibilities, for the fulfilment of which she must be endowed with a certain degree of corporate freedom. Her life is incomplete, checked, so to speak, in its outflow, so long as her growing consciousness of her own aims and destiny cannot translate itself into action. We claim that the power of self-government is essential to the life of the Church, and that, from this point of view, what Parliament does or does not do is immaterial, unless Parliament can be regarded as the Church's organ and as empowered to express, not merely accidentally, but necessarily, the will of the majority of churchmen.

That this is not the case at present, whatever it may have been in the past, needs very little proof. Every one knows that, by the gradual removal of constitutional restrictions, Parliament, which was formerly composed of churchmen alone, can and does now include men of any and of no religious belief and denomination. The point is too obvious to need further labouring, but it has less frequently been noticed that, besides what may be called its unfitness owing to individual constitution, the representative character of Parliament would seem to disqualify it from acting as the organ of the Church of England. Two hundred years ago Parliament was a purely English assembly, and as such might fairly be considered to represent the national Church of England. Now it is the legislative assembly for three kingdoms, of which one has no national established church at all, and another an establishment wholly separate from the Church of England, and differing from it in many important, indeed vital, respects. Whatever the *personnel* of the English section of Parliament might be, the fact that it has to deal with Scotch and Irish affairs, and that Scotch and Irish members have the right of voting on English measures, unfits it for governing a Church with which Scotland and Ireland, constitutionally speaking, have nothing to do. There seems to be very little logic

Self-government of the Church

or principle in the system by which local affairs are separated from imperial affairs, and it is easy to point to cases in which the time of Parliament is taken up with matters apparently affecting only one kingdom or even one locality; but there is at least sufficient precedent to allow politicians to admit that the time has come for giving to the Church of England a power of self-government similar to that already possessed by local municipalities and by some of the great departments of the State.

When this claim is put forward, under all the various objections that are made to it there may be discerned, though it is not always expressed or even realized, the feeling that the Church is incapable of self-government, not because she is a religious body—the facts are too strong for such an assertion—or because she is established, though that is often confusedly argued, but because she is a purely clerical body. Parliament retains its grasp of church affairs, because after all there is no other body competent to deal with them. Whatever you may say about the unfitness of Parliament, it is the only lay assembly of the Church of England, and it is quite certain that the country is not going to entrust the management of the Church to any body or bodies in which laymen are not largely, or indeed overwhelmingly, represented. Now, no clear-sighted person can doubt that if we are to establish our claim to self-government, or even to bring it into the arena of serious discussion, we must be prepared to recognize and to deal with this feeling. However far Parliament may now have travelled from its original position and constitution, it possesses still the memory of its past history when, for good or ill, it was the lay house of the Church of England. Its ecclesiastical functions were none the less real because they were then exercised in constitutional co-ordination with the provincial synods of the clergy; they are none the less constitutional now, although the authority of those synods has been unconstitutionally absorbed into them. Unless it is shown that the ecclesiastical jurisdiction of Parliament can be transferred, in whole or in part, to a body representative of the whole Church, in which both the lay and the clerical element shall have its due share, we may take it as certain that the country will not listen to any scheme of self-government. In other words, before designing any plan for freedom of legislation, we must be ready to give to the laity of the Church their share in governing it.

In dealing with this indispensable preliminary to our main subject, I must be allowed to assume the results of the historical and canonical discussions which will be found elsewhere in this volume. That is to say I assume that there is nothing in the doctrine or the history of the Church which forbids the laity to take part in the management of ecclesiastical affairs. In the words of the Bishop of Durham[1] 'the organization at which we aim corresponds with precedents in the New Testament and in the early Church, and is involved in the essential idea of Christianity,' and 'the judgement of the whole Church, clergy and laity together, has been effective in the past.' The fuller discussion of this, from the

[1] Address to Durham Dioc. Conf., Oct. 20, 1897. Church Ref. League Paper, No. 10, p. 3.

historical point of view, will be found elsewhere; I do not attempt to touch it. But whatever the historical or doctrinal justification for the proposal may be, the circumstances of the present make its practical accomplishment less simple than may appear at first sight. We are to admit the laity to a share in the government of the Church. Yes, but who are the laity? and what is to be their share in church matters? These are the two questions which must be answered before any practical solution of the problem of self-government can be found. In venturing to suggest answers to them I do not claim to speak for any one but myself, and I am too conscious of the difficulties surrounding them not to be very ready to give way to the declared opinion of the majority of churchmen on the subject.

Who are the laity? It is clear that the very demand that we are making for self-government sets aside the old answer—still given by some churchmen—that all citizens of the State are members of the national Church, and therefore must share whatever privileges are conferred upon the laity. If this were allowed, *cadit quaestio;* Parliament would be fully competent to deal with the Church, as with other national institutions. That self-government is claimed means that the Church is not conterminous with the nation, and it therefore becomes necessary to lay down some principle, some definition, by which the body to be governed and the persons who are to govern it shall be distinguished from the nation. At the very least, baptism, and not merely the assumption but the proof of baptism, must be required of all who desire to be reckoned as churchmen and to exercise the privileges of churchmen. It can hardly be necessary to spend time in discussing this. The distinction between the baptized and the unbaptized has always been recognized as vital from the religious point of view, while, as a practical matter, it seems absurd to entrust any Christian privileges or duties to those who have given no assurance, even vicariously, that they know or wish to know anything about Christianity. So far there will be, if not absolute unanimity, at least an overwhelming *consensus* among churchmen and, I take it, among all thoughtful practical persons. There will be less agreement as we advance; nevertheless, it seems to me clear that, under the present conditions, comparatively little would be gained were we to rest satisfied with the definition of a layman as a baptized person. There is needed some evidence, however slight, of personal participation in church life and church responsibilities, of personal interest in the objects and methods of the Church, of personal acquaintance with the truths which she teaches. Such evidence is afforded by confirmation. There are several subordinate reasons for requiring proof of confirmation from all who desire to be reckoned as lay churchmen. In the first place, confirmation has always been regarded in theory, and among those of the Orthodox Church in practice, as the necessary complement of baptism, which is held to be incomplete without it. In the next place, it is a condition which, though easily fulfilled by bona fide and duly qualified persons, can be equally easily and justifiably withheld from any who are suspected of desiring it from wrong motives. Baptism, as usually

Self-government of the Church

administered, affords no opportunity for testing the motives of those who are baptized, but the universal practice of preparation for confirmation, with the instruction and questioning which are recognized as essential to it, provides an obvious machinery for preventing the abuse of the ordinance for the sake of a merely political object. Then again, in comparison with some other conditions which have been proposed, confirmation can be easily and indisputably proved, with little or nothing of the invidiousness or the inquisitorial character which is sometimes resented in inquiries as to religious status or profession. No one can reasonably object to producing a certificate either of baptism or of confirmation, and there can be no dispute as to the fulfilment of a condition which consists in a single well-defined act. For these subordinate reasons confirmation would seem to be marked out as a natural and effective test of church membership; but the main consideration which I would urge is that, unlike baptism, it represents the personal act by which the full responsibilities of the Christian life are undertaken, and the full privileges claimed. Apart from the instrumental force which the Church ascribes to the laying on of hands in confirmation, great, indeed almost undue importance is attached by the Prayer Book and in the common teaching of our Church to the part taken by the confirmed person, who is evidently regarded as then and thereby entering, by his own definite act and choice, upon the full Christian life. Every one who has been confirmed, at least as the rite is now administered, has publicly and definitely declared himself a member of the Church, has been instructed and examined in the necessary rudiments of the Church's faith, and is entitled to receive the complete privileges of a churchman. Here, then, we have a test which is open to none of the objections usually urged against religious tests, and which more or less adequately fulfils the purpose in view.

The laity would thus consist of baptized and confirmed persons. Is any further requirement to be made of those who wish to share in the government of the Church? We are here of course confronted with the very difficult question of the communicant qualification, a question on which the arguments on each side seem to me almost exactly balanced. It should be kept in mind that we are not now considering who shall be the representatives, but the represented, the voters. Is the church franchise to be limited to communicants, or are we to be content with the less stringent qualifications which I have discussed? The really important arguments can, I think, be reduced to one on each side. For the limitation it is urged, with unquestionable force, that according to the true conception of the Church, only those can be reckoned as active members who exercise their church privileges and receive the needful grace promised to them in the mode ordained by our Blessed Lord. Others, so to speak, voluntarily hold their privileges in abeyance, and until they take them up, cannot be considered as entitled to act with the true members who are not only potentially but actually in communion with the Church. To allow them to share, even indirectly, in the government of the Church would be to lower the conception of the Church, and to intensify

Self-government of the Church 135

the evils from which we are at present suffering. Those evils spring, it is urged, from the undue laxity with which the idea of the Church has been interpreted, and from the attempt to include as many as possible within it. We now need concentration rather than extension, to define and limit rather than to include. A measure of self-government, based on an inadequate definition of church membership, will be directly opposed to the only sound policy, the policy of concentration, and will therefore be injurious to the true interests of the Church. There can be no question that this argument, founded as it is on the primitive and catholic conception of the Church as a body whose life and unity are derived from its Head through the sacraments, has very great weight, and leads many who are the reverse of narrow in their sympathies to hesitate before entrusting any active share in church government to non-communicants. On the other hand, the recollection of past abuses supplies an equally powerful argument against any employment whatsoever of the Holy Communion as a test or qualification even of an ecclesiastical kind. The odious mockery of the 'sacramental test,' lasting as it did almost into our own generation, has bequeathed to us an unconquerable dislike of any similar method of defining church membership, however safeguarded. If to admit non-communicants to a share in church government would be a degradation of the true idea of the Church, to use the Holy Communion as part of the machinery of registration would be equally to degrade the sacrament and through the sacrament the Church herself.

Between these two opposing considerations I must confess the choice seems to me extremely difficult. Each alternative has its special disadvantage. It may even be argued that the whole proposal for lay representation is thus condemned; it is better to remain as we are than to incur these fresh risks. But one of them, at least, is not fresh. Without any definite system of lay government most of us do, as a matter of fact, entertain that lax conception of the Church which results from ignoring the close relation between the Holy Communion and true church membership. At the present moment the average churchgoer would stare if he were told that because he is not a communicant he is not a member of the Church, and his easygoing complacency would be very little increased if, in addition to the existing privileges of a churchman, he were to acquire the right of voting for a representative in the lay house. We should, in fact, be no worse off than we are now, though it may readily be admitted that we ought to aim at being better, at raising rather than acquiescing in the low conception of the Church which at present obtains among us. Still we should be no worse off, whereas if the other alternative were adopted it seems clear that a very serious risk would be incurred, not indeed of an altogether fresh kind, but one from which we have, though with some difficulty, managed to shake ourselves free. On the whole then it seems advisable not to adopt the communicants' qualification for the lay franchise, but to rest content with a careful enforcement of baptism and confirmation, with perhaps the additional safeguard of a written declaration of membership. From those, however, who aspire to hold any office, even if it be only that of a representative on the parish or diocesan council, it should be required that they must be communicants. By some such compromise as this it seems that the problem, the difficulties of which I hope I have not ignored, can best be solved [1].

There remains the question, on what subjects is the Church to be free to legislate? It may be taken as certain that the State will not part with the whole of its control over ecclesiastical matters. In theory, indeed, nothing can be removed from the authority of Parliament, which will thus retain its power to deal with the Church as with all other bodies in the realm. We may assume, however, that this general and inherent authority will not, unless in very exceptional crises, be exercised by Parliament. The great council of the nation will, indeed, probably be glad to be rid of the troublesome ecclesiastical business which still occasionally occupies its time. But, apart from the constitutional supremacy of the State 'over all persons and causes within its dominions,' it is not to be supposed that it will give an unlimited power to any body representative of the Church to deal with ecclesiastical matters. In one way or another, either by positive or by negative definition, there will be some limit set to the authority of the Church, and the question that has to be faced is, what restrictions ought we as churchmen to be willing to accept, and what, on the other hand, are to be regarded

---

[1] It is perhaps advisable to make it clear that, in all that is said in this essay as to the definition and the functions of the laity, the term 'laity' is intended to include women.

as encroachments on the just freedom of the Church? There are conceivable reservations and limitations which might make the whole concession of self-government valueless. This does not, however, apply to one large and important class of subjects over which the Church must be prepared to resign any legislative control. Questions affecting property are naturally and rightly within the special jurisdiction of the State, and as even the seceders from the established Church of Scotland were willing to submit all such matters to the control of Parliament and the civil courts [1], the Church of England can hardly claim to reserve them for the decision of her own legislative body. Under questions of property we must further expect to see patronage placed. Rights of presentation which, legally speaking, are real property, cannot be taken away, or even limited, by any authority short of that of Parliament. This is of course a wide and far-reaching exception, and it may be said that if such matters as those dealt with by the patronage clauses of the Benefices Bill of 1896 are to be removed from the jurisdiction of the Church, the right of self-government will be little more than illusory. It is true that patronage is a matter very closely connected with the efficiency of the Church, and one on which most churchmen feel deeply. We should all like to deal with the system of patronage if we could. But it is one of the conditions, not of establishment only, but of any ancient institution which is closely connected with questions of property, that in regard to those questions it is necessarily more or less bound up with the State, and must submit to

[1] See Hanna's *Life of Dr. Chalmers*, vol. iv. pp. 18, 95, 145.

Self-government of the Church 139

State interference. The Church, therefore, cannot reserve to herself the right of dealing with patronage, but it is not true to say that her freedom would in consequence be only illusory. The chief reason at present why Parliament cannot settle the patronage question satisfactorily is that it is impossible to ascertain what the great body of churchmen really desire, and this difficulty would be removed were there a truly representative church body able to vote upon questions submitted to it, even though the final decision were not in its hands. The assemblies that now profess to speak for the Church are not really representative, and further are almost entirely without the sense of responsibility that comes from the possession of practical power. A church council, exercising legislative authority on most ecclesiastical subjects, would be able to convey its opinion to Parliament on the few reserved questions in a way which, in nine cases out of ten, would ensure the acquiescence of the legislature. Freedom of action in certain matters would give great weight to opinion on others.

It would thus be in practice less hampering to the Church than appears at first sight were all questions of property and patronage reserved for parliamentary legislation, and on all other matters the Church might fairly claim to exercise her own judgement and to carry out her own declared will. It is well to anticipate the opposition which is certain to arise as soon as the scope of this proposal is realized, by specifying certain classes of questions which would thus come within the jurisdiction of the representative church body, subject only to the veto of Parliament. Nothing will be gained by leaving it, even for a short time, vague and ill-defined. I submit, therefore, that the Church ought to claim for herself such subjects as the revision of the Prayer Book and of other authorized formularies, the conditions of clerical work and the terms under which clergy are to retire, the subdivision of parishes—except in so far as rights of property, i.e. of patronage, are thereby affected—and the creation of new bishoprics. It is not of course asserted that legislation on all, or indeed on any, of these matters is immediately required. All that is claimed is that the Church, through her representative body or bodies, should be free to legislate upon them when occasion arises.

So far as regards questions reserved by the State; it is also necessary to consider whether some reservation and limitation should not be made within the church body itself. The only real question here is as to the competence of the laity to discuss and pronounce upon matters of doctrine. It appears that among the churches in communion with our own, there is some diversity of practice in this; but in some, at least, absolute equality obtains between the different orders with regard to the discussion and the initiation of changes bearing on doctrine. It is also a principle of church government, recognized from the earliest times, that definitions of doctrine, though drawn up and passed by assemblies of bishops, yet become catholic dogmas by the acceptance, gradually and informally given, of the whole Church, in which of course the faithful laity are included. In the words of an important declaration of thirty-one Greek bishops in 1850, 'the unvarying constancy and

Self-government of the Church

unerring truth of Christian dogma does not depend upon any hierarchical order; it is guarded by the totality, by the whole *people* of the Church which is the Body of Christ[1].' Now the position here assumed differs to some extent from that taken by those churches which have given to the laity equal rights in respect of doctrine with the clergy. The difference will be best indicated by reference to the well-known words of Cyprian, 'I have determined to do nothing without your counsel and without the consent of the laity, on my own private opinion.' There is here implied a distinct difference of function; the bishop must initiate, propose, set on foot; the priests and deacons are to discuss and advise; the laity to accept or reject. Thus they can truly be said to 'guard' the doctrine of the Church, even though their function is strictly limited and differentiated from that of the other orders. I do not believe that in practice, if we may judge from the experience of other churches, it would be found dangerous to give to the laity co-ordinate rights in all respects with those of the clergy. It is said that in doctrine, as in other matters, the laity are the conservative element. If there is any danger, it becomes practically nil when each order votes separately, and the consent of each is necessary before any change can be introduced. It may further be urged that it is difficult, if not impossible, to draw the line between doctrine and other ecclesiastical questions; to define, for instance, the respective provinces of doctrine and ceremonial; and that to give the laity a voice in the one and to silence them on the other, would be to breed

[1] Quoted by Bp. Westcott, l. c., p. 7.

endless confusion and perplexity. If, however, it should seem better to follow ancient precedent, the words of Cyprian and the recognized custom of the Church point to the just compromise, by which the laity would have the right of assent or dissent, but not of initiation, in respect to all matters of doctrine. At the same time it should be pointed out that a strict adherence to catholic precedent would equally deprive priests and deacons of anything but a consultative part in such questions, and would entrust the final decision and sole responsibility to the episcopate alone. But whatever the ultimate solution may be, it seems clear that there must be some definition of the functions of each order, unless each is to have equal powers with the others; and if there is such a definition, it must deal with doctrine, either removing it altogether from the authority of the laity, or, and in my opinion preferably, giving to the laity the right to accept or reject doctrinal changes otherwise initiated.

The due definition of the laity, and of their functions in regard to ecclesiastical matters, supplies us at once with what may be called the requisite material for the body or bodies which, according to the scheme we are considering, will constitute the legislature of the Church. It only remains to consider the method of legislation, and the relation between the legislature of the Church and that of the State. The question is often discussed as if it only related to the convocations or to a general assembly of the whole Church. But though the constitution and methods of subordinate bodies lie outside the subject of this paper, the self-government of the

Church cannot be usefully discussed without an explicit statement that in some degree or other the diocese as well as the province, the parish as well as the diocese, must take part in it. No scheme of church legislation or of lay representation can be effective that ignores the foundation of church life, the true unit of church force. That unit is the parish. Without parish councils, duly constituted and recognized, and entrusted within defined limits with statutory powers of control over parochial church affairs, the most elaborate and well-ordered scheme of representative government will fail for want of motive force, of that interest in church questions among the laity which is only to be obtained by entrusting them with real power and responsibility in those parish matters which come home 'to their business and their bosoms.' The State, for one thing, will only consent to entrust a certain measure of legislative freedom to the Church if the body which is to legislate is truly representative; and it will be no more representative than the existing lay houses or diocesan conferences unless the interest of churchmen in the parishes is aroused. At present, hardly one churchman in ten knows that there are lay houses at all, and the consequence is that they are only nominally representative. But once constitute parish councils and every churchman in the country would know of their existence, and lay houses elected by the parish councils—after the fashion of the established Church of Scotland—would really represent the great mass of the Church. It is not my business at present to consider further the constitution of the parish councils or their relation to the diocesan and to the provincial councils, but it may be assumed that some relation there must be, and the more direct the better. Nor have I to deal with the reform of convocation in the narrower sense of the word, that is with the constitution of the clerical houses of the church legislature. Here again it may be taken for granted that convocation must be made really representative of the whole body of the clergy, and not of the beneficed clergy alone. To convocations reformed in this way, and associated with legally constituted representative houses of laymen, it is proposed to entrust a certain measure of legislative freedom in church matters, limited as we have already seen, and subject to the veto of Parliament.

With regard to the method of legislation there seems to be little practical difficulty. The principle of devolution is already at work in so many departments of the national life that it might readily enough be applied to the Church. Bills discussed and passed in the three houses of the church legislature—for the final stages of which process the representatives of both provinces would probably be empowered to sit together in a national synod—would be laid upon the table of both Houses of Parliament, and would be presented for the Royal assent after a certain period unless in the meantime an address were voted calling on the Sovereign to withhold that assent. In short the proposal is that the system now applied to the schemes of the Charity Commissioners and other bodies should be applied to measures passed by the church representative assembly. In this way both the requisite freedom of legislation and the

Self-government of the Church

veto of Parliament would be secured in a recognized and constitutional manner.

Against the proposal for ecclesiastical self-government thus sketched there are certain obvious objections which may be referred to in conclusion. First, of course, stands the well-worn argument that self-government is impossible in an established Church, and that we must be content to have our laws made by Parliament so long as we enjoy the benefits of our connexion with the State. It is, however, enough to point to Scotland in order to show that the principle of establishment is not *per se* inconsistent with a very considerable measure of self-government. For nearly three centuries the presbyterian Church of Scotland, although established, has enjoyed a greater freedom than we are claiming for the Church of England. If an established Church can be free in Scotland, why not in England? The argument in fact is thoroughly insular, not to say provincial, and is possible only when it starts from, and assumes, the most complete ignorance of other conditions than our own. It may, however, be urged that though in itself establishment is not inconsistent with self-government yet the conditions of establishment in England make self-government impossible here. But what are the conditions of establishment in England? Leaving aside a few lesser matters, which do not affect our present subject, such as the presence of the bishops in the House of Lords, the conditions of establishment seem to be twofold. In the first place, the endowments of the Church have been recognized, sanctioned, and protected by the State from very early times. For the sake of argument it might be conceded that in regard to one kind of endowment, the tithes, the State has gone further and actually granted them to the Church. But even if this be admitted, why should it place the Church of England in a more fettered condition than the Church of Scotland, or many other Churches? They also have endowments recognized, sanctioned, protected, and in many cases directly granted by the State; yet they are free to manage their own affairs. It is impossible to prove that the process by which the English Church has been endowed gives the State a greater right to control her than is the case with the Church of Scotland, to say nothing of the Church in France and other continental countries; I believe it would not be difficult to prove the direct contrary. So far then as endowment goes, the opponents of self-government have no logical ground on which to resist our claim. Will they oppose it on the ground of the system of patronage, which is the other main condition of establishment in England? Now whatever may fairly be urged against the system by which the State appoints to all the chief offices in the Church, it cannot be said to make the Church dangerously independent. On the contrary, it gives the State a most powerful means of control over the Church, not less, if not more powerful than the legislative control of Parliament, and therefore it makes the gift of self-government far less objectionable, from the State point of view, than it would otherwise be. Apart from the immense indirect influence in church matters which the crown patronage gives to the State, an influence extending into every department of church life, it would afford

Self-government of the Church

a direct means of controlling ecclesiastical legislation, in that every member of one of the three legislative houses would be a nominee of the Crown. So long as the bishops, who, under the proposed scheme, would have a veto on legislation, are virtually, if not nominally, appointed by the State, it is absurd to anticipate any danger to the State from whatever measure of self-government may be conceded to the Church. It is quite possible for churchmen to consider the system of crown patronage an intolerable bondage ; it is not possible for politicians to make it a fair ground for refusing any freedom in other directions.

From the point of view of the State, then, the scheme of self-government, guarded and limited as has been suggested, has nothing dangerous in it; but there are other objections which proceed from churchmen. It is said that the only obstacle in the way of church legislation in Parliament is that churchmen cannot agree on what they are to demand from Parliament; once agreed, they would have no difficulty in obtaining the measures they want. And it is argued that the same incapacity would prevent any practical legislation in a church council. I have already in passing indicated the answer to this objection. The difficulty arises from the want of that very representative system which we propose to institute. The Church has no means of ascertaining her own mind, and consequently she has no means of effectively formulating her demands. Her representative bodies do not represent, and even if they did their lack of practical power would make their conclusions almost inoperative. But a Church which, by a chain of representative bodies extending from the parish to the province and the national synod, could collect the opinions of her members, and could give them practical effect, would be in a very different position, and the difference would lie precisely in that point which at present constitutes the obstacle to legislation. It is not of course to be expected, or indeed hoped, that any representative system will make a vast body of men unanimous, but the experience of Englishmen for centuries, an experience reaching into every corner of the national life, has shown us that the principle of representation is all-powerful in inducing the minority, after full and frank discussion, to acquiesce in the opinion of the majority, and there is absolutely no reason to suppose that these ecclesiastical assemblies will fail where all other English assemblies have succeeded.

It is this consideration which supplies an answer to the last, and perhaps the most formidable objection that has to be considered. Your scheme is all very well, it it is said, on paper, but practically it will be shattered by the party differences which are the bane of our Church. It will not work, and the attempt to work it will break up the Church itself. The first majority vote on a party question will precipitate a schism. I am by no means blind to the danger thus described, which is a very real one; so real, indeed, that but for my conviction that continued legislative impotence means eventual lifelessness, and that lifelessness is the worst of all dangers for a Church, I should hesitate before supporting a scheme which must bring the various parties in the Church into practical, and not merely

Self-government of the Church

controversial, opposition to each other. But real though the danger is, I believe the responsibilities of self-government would do more than anything else to avert it. So long as men have no practical power over their own concerns they will wrangle; the hostilities of a debating club are far more uncompromising than those of Parliament, for there is no need to bring them to a conclusion. Once entrust a body of men with the power of translating their opinions into action, and they will find some means of coming to a decision. It may be by the simple process of the submission of the minority to the expressed wish of the majority, or it may be by the favourite English method of compromise; in one way or another a practical way out of the partisan deadlock will be found. And in the process I am sanguine enough to hope that much of the bitterness of party spirit, which arises in great measure from want of intercourse, will be allayed. Men engaged in a common work, and discussing every detail of it in common, seldom fail to be brought nearer together than they were, even in opinion. At all events the risk is worth incurring for the sake of that for which alone this scheme of self-government is proposed, and which all alike hold dear, the life and work of our Mother Church.

VI

LEGAL AND PARLIAMENTARY POSSIBILITIES

By the Hon. Mr. Justice Phillimore

I ASSUME that the other essays in this volume have sufficiently shown the need for certain reforms in church administration. My task is to show how these reforms could be effected.

'Act of Parliament,' says some one. 'You can do anything by Act of Parliament': and so in a sense you can.

But here there are three objections:—

(1) You do not want the Church to be driven back upon any secular body, however venerable, for her title. It is true that we are mainly dealing with matters of administration, of the adaptation of worldly means and instruments to spiritual ends, and we are not trenching upon the great commission which the Head of the Church gave to His Apostles and to their successors.

But still it is sometimes difficult to disentangle the lines of the complicated skein of an established church, and trace each to its true source.

Moreover, you do not want the enemy to blaspheme,

Legal and Parliamentary Possibilities 151

and the lukewarm believer to suppose that religion is after all a mere matter of State, of governmental regulation and state policy, to look at the Church and defend it as the statesmen of Louis XIV and the bishops of the first Georges did in France and England in the early part of the eighteenth century, with the disastrous results which accrued in the latter part.

(2) Parliament is unfitted. It contains indeed in its Upper House most of the bishops and in its other House many devout laymen; but of the order of priesthood none.

In 1553 the House of Commons resolved: 'That any person having a voice in the Convocation House cannot be a member of this House [1]'; and ultimately the matter was carried further, till Blackstone speaking of the qualification of persons to be elected members, says that 'they must not be of the clergy for they sit in the Convocation [2].'

But, if Convocation is not to be the legislature or at least part of the legislature to decide these questions, the resolution of the House of Commons is a mockery.

Moreover, a large number of members of both Houses do not belong to the Church, but to different and sometimes hostile religious bodies. These members if not actually opponents of church reform are, as experience has shown, often critical to the extent of being captious, act without serious sense of responsibility, and what is

---

[1] Commons Journals, Oct. 13, 1553. Phillimore's *Ecclesiastical Law*, p. 1537.

[2] *Commentaries*, vol. i, p. 175; Phillimore, ibid. p. 480. See the Act for Horne Tooke in 1801, 41 Geo. III, c. 63, excluding even deacons.

for our purpose as important, resent the introduction of church matters as taking up the time of Parliament, and so delay, postpone, or obstruct them. Worse still, they may be induced to combine with imperfectly educated church people to legislate in a wrong direction, and pervert useful measures brought before them into positive mischief.

(3) Lastly, Parliament has not the time. It is a commonly admitted fact that the House of Commons is overburdened by the multitude of its ever increasing business. It has perhaps not been so clearly noticed, but it is nevertheless an important fact that the delay occasioned by the multiplicity of business is itself multiplied by the number of the doers of the business, and that the very circumstance that in these days every member of the House of Commons is expected by his constituents to be active and attentive, enormously increases the difficulty of getting business done.

It may be going too far to say that each of the 670 members has to give his separate opinion; but at any rate the number of the contributors of suggestions and criticisms is now very large, and the necessary obstruction almost incalculable.

In these circumstances anything that encourages *legislation by devolution* must be welcomed.

On these grounds, therefore, I should assume *a priori* that church reform cannot be satisfactorily carried out by Parliament: and the experience of Her Majesty's reign confirms it.

The Church Discipline Act of 1840[1] was so crudely

[1] 3 & 4 Vict. c. 86.

Legal and Parliamentary Possibilities

and badly drawn that its interpretation by the law courts must have cost tens of thousands of pounds; but it was impracticable to amend it till the Clergy Discipline Act of 1892[1]. With what difficulty and after what entreaties of the archbishops and bishops this latter Act got itself through Parliament most of us can remember. Amendments which ought to have been made in it could not be made for fear of delaying it; and in the result it has always seemed to me a badly drawn and in many respects unsuitable measure.

So far we have an illustration of the objections, which I have numbered (2) and (3).

In the interval between these two Acts a fire of religious intolerance burst forth, and led to the passing of an Act for clerical discipline in the solitary matter of ritual—the Public Worship Regulation Act, 1874[2]—which as it came to be worked, by its assumption of hard secular dictation to spiritual men in spiritual matters, nearly rent our Church in twain, drove as it was many clergy and laity to other folds, and led to the scandalous spectacle of five priests of devoted and blameless lives being thrown into prison for their conscience sake. This is an example of objection (1); and when I add that the Act was after all used in only nine cases, and that owing to the uncertainties of its ill-drawn clauses and the loopholes which they left, the cost of litigating these few cases certainly ran into many thousands of pounds, I think the Public Worship Regulation Act may also be treated as an example of objection (3).

As to patronage, my father, Sir Robert Phillimore,

[1] 55 & 56 Vict. c. 32.   [2] 37 & 38 Vict. c. 85.

in 1853 and 1854 brought in a bill to prevent the sale of next presentations; and ever since 1874, there have been attempts made to get Parliament to reform 'abuses,' some of which are now officially styled as 'recognized[1].' Latterly the attempts have become annual. But as yet nothing has been done.

The result then is, as regards head (3) of objections, that church reform by regular Parliamentary legislation with bills proceeding through first and second readings, committee, report, and third reading in both Houses, is as impracticable as, for the reasons given under heads (1) and (2), it is undesirable.

Abandoning regular Parliamentary legislation as hopeless, I proceed to discuss other alternatives. In so doing, I do not derogate from the supreme controlling power of Parliament, but I inquire how that power can be worked as one of general control and not of constant interference.

Much effective church legislation, as I shall show, has been in former times done by Convocation only, and remains in the Thirty-nine Articles and in Canons; and if this course of legislation had not been interrupted, it could still be pursued. The old canons might have been amended and supplemented, and being assented to by the Crown would have had authority sufficient without recourse to Parliament. For instance, the Canons of 1603 provide for residence of cathedral dignitaries (canons 42–44), admission to Holy Orders, the licensing and discipline of curates (canons 31–37,

---

[1] Queen's Speech at opening of Parliament, Feb. 8, 1897. See the *Guardian*, Feb. 9, p. 180.

Legal and Parliamentary Possibilities 155

48), and the regulation of the ecclesiastical courts (canons 92-98). But a series of Statutes from 13 Anne, c. 11, on the subject of curates, Statute 1 & 2 Vict. c. 106 on the subject of cathedrals, and the Clergy Discipline Acts which I have mentioned as dealing with the ecclesiastical courts, have engulfed and submerged these canons; and instead of a malleable body of its own constituting, which Convocation could have modified, we have now statutes which cannot be touched except by Parliament.

During the discussions on the Public Worship Regulation Act, I at the request of some friends prepared a bill repealing the Church Discipline Act of 1840, making a few necessary provisions, and then leaving it to Convocation to enact by canon all reforms it might deem necessary. It would have been a bold course, but for reforming purposes a very useful one.

As things stand, however, the patchwork of legislation is so made up of canon and statute that it is difficult now to have any effective legislation by canon alone.

Then comes the next alternative; let the Convocations pass canons, and Parliament pass statutes confirming them. This is even more hopeless. With such a legislature the utterest abuse, the veriest eyesore, would remain unaffected.

In the kingdom of Sweden the four estates of the realm, nobles, clergy, burghers, peasants, used to have each a separate house; and laws had to pass all four, and little business could be done. How much worse would it be here, with six houses, two from Canterbury, two from York, the House of Lords and the House of

Commons! and how much worse still when we remember that it has been already shown that ecclesiastical legislation can hardly as it is push its way through the Houses of Lords and Commons.

What then is to be done?

In a paper which I read before the Church Congress at Shrewsbury in 1896, I advocated the following method:—

'First, let the ministers of the Crown recur to the older practice and encourage the Convocations to legislate as much as possible by canons, offering the assistance of the Crown lawyers or other skilled draftsmen to put the intentions of Convocation into the best legal form.

'Secondly, let ministers entertain representations from the heads of the Church and give to the Convocations "letters of business" on any church subject where change or reform is needed. Let them confer with the Convocations as to the ultimate legal form in which the change is to be carried out; and let them submit to Parliament, if an Act be necessary, one complete scheme, a schedule to a bill in one clause, and let it be a Government bill, backed with all the power of Government if taken up at all.'

This would represent the *minimum* of change in our present system of legislation; but even so it would require considerable courage and determination on the part of the Ministry of the day; and as yet no signs have appeared of any readiness to take such a course.

The only other course which I know of, the only remaining chance of getting anything done is that upon which church reformers seem now all to concentrate. It is to apply that principle of *devolution*, which has been

Legal and Parliamentary Possibilities 157

so largely adopted in civil legislation, to our ecclesiastical law-making.

A barrister of much learning has well expressed this in the following words:—

'Parliament, either to avoid unnecessary discussion by the representatives of the nation of matters which affect only particular classes, or because in particular cases the saving of time may be of essential importance, or because it may well be that certain public authorities may fairly be considered most competent to deal with special questions which may arise, has in many cases delegated its powers to a greater or less extent. The schemes, of which there are considerable variety, consist in one act which is common to all, the grant to some council, board or committee, some department of State or a minor public authority of the right to make rules, orders or byelaws, which when promulgated are to be of as much power and effect as if directly enacted by Act of Parliament. Sometimes the power given is unhampered and absolute. The authority may issue within the assigned limits of its orders, and thereupon such orders are of full force and validity. More frequently a check is placed on execution of the power bestowed, and this may be of two kinds. It is not unusual to make provision that before the particular regulations are formulated such notice shall be publicly given as will enable all parties interested to raise any objections which they may think are of force; and in one way or another the opportunity is given for effect to be given to these objections. A common course of procedure laid down is for Parliament to reserve to itself the right of pronouncing for or against the validity of the rules or orders; and there are two principal ways in which this may be effected. Either the "provisional orders," to use a phrase in common

158 *Legal and Parliamentary Possibilities*

use, may be made valid unless objected to by Parliament, or they may be valid after a certain interval of time, unless Parliament sees fit to annul them.'

The Church Reform League has put forth a 'Suggested Draft of a Bill for the better Government of the Church of England,' which runs as follows:—

'If Her Majesty shall be pleased to grant letters of business, the Convocations of Canterbury and York may prepare a scheme, whereby representatives of the laity of the said Church in every ecclesiastical parish may be elected to assemblies, to be called houses of laymen, for advising in the general management of the said Church.

'Further, the Convocations of Canterbury and York may prepare a scheme granting to reformed Convocations, in conjunction with such houses of laymen, legislative freedom and authority, exercised as hereinafter described, in all matters of discipline, organization, administration and worship in the said Church.

'And when such scheme, or any subsequent scheme, prepared under the powers given by the first scheme, shall have been presented to Her Majesty by the Presidents of the said Convocations, Her Majesty may, if she see fit, cause the same to be laid before her two Houses of Parliament for forty days during their session; and if, within such forty days, neither House address Her Majesty, praying her to withhold her assent from such scheme, or any subsequent scheme prepared under the powers given by the first scheme, Her Majesty may, by Order in Council, if she see fit, signify her approval thereof, and cause such approval to be published in the *London Gazette*, whereupon such scheme, or such subsequent scheme, shall have the force of law, as if it had been enacted as part of this Act.'

Obviously this draft is merely a sketch. It does not define what 'reformed Convocations' are, or how they are to be reformed. It leaves much that is uncertain in the powers suggested for the laity of 'advising in the general management of the Church.'

But the value of this draft lies in three things:—

First, it points to a special voice in the preparation of church schemes being given to the laity of the Church.

Secondly, it marks the need of reforming Convocations, presumably both by the admission of representatives of the curates—a matter upon which I venture to refer to my Church Congress paper at Shrewsbury—and by some addition and redistribution of seats which would give a larger number of representatives to the greater dioceses.

Thirdly, it strikes out a bold path of devolutionary law-making 'in all matters of discipline, organization, administration and worship.'

Are these words too wide? Roughly speaking I think they are not. They may not be precise enough; they are not very good parliamentary words; but the idea underlying them seems right.

The fullest protection will be wanted for three external interests: (1) those who have civil rights in church property, from the Crown itself down to the holder of a faculty pew; (2) incumbents of benefices with vested interests, from the bishop to the perpetual curate; (3) Nonconformists of all kinds. If these are protected, the Church in and by her assemblies ought to have the widest powers of self-government and home rule.

160 *Legal and Parliamentary Possibilities*

The Established Kirk of Scotland has very large powers of self-management; it passes from time to time as seems good to it its 'Acts.' In 1711 it appears to have regulated its own formula of subscription for ministers elect and for elders[1]. In 1834 it appears to have consolidated the whole law as to probationers, that is candidates for ordination and appointment to a particular kirk[2].

In the great patronage contest in which its powers were restricted in 1839, Lord Brougham delivering judgement in the House of Lords yet said, ' It is the province of the General Assembly and the inferior church courts to take cognizance of church matters and to make regulations binding ecclesiastical concerns and ecclesiastical concerns alone[3].'

Why should not the Church of England have similar power? Can it be denied that self-reformation is the best? Can it be contended that it is not for the interest of the whole nation that a great organism such as the Church shall be sound, and capable of doing its best work in the best way? It is sometimes said that so much power is conceded to the General Assembly of the Kirk, because it consists of laity as well as clergy, though indeed the ruling elders who are called the laity are ordained persons, ordained it is true for limited functions. Well, we have the houses of laymen attached to the two Convocations[4]. Nothing, I have observed, is so irritating to some people as the mention of the houses of laymen. Such people assert that the House of Commons is the true

[1] *Law of Creeds in Scotland*, by A. Taylor Innes, 1867, p. 88.
[2] Ibid. p. 89.   [3] Ibid. p. 174; Auchterarder case.
[4] As long ago as 1873 (*Union Review*, May, 1873, p. 241) I advocated the creation of a house of laymen.

house of laymen! But how absurd this is has been already shown. Why, from the time of the Act of Union with Scotland the House of Commons has officially consisted of the laymen of two established religious bodies, and might as well assert itself as a house of laymen for Scotland as for England. But indeed before this, from the first Toleration Act, it ceased to represent necessarily the laymen of the Church.

And we may go still further back. Supposing that the House of Commons did consist of nothing but church people elected only by church people, still it would not be elected for purposes of church government or show any *a priori* aptitude for them.

As well *in fine* might you call the County Council the house of laymen for London as the House of Commons the house of laymen for England.

The houses of laymen in the two provinces are not yet altogether sufficient and satisfactory. Perhaps this is due to the mode of election; perhaps to their want of real power. They are still experimental bodies, and may want reform as well as Convocation. But let there be a chance that the lay and clerical bodies will be permitted to do sufficient real work, and they will become both in form and in fact truly representative.

To Convocation, or rather to the two Convocations thus reformed and supplemented by their lay houses, let power be given by Act of Parliament to frame *schemes* (I prefer to keep the word 'canon' for canons proper) on any matter which may come under the head of 'discipline, organization, administration, and worship.' It is a draftsman's question how this shall be best expressed. It may be expressed by general words or by enumeration, thus :—

The creation of new bishoprics, the division or alteration of dioceses.

The enacting, repealing, or amending of cathedral statutes.

The creation of new cathedral bodies for new dioceses.

The creation and alteration of archdeaconries and rural deaneries.

The creation of new benefices and the division or alteration of old ones.

(All the powers now exercisable by the Ecclesiastical Commissioners by schemes confirmed by Order in Council.)

Removing 'certain recognized abuses in connexion with church patronage [1].'

Altering the conditions of tenure of benefices, making them, if thought advisable, no longer for life, and making any amendments in the law of dilapidations.

Amending the ecclesiastical courts and the procedure before them both in respect of discipline, whether lay or clerical, and in such matters as faculties and marriage licences.

Redistributing the work of Queen Anne's Bounty and the Ecclesiastical Commissioners, or amalgamating the two offices (an object which I have had long at heart).

Where churchwardens are purely ecclesiastical officers, as they are in new parishes and now in old rural parishes, amending the mode of their appointment, their qualifications, and the qualifications of their electors.

[1] See page 154 supra.

Legal and Parliamentary Possibilities 163

Establishing and empowering parochial church councils, if thought advisable.

As to the mode of preparing and passing these schemes, I would make the following suggestions:—

No scheme shall be framed except upon the previous grant of 'letters of business,' the old form in which the Crown has been wont to authorize Convocation to treat of and discuss any special matters.

When a scheme has been passed by the three Houses in each province, it shall be certified under the hands of the two Archbishops, or other Presidents of the Convocation[1], as a *provisional scheme* to the Secretary of State; and the archbishops shall at the same time certify to the Secretary of State that a joint Executive Committee has been formed out of the Convocations of the two provinces to receive and consider any alterations which he may desire to have made and to confer with him thereupon.

Any amendments made by the Secretary of State shall be considered by the Executive Committee.

The scheme as amended and recommended by the Executive Committee shall be submitted again to the two Convocations, and after being assented to by them shall be submitted to the Crown for ratification.

If Her Majesty is advised to ratify the scheme, it shall be the duty of the Home Secretary, before she actually ratifies, to lay the same upon the tables of both Houses of Parliament; and either House shall be at liberty within forty days to address Her Majesty praying her to withhold her ratification. But if neither House so address her,

[1] The Canons of 1603 were passed when there was no Archbishop of Canterbury, under the presidency of the Bishop of London.

164 *Legal and Parliamentary Possibilities*

Her Majesty may ratify, and on her ratification it shall become law.

Such are the outlines of a scheme. I desire briefly to explain how the matter would work.

In the first place the Convocations must obtain the aid of professional draftsmen. Neither clergy nor members of the house of laymen will *ex necessitate rei* have any gift that way. It is one thing to see an abuse, and even to see how it should be rectified, and quite another thing to put it in legal language, or to foresee and provide for all the necessary legal contingencies. The provisional scheme must be prepared with legal assistance, and the Executive Committee must have a lawyer present with them.

The Home Secretary would, I take it, refer the provisional scheme to the law officers of the Crown, with two main directions: first, to see that the three interests which I have mentioned above[1] are protected; secondly, to see that the scheme is effective and workable.

The double procedure of passing the scheme twice through the Convocations may seem cumbrous. But I contemplate the second passing as being almost always a matter of course. The Convocations must treat their Executive Committee as plenipotentiary, and ratify its acts *en bloc*, unless there is very grave reason to the contrary. It is somewhat in this way that our present Prayer Book was constructed in 1662.

Either House of Parliament will be able to stop the scheme from becoming law. Thus Parliament will have full control. But the differences in legislative facility are

[1] Supra, p. 159.

Legal and Parliamentary Possibilities 165

enormous, as all experience shows. (1) The matter is simultaneously before the two Houses instead of making a procession through both in order. (2) Positive action is needed, not to urge on but to stop. (3) The measure is not taken piecemeal; the amendments of each individual member of Parliament do not need to be considered. It must be rejected (if there are faults enough in it) or accepted as a whole.

One other matter requires to be considered and faced. Parliament has so often attempted projects of church reform that further reform will not infrequently mean modification or repeal of particular provisions in previous Acts of Parliament. Will it be possible, except by direct Act of Parliament, to repeal an Act of Parliament? It could be done; and there are precedents. Some Acts relating to the colonies or to treaties with foreign Powers have been made by other Acts repealable by Order in Council. But probably it will be unwise to ask for as much as this.

I should propose that every scheme when laid on the tables of the two Houses shall be accompanied by a certificate by the law officers of the Crown, stating whether it alters or supersedes any provision in an Act of Parliament, and if it does, setting out each provision in detail; and that it shall be the duty of the Secretary of State forthwith to bring in a bill to repeal all the provisions so affected; and till such bill has passed into law, such provisions shall not be deemed to be in any wise repealed.

I should hope that such a bill would not be contentious. I think that the two Houses might alter their standing orders so as to give it an easier passage. At any rate it need not be necessary to give the additional stage, which I believe is required of some church bills in the House of Commons, that of moving for leave to bring in a bill in Committee of the whole House. But I do not see how more can be done to make reforming legislation easy.

At best it will be a laborious task. But at least these proposals should relieve reformers from that rolling of the stone of Sisyphus which has so long been their fate. And so my proposals are finished; and the reader is not invited to dwell on the dry passages which follow. But lest any one should consider the innovation too bold, I have collected in a sort of Appendix the precedents and instances of similar legislation by devolution.

I. THE ECCLESIASTICAL COMMISSIONERS.

The first Act forming this Commission (A.D. 1836)[1] recites in its preamble the great changes which it proposes to effectuate entirely by schemes framed by the Commissioners and approved by the Queen in Council. The preamble is of great length. I make the following extracts:—

'Whereas His Majesty was pleased . . . to issue two several commissions to certain persons therein respectively named, directing them to consider the state of the several dioceses in England and Wales, with reference to the amount of their revenues, and the more equal distribution of episcopal duties and the prevention of the

[1] 6 & 7 Will. IV. c. 77.

Legal and Parliamentary Possibilities 167

necessity of attaching by commendam to bishopricks benefices with cure of souls, and to consider also the state of the several cathedral and collegiate churches in England and Wales with a view to the suggestion of such measures as may render them conducive to the efficiency of the Established Church, and to devise the best mode of providing for the cure of souls, with special reference to the residence of the clergy on their respective benefices. And whereas the said commissioners have, in pursuance of such directions, made four several reports: ... And whereas the said Commission have, in their said reports, amongst other things, recommended *that commissioners be appointed by Parliament for the purpose of preparing and laying before His Majesty in Council such schemes* as shall appear to them to be best adapted for carrying into effect the following recommendations; and that His Majesty in Council shall be empowered to make orders ratifying such schemes, *and having the full force of law;*' ...

(Then follows a description of the redistributed areas proposed to be assigned, by counties and parishes, to the several dioceses.)

'And that all parishes which are locally situate in one diocese, but under the jurisdiction of the bishop of another diocese, be made subject to the jurisdiction of the bishop of the diocese within which they are locally situate; and that such variations be made in the proposed boundaries of the different dioceses as may appear advisable, after more precise information ... and that the bishops of the two newly erected sees be made bodies corporate, and be invested with all the same rights and privileges as are now possessed by the other bishops, ... and that the collegiate churches of Manchester and Ripon be made the cathedrals; ... and that the members of these and of all other cathedral churches in England be styled dean and canons; ... and that the jurisdiction of the bishop's court in each diocese be coextensive with the limits of the diocese as newly arranged; and that such arrangements be made with regard to the apportionment of fees payable to the officers of the several diocesan courts as may be deemed just and equitable, for the purpose of making compensation to those officers who may be prejudiced by the proposed alterations; and that such alterations be made in the apportionment or exchange of ecclesiastical patronage among the several bishops as shall be consistent with the relative magnitude and importance of their dioceses when newly arranged, and as shall afford an adequate quantity of patronage to the bishops of the new sees; and that in order to provide for the augmentation of the incomes of the smaller bishopricks, such fixed annual sums be paid to the commissioners out of the revenues of the larger sees respectively as shall upon due inquiry and consideration be determined on, so as to leave as an average annual income to ... and that out of the fund thus accruing fixed annual payments be made by the commissioners, in such instances and to such amount as shall be in like manner determined on, so that the average annual income of the other bishops respectively be not less than £4000 or more than £5000 ... and that fit residences be provided for (certain) bishops; ... and that for the purpose of providing the bishop of any diocese with a more suitable and convenient residence than that which now belongs to his see, sanction be given for purchases or exchanges of houses or lands, or for the sale of lands belonging to the respective sees ... and that new archdeaconries of ... be created, and that districts be assigned to them, ... and that the limits of the other existing deaneries and arch-

Legal and Parliamentary Possibilities 169

deaconries be newly arranged, so that every parish and extra-parochial place be within a rural deanery, and every deanery within an archdeaconry, and that no archdeaconry extend beyond the limits of one diocese; and that all the archdeaconries of England and Wales be in the gift of the bishops of the respective dioceses in which they are situate; and that all archdeacons have and exercise full and equal jurisdiction within their respective archdeaconries' . . .

The list of powers proposed to be devolved is, then, enormous. The actual authority is thus conferred (sect. 10):—

'The said commissioners shall from time to time prepare and lay before His Majesty in Council such schemes as shall appear to the said commissioners to be best adapted for carrying into effect the hereinbefore recited recommendations, and shall in such schemes recommend and propose such measures as may upon further inquiry, which the said commissioners are hereby authorized to make, appear to them to be necessary for carrying such recommendations into full and perfect effect: Provided always that nothing herein contained shall be construed to prevent the said commissioners from proposing in any such scheme such modifications or variations as to matters of detail and regulation as shall not be substantially repugnant to any or either of the said recommendations' . . .

By section 12, if His Majesty in Council approves a scheme, he can issue an Order ratifying the same, specifying the time for the scheme to take effect, and directing the Order to be registered in the registers of the dioceses affected.

By section 13 every Order is to be published in the *London Gazette*.

By section 14 it is thereupon to be of full effect.

By section 15 copies are to be laid before Parliament every year.

The next Act[1] adds the duty to give notice to any corporation proposed to be affected, which has thereupon a right to be heard by the Privy Council.

II. THE LAW COURTS AND THE PROCEDURE THEREIN.

By the Judicature Act, 1875[2], Her Majesty may—

'At any time after the passing and before the commencement of this Act, by Order in Council, made upon the recommendation of the Lord Chancellor' (the principal judges are then enumerated), 'or any five of them, and the other judges of the several Courts, or a majority of such other judges, make any further or additional rules of court for carrying the principal Act and this Act into effect, and in particular for all or any of the following matters, as far as they are not provided for by the rules in the First Schedule to this Act; that is to say—

'1. For regulating the sittings of the High Court of Justice, of any divisional or other Courts thereof, and of the judges of the said High Court sitting in chambers; and,

'2. For regulating the pleading, practice, and procedure in the High Court of Justice and Court of Appeal; and

'3. Generally for regulating any matters relating to the practice and procedure of the said Courts respec-

[1] 3 & 4 Vict. c. 113, s. 83.   [2] 38 & 39 Vict. c. 77, s. 17.

tively, or to the duties of the officers thereof, or of the Supreme Court, or to the costs of proceedings therein.

'From and after the commencement of this Act the Supreme Court may at any time, with a concurrence of the majority of the judges thereof present at any meeting for that purpose held (of which majority the Lord Chancellor shall be one), alter and annul any rules of Court for the time being in force, and have and exercise the same power of making rules of Court as is by this section vested in Her Majesty in Council on the recommendation of the said judges before the commencement of this Act.

'All rules of Court made in pursuance of this section, if made before the commencement of this Act, shall from and after the commencement of this Act, and if made after the commencement of this Act shall from and after they come into operation, regulate all matters to which they extend, until annulled or altered in pursuance of this section.'

These powers have been extended by later Acts[1].

By the County Court Act, 1888[2]:

'The Lord Chancellor may appoint five judges, and from time to time fill up any vacancies in their number, to frame rules and orders for regulating the practice of the Courts and forms of proceedings therein, and scales of costs to be paid to counsel and solicitors, and from time to time to amend such rules, orders, forms, and scales; and such rules, orders, forms, and scales, or amended rules, orders, forms, and scales, certified under the hands of such judges, or any three or more of them, shall be submitted to the Lord Chancellor, who may allow or disallow, or alter the same; and the rules,

[1] See 39 & 40 Vict. c. 59, 57 & 58 Vict. c. 16, among others.
[2] 51 & 52 Vict. c. 43, s. 164.

orders, forms, and scales, or amended rules, orders, forms, or scales, so allowed or altered subject to the concurrence of the authority for making rules of the Supreme Court, as in the Supreme Court of Judicature Act, 1884, provided, shall, from a day to be named by the Lord Chancellor, be in force in every Court. Such power of making rules and orders shall extend to all matters of procedure or practice, or relating to or concerning the effect or operation in law of any procedure or practice, in any case within the cognizance of County Courts, as to which rules of the Supreme Court have been or might lawfully be made for cases within the cognizance of the High Court of Justice.' . . .

By the Public Worship Regulation Act, 1874 [1]—

' Her Majesty may by Order in Council at any time either before or after the commencement of this Act, by and with the advice of the Lord High Chancellor, the Lord Chief Justice of England, the judge to be appointed under this Act, and the Archbishop and Bishops, who are members of Her Majesty's Privy Council, or any two of the said persons, one of them being the Lord High Chancellor, or the Lord Chief Justice of England, cause rules and orders to be made for regulating the procedure and settling the fees to be taken in proceedings under this Act, so far as the same may not be expressly regulated by this Act, and from time to time alter or amend such rules and orders. All rules and orders made in pursuance of this section shall be laid before each House of Parliament within forty days after the same are made, if Parliament is then sitting, or if not, then within forty days after the then next meeting of Parliament; and *if an address is presented to Her*

[1] 37 & 38 Vict. c. 85, s. 19.

Majesty by either of the said Houses within the next subsequent forty days on which the House shall have sat, praying that any such rules may be annulled, Her Majesty may thereupon by Order in Council annul the same, and the rules and orders so annulled shall thenceforth become void, without prejudice to the validity of any proceedings already taken under the same.'

Rules made under this section stood the severest strain, and were held valid by the Courts in one of the leading Ritual prosecutions[1].

By the Clergy Discipline Act, 1892[2]—

' 1. The Rule Committee, that is to say the Lord Chancellor, the Lord Chief Justice of England, the judge of the provincial Court, and the Archbishop and Bishops who are members of the Privy Council, or any three of the said persons, two of them being the Lord Chancellor and one other of the aforesaid judicial persons, may make rules for carrying this Act into effect, and in particular for regulating all matters relating to procedure, practice, costs, expenses, and fees under this Act, including the appeals (so far as rules made by the Privy Council or the Judicial Committee do not extend), the electing and choosing of assessors, the place of sitting of the Court, the giving of security for costs, the passing of sentences, the validity of proceedings, notwithstanding defects of form or irregularity, the application of this Act to a clergyman who cannot be found or holds no preferment, or several preferments, the liability to and recovery of costs and expenses, the forms to be used, and all matters incidental to or connected with the administration of justice under this Act.

---

[1] Dale's Case, Law Reports, 6 Q. B. D. p. 376.
[2] 55 & 56 Vict. c. 32, s. 9.

'2. Every rule purporting to be made in pursuance of this section shall be forthwith laid before both Houses of Parliament, and *if an address is presented to Her Majesty the Queen by either House within the next forty days thereafter on which that House has sat, praying that any such rules may be annulled, Her Majesty in Council may annul the same*, without prejudice to the validity of anything done in the meantime in pursuance thereof; but subject as aforesaid, *every such rule shall, while unrevoked, be of the same validity as if enacted in this Act.*'

III. THE NEW BISHOPRICS ACT, 1878[1].

'Whenever the Ecclesiastical Commissioners certify to Her Majesty under their common seal, with respect to the endowment fund of any new bishopric mentioned in the schedule to this Act, either that'... (here follow provisions for ascertaining the endowment to be considered sufficient).

'Her Majesty by Order in Council, may found that new bishopric with a diocese and cathedral church, in accordance with the schedule to this Act, and may declare the time at which such order founding the bishopric is to come into operation.

'Her Majesty by the same or any other order in Council may constitute the bishop of such bishopric a body corporate, and invest the bishop with all such rights, privileges, and jurisdictions as are now possessed by any other bishop in England, or such of them as to Her Majesty may seem meet, and may subject such bishop to the metropolitan jurisdiction of the Archbishop in that behalf mentioned in the schedule to this Act'...

[1] 41 & 42 Vict. c. 68, s. 4.

IV. THE CHARITY COMMISSIONERS.

From the earliest Acts onwards some power of direct legislation by means of schemes has been given to these Commissioners [1], and a further power of provisional legislation in other cases to be confirmed annually by Parliament [2]. But it is in connexion with Endowed Schools that the best known and most remarkable powers were given to the Endowed School Commissioners, and then transferred to the Charity Commissioners [3].

By the Act of 1869 [4] the Commissioners may prepare draft schemes, which they are to print and send to the governing body and the principal teacher of the school, and to publish and circulate. During three months they are to receive objections and alternative schemes. After the three months they may hold an inquiry, and after considering everything they may frame a scheme and submit it to the Committee of Council of Education. This body is to consider, and may approve, or frame another scheme. When finally approved the scheme is laid before the Privy Council; then the governing body may appeal to the Privy Council. Supposing there to be no appeal, or the Privy Council to confirm the scheme, it is then laid before Parliament, and if within forty days no address against it by either House is presented to the Crown, the *scheme becomes law*.

It is well known how great have been the changes,

[1] 16 & 17 Vict. c. 137 (1853), 18 & 19 Vict. c. 124 (1855), 23 & 24 Vict. c. 136 (1860), 45 & 46 Vict. c. 66 (1882).
[2] 16 & 17 Vict. c. 137, ss. 54-60.
[3] 37 & 38 Vict. c. 87 (1874).
[4] 32 & 33 Vict. c. 56, ss. 32-45 (1869).

how drastic the reforms, which these schemes and those under the Welsh Intermediate Education Act[1] have made.

The last instance I would mention, though I will not enter into detail, is the remarkable power conferred by THE FOREIGN JURISDICTION ACT, 1878[2], upon the Queen in Council.

I will conclude by observing that *legislation by devolution* has now become so much part of the constitution of the country that one law of procedure for all these cases has been made generally applicable, and reduced to a code, by the RULES PUBLICATION ACT, 1893[3].

There need therefore now be no jealousy of its extension, no shrinking from empowering the Church to make those by-laws for its internal management, which are found necessary to the life of any great organism.

[1] 52 & 53 Vict. c. 40 (1889).
[2] 41 & 42 Vict. c. 67, s. 3.
[3] 56 & 57 Vict. c. 66.

VII

PAROCHIAL CHURCH COUNCILS

By H. J. Torr

THE formation of parochial Church councils is a measure of church reform that has a very special claim on the consideration and support of churchmen, because it is one which we have the power to carry out ourselves without reference to any external authority. To secure self-government, however restricted, to remove the scandals, however gross, now connected with the sale of patronage, or to raise, however slightly, the standard of discipline, we must first win the assent of others. Here, on the contrary, we are our own masters. We have a free hand, and with it an invaluable opportunity for proving the sincerity of our desire for reform. And further, surely nothing will so effectually remove the suspicion with which many still regard church reform as the proof which such a practical measure as this may afford, that our principles are neither academic nor revolutionary, but are such as the general intelligence of the nation may recognize as being moderate, just, and in accordance with the best traditions of the past.

From this it follows that a very grave responsibility will rest on those who are the pioneers. Incalculable harm may very easily be inflicted on the whole reform movement, and our success deferred many years, by injudicious action here. Found these councils on wrong lines, to be exhibitions either of ecclesiastical exclusiveness or of lay incompetence in the exercise of powers too comprehensive for the inexperienced laymen of to-day, and their failure is inevitable. Therefore—strange plea in the mouth of reformers—our first appeal must be for caution. But it would seem highly desirable that the formation of these new councils should not be left entirely to the private initiative either of individual clergy or of particular parishes. The bishops have already shown that they are fully alive to the importance of this question by the resolution passed unanimously last May in the Upper House of the Canterbury Convocation, that—

'The formation of parochial Church councils will tend to quicken the life and strengthen the work of the Church.'

It is therefore natural to appeal to them to indicate the lines on which they would welcome, each in his own diocese, the formation of these councils. It is not necessary nor even advisable that these lines should be identical in all dioceses, nor that they should be stereotyped even throughout any one diocese; but the same broad principles may well form the basis of all diocesan schemes; and though each scheme in itself should afford ample scope for the recognition of the peculiar characteristics and needs of the different parishes, it may well impose limitations which shall check personal eccentricity both in pastor and in parish. Further, the authority of the diocesan is necessary to secure some degree of permanence. The councils are little likely to succeed if their

Parochial Church Councils

continuance is entirely dependent on the tenure of any particular incumbent.

The first stage must necessarily be experimental. We have so completely lost the art of self-government in our Church that the use of even such rudimentary powers as are involved in the action of a parochial Church council must be painfully re-learnt. Therefore there should be no haste to have our council schemes sealed by law. Let us work them as voluntary organizations until we ascertain by experience what constitution and powers are best. Ultimately they must be consolidated as an integral portion of our ecclesiastical constitution, with clearly defined functions and legal obligations; they will be indeed the pillars on which it must all rest. But for the present our work is to prepare the ground only, so that the final scheme may rest not on theory but on practice.

What, then, are the lines on which Church councils should be formed? The answer depends on that to another question, What is our object in forming these councils? Different minds will give different answers here, but entering into all will, we think, be found this common and predominant factor,—the pressing need for the re-establishment of the church citizenship of the laity, and the enlistment of their active interest and co-operation by the frank recognition of their responsibility. We fully admit the fact that to-day it is the laymen who are to blame in refusing to take advantage of such opportunities as are even now open to them for the exercise of their citizenship. Yet, granting this, we believe that their apathy is far less due to inherent indifference than to the fact that few of these opportunities involve any real responsibility for action, and that they have never been taught that any duty attaches to citizenship except that of paying taxes. We have heard many sermons, but one only within our memory on our citizenship in the Church, and that by special request. In Congress speeches we readily recognize the comradeship of 'clerical members' and 'lay members,' but in private life we still speak of 'going into the Church' as the equivalent of ordination. For comradeship we have substituted tutelage, the natural order for mediaeval Rome or the Church of the Russian serf, but utterly unworthy of the capacity of a free people that has long since won and justified its citizenship in civil life. We would indeed plead very earnestly for the complete recognition of this principle in the work that lies before us. The Church has need of her laity. She has need of more than the respect with which they now regard her. She needs their interest, their sympathy, their love. Love cannot be given by the stranger or the servant, it is the prerogative of the son. The hireling fleeth because he is an hireling; it is the son alone who will stand by and for his Church against all the world. Some indeed she treats as sons to-day, and receives in return a devotion and a service that knows no limitations. But it is not for these we plead. The battle lies not with the feudal leader now, but with the men of the city and the field who form the privates in the army. It is they who make the State what it is, it is their aid we need for the Church in the ever-thickening strife with evil. Here, it seems to us, is the true aim and purpose of 'church reform'—the provision of opportunity for the recognition of the citizenship and sonship of all church people: the status which is their birthright from the moment when their Church set her seal upon them in baptism. Church councils will be valuable exactly in proportion as they are based upon this principle. Emasculate them so as to make them mere advisory boards of finance, and they may indeed here and there keep the rats out of a church or provide the curate's stipend, but they will still leave the whole weight of the Church's battle to be borne by the officers, while the rank and file stand idle spectators, ready victims for the weapons of the foe.

We must also remember that Church councils whose chief interest is finance will inevitably become the happy hunting-grounds of the plutocrat. On them the poor man is of no account, and their inevitable end is the tyranny of the rich man over clergy and congregation alike. The remedy lies in recognizing other interests. It is service we want, not money: this the poor can give equally with the rich, and the best council will be that which gives him most opportunity for doing so.

The second great function these parochial councils will have to discharge is that of being the foundation on which the higher councils will rest. Direct election over necessarily wide areas with its complicated machinery is hardly possible, and consequently the members of the future ruri-decanal, diocesan, and provincial councils will in all probability have to be chosen by the parish councils. The elections to these will therefore be doubly important, for not only will they be the only instrument by which the wishes of the great mass of our citizens can be weighed, but also it is in connexion with them that the thorny question of the church franchise must be settled, a question which lies at the very root of all constitutional Church reform.

So far as we know the minds of the bishops at present through the Convocation resolutions, they are evidently inclined to encourage a wide franchise. 'The electors,' they declared, 'shall be *bona fide* members of the Church of England of full age resident in the parish'; the words, 'on their own declaration,' being added in the report of the committee on which this resolution was based. The debate turned entirely on the residency clause; the question of the 'communicant' standard not being raised at all, we gather, because it was believed to be impracticable in face of Parliamentary prejudice. In most of the colonial churches signature of a declaration of membership, followed by enrolment in the churchwarden's book, seems to be the basis of church membership. For instance, in New Zealand by the tenth section of the fifth Canon, 'Every man of twenty-one years old, resident in any parish, and who shall have been registered for a period of not less than two months in the churchwarden's book as having made and subscribed this declaration, viz. I, A. B., do hereby declare that I am a member of the Church of the Province of New Zealand, commonly called the Church of England,' shall be entitled to attend and vote at parish meetings, and to vote at the election of synodsmen for the parish. The Church of Ireland accepts a similar declaration as sufficient, provided that it is made either by an owner of property in the parish of £10 yearly value, or by one 'usually resident in the parish,' or by 'an accustomed member of the congregation . . . for the three calendar

Parochial Church Councils 183

months last past.' The Episcopal Church of Scotland, on the other hand, only entrusts the franchise to 'male communicants,' and, like the others, insists on all who are elected to sit on any council being communicants.

To very many the practice of the last-named Church will alone seem to be in accordance with the demands of our Prayer Book. But, on the other hand, the adoption of this standard brings with it the danger of Holy Communion being attended for electoral purposes, an evil of which we have had bitter experience in civil life. To avoid this danger is the principal cause of the other churches having almost universally substituted other standards of membership, and we believe that we should be wise to follow their experience. It would seem to be sufficient to insist upon Baptism and Confirmation as the minimum, and to rely upon the growing earnestness of our people to teach them how much they lose by not accepting the higher standard of the Prayer Book. We believe, indeed, that the Church herself would lose in fighting strength if she refused these recruits. The volunteers may not have the discipline of the line, but we should be badly off in England if they were disbanded.

The question of residence also is an important one, and with it that of the area over which the council's authority should run. In country districts the council would naturally be for the whole parish and the electors would be residents, but in towns it would certainly be inexpedient that where congregations are now drawn together by common sympathies they should be liable to interference from any captious person who might happen to live in the neighbourhood. Similarly equal harm would be done by the interference of outsiders in the affairs of churches which the church-going parishioners are compelled to attend owing to the absence of any alternative church within range. The solution of the difficulty may possibly be found in the authoritative recognition of the distinction between two types of church, 'the congregational' and 'the parochial,' the residency qualification being demanded only in the latter case.

From the electors we come to the elected, and again it is inadvisable to lay down any hard and fast rule, except that all councillors should certainly be communicants. The councils may well be annually elected at special meetings at Easter time, which would practically take the place of the ' Easter vestry ' already shorn of its ancient civil powers. The councils should be large enough to permit of all classes being represented, and it would be well if in every scheme a memorandum emphasizing the importance of this were inserted, and, if practicable, definite provision made limiting the representation of any one class. The incumbent would naturally be the chairman, and the vice-chairman might conveniently be the people's warden. *Ex officio* members should be freely welcomed in the representatives of any special branches of church work, i.e. the curates, schoolmaster, choirmaster, school managers, deaconess, &c., provided only that the elected members were in a clear majority. Subject to this also, the incumbent and churchwardens, who would form a sort of cabinet, might well have the power of nominating certain additional members. One warden being appointed by the incumbent, this nomination would largely rest in his hands, but the association of the wardens with him would safeguard the interests of the parish and avoid the possible unpopularity often attaching to personal appointment. The right itself is valuable alike as a security for the incumbent's position and a guarantee of the rights of any minority on whose behalf it should be freely exercised.

Here also we have to decide whether or not women should be eligible for election. The resolutions of the bishops place the sex in the same position as 'non-communicants.' They may vote but may not be voted for. As they may, and in some known cases do, even now act as churchwardens, this proposal amounts to disfranchising them—a sorry reward for their loyal efforts in the past to do the work the lay*man* has neglected. As Chancellor Espin well said at Nottingham—

' I should be ashamed if, looking to the fact that when help is wanted for any purpose in a parish we always go first to the women, who support us with readiness, efficiency, and zeal, it is to be said that women are to have no vote and no place on our parochial councils. I once had a woman churchwarden, and she was one of the most efficient church officers I ever had.'

And not only would exclusion, we believe, thus be unfair, but it would also be a practical mistake. We want their aid, and never more than now, when the dividing line between social work and religious work is daily becoming fainter. We want all their keen sympathy with suffering and their generous indignation against wrongdoing, if our Church is to play her proper part as the friend of the poor and of the oppressed.

We have said that hard and fast rules are inexpedient, but in leaving this branch of our subject we would modify this by urging that non-attendance, alike at parochial, ruri-decanal, diocesan, and provincial councils, should be without exception a bar to re-election. Our diocesan conferences to-day are half empty because those who take little or no interest in their work are persistently re-elected on account of their social position, to the exclusion of many better men.

Having thus considered why these councils should be created and how they should be constituted, our next task is to discuss what they should do—what duties should they perform? I do not say, what rights should they exercise, for it is the ideal of duty and not that of rights which should be set before these councils. We do not want our laity to come to their work eager to vindicate 'their rights.' We care nothing whatever for their 'rights'; what we want is that through responsibility they may realize their duties. The new order has enough difficulties to overcome already; and if the change from autocratic to constitutional government is to be based on a clamorous insistence on rights, then failure is inevitable. But while this conception of the council's work is made clear, it is equally important that it should have a real responsibility for the discharge of its duties. It is of course not easy to say exactly how far this responsibility should extend, but certainly it is better that we should err in making it too complete rather than in curtailing it unduly. It is responsibility more than anything else that breeds interest and work. The men whose work and guidance

Parochial Church Councils

is worth having, have neither the time nor the inclination to take part in the proceedings of a debating society or a mutual admiration show. Nay, further, it is the absence of responsibility for action that creates the danger of wild talk and ill-considered proposals that may captivate popular fancy and end only in bitterness when the inevitable failure follows. From the first, then, these councils should be encouraged and even compelled to accept responsibility in every possible way. Let the clergy never override them within their allotted sphere even when obviously in error; for it will be generally better that they should learn wisdom by their own mistakes. A good plan was sketched by one speaker at the Nottingham Congress. Our *lex non scripta*, he said,

'is this, that in case of disagreement between the vicar and the council the matter shall be adjourned; if no agreement is then arrived at, the matter shall be postponed twelve months; and if that does not remove the obstacle, it shall be referred to the Diocesan for settlement.'

On such a plan a real responsibility rests with the councils, and one which can easily be further extended as experience proves their fitness, and yet ample provision is made for the avoidance of any deadlock. But, whatever plan be adopted, this is certain, and should mainly guide our decision, that trust begets trust, and that the more completely a council is trusted the more readily will it reciprocate that trust.

The first duty that the council will have to perform will naturally be that of 'assisting the incumbent in the initiation and development in the parish of all forms of church work.' Here we believe that the principle to be adopted is the simple one, that nothing is either too important or too trivial to be submitted to the consideration of the council. Our model should be a council of war. The whole plan of campaign should come before it. The full meaning of every portion of the common work should be fully explained and considered in common— what services allowed by proper authority are most helpful, what hours are best, what missions are possible, how can daily service secure a congregation, what arrangements of choir and of music will make the service most congregational, what extra parochial work can be supported, how can diocesan life be fostered, how can church and churchyard be made most worthy, what can be done for the young men and boys, how can the girls of the village be helped upwards, how can the schools be made the nursery of a strong and healthy future, how can co-operation with other Christian bodies in common action against common enemies, drink, vice, insanitation, infidelity, best be organized? There is not a single department of church work which would not gain in vigour and efficiency from the adoption of such a policy. The council should feel they are the non-commissioned officers of the army: that the work is not the 'parson's job,' for which he is paid so much a day, but that it is a common work in which he and they may labour together, not as master and pupils, but as comrades.

Then again, if instead of having half a dozen independent and often divergent committees, the offspring of the incum-

Parochial Church Councils

bent's *ipse dixit*, each to manage some particular branch of parish work—reading-room, schools, school treats, temperance work, clubs, guilds, &c.—we had so many sub-committees of the same council, would not the whole gain immensely in unity of purpose, just as the various independent diocesan organizations are being gathered up under the authority of the Diocesan Conference with such good result? It may be fanciful, but we conceive that even so light a duty as that of decorating our churches for festivals would have a new interest and meaning to our people if it were 'our' council which were responsible rather than one or two kindly ladies, the lieutenants of the vicar's wife. And then, when the wider question of repairs or improvements comes to be discussed, let the plans of the artist or architect come before the council, and depend upon its decision. We often declare our desire that our folk should realize the church as their own. Let them have the building of it then, and the beautifying of it. It may be that many will as yet cling to the whitewashed barn and the drawing-room pew, and if so, then let their teacher prove his metal, not by overriding them but by educating them to a love of better things. Autocratic action here as always is the last refuge of incompetency. It is the master mind alone that can convince. Closely connected with these duties is that of representing the wishes of the congregation, when questions arise in connexion with the alteration of the accustomed ritual. The present uncontrolled position of our clergy is of very modern origin, for it is largely due to three events of our day which had other results than those anticipated by their authors.

The abolition of church rates destroyed the control of the parish, the Gorham judgement destroyed that of the bishop, and the Public Worship Regulation Act destroyed that of the State. The judgement practically made the patron omnipotent as against both bishop and parish, and removed almost every check on the original appointment. Once appointed, the unchristian procedure and barbarous penalties of the Public Worship Regulation Act effectually prevented any self-respecting congregation from invoking its aid, while the disappearance of the church rate deprived them of the checks they had themselves previously possessed through their control of the parish purse. To-day, therefore, a congregation is doubly helpless against either eccentricity or indolence on the part of the pastor, or misguided enthusiasm or criminal negligence on the part of the patron. It is now twenty years since Mr. Gladstone, 'the one untiring and passionate opponent' of the Public Worship Regulation Act, declared in his alternative resolutions—

'It is to be desired that the members of the Church having a legitimate interest in her services, should receive ample protection against precipitate and arbitrary changes in established customs by the sole will of the clergyman or against the wishes locally prevalent among them, and such protection is not afforded by the provisions of this bill.'

The events which followed the passing of this unhappy Act by his ecclesiastical opponents proved alike the truth of his statement, and the accuracy of his prediction. These events now are but memories of the past. Let us make their recurrence for ever impossible by the adoption

Parochial Church Councils

of such constitutional safeguards as shall remove all opportunity for such misunderstandings between pastor and people. It is perhaps well that this question has not been settled before. When party passion ran higher and mere panic bred of ignorance was more prevalent, probably no permanent settlement was possible. Too many desired our Church to be exclusive rather than inclusive. But now, when the Lambeth judgement has helped to place the magnificent comprehensiveness of the English Catholic Church beyond reach of attack from any section or any party, we may well ask for a more generous recognition of the difference between things lawful and things expedient. For nineteen hundred years, as Bishop Lightfoot said so well, some men have been 'of Paul,' some 'of Apollos,' and some 'of Cephas,' different architects raising on the same foundation different types of building to satisfy different moods of the human soul, to the great gain of the Church. Since, then, the foundation has been once for all laid and the main design approved, assuredly the opinion of the worshippers should have no small weight in determining the details of the superstructure. The exact limits within which their opinion should be accepted need not be settled now. We contend only for the acceptance of the principle that it should have great weight, that it should be expressed through the Council, and that it should cover sins of omission as well as those of commission.

In the Church Reform League proposals, this principle is set forth in the following words :—

'The communicants of every parish should have a

recognized power to prevent the arbitrary alteration of lawful customs in ritual.'

Here we note as very important the three words 'recognized,' 'arbitrary,' 'lawful.' First, 'recognized' clearly implies that the power is not an absolute one. No one we suppose who supports this proposal ever dreams of investing the parish council with the means of vetoing all change and crushing all individuality. Far from it, the only absolute veto the council should have is that on neglect of duty. Too great zeal may be inexpedient, but too little is criminal. Then the use of the word 'arbitrary' in itself suggests and condemns the kind of action which is contemplated. What right has the disciple to set himself above his master? From the first day of His ministry to the last Christ's work was one continued witness against such action on the part of a Christian teacher. Every argument which would justify a vicar 'arbitrarily' altering lawful customs in ritual, would equally have demanded the extinction of the Temple ceremonial by the Divine power. Once for all Christ showed us that education has a more permanent power than brute force. Not one 'lawful' custom should be overthrown until it disappeared by the wishes of the people themselves, this being the final proof of the teacher's success. Lastly, the qualification 'lawful' secures on the side of the congregation the whole authority of the Church. When her law has recognized any custom, he must indeed have a high opinion of his own wisdom who shall declare it to be so injurious to the spiritual welfare of his

Parochial Church Councils

congregation that it must be altered, even at the cost of the loss of their allegiance.

The third duty which should be imposed on the council is that of sharing in the appointment of the incumbent. Mr. Lyttelton's Benefice Bill stipulates that

'The bishop shall not institute any person to a benefice until the expiration of one month after notice . . . has been served on the churchwardens, who shall publish the notice, &c. Any three parishioners may serve on the bishop a representation objecting to the institution on any ground on which the bishop is empowered to refuse institution.'

The duty of representing the congregation should not, we believe, be thus thrown on irresponsible individuals who may well be animated by personal rather than by public motives. The proper body to act is the council, which should either have the duty of making representations direct to the bishop, or should nominate certain representatives to sit on the Diocesan Patronage Council *ad hoc*, as in the Church Reform League patronage proposals. And a unanimous recommendation from either the parochial council or from the above-mentioned Diocesan Patronage Council should be itself a 'legal ground' entitling the bishop to refuse institution, the patron in that case being free of course to submit another name. Will the critic kindly note here that this means neither popular election by the council or congregation nor a patronage board after the Irish model, but simply the reduction of the patron's right within its original limits as a right to 'present' a name only; while the bishop's original right to reject all names is restored, subject to its being exercised with the approval of the parish. Again, no 'exchange' should be sanctioned by the bishop until it has been considered by the council. We have too many rolling-stones ruining parish after parish to-day, their opportunity being found unfortunately in the eagerness of their victims to escape by facilitating their descent on another diocese. If the sale of souls by auction is bad, this barter is worse, for it is secret, so that the sufferers cannot even escape by themselves competing for the purchase of their own rights.

Then, fourthly, these councils should have a very complete responsibility for all parochial finance, and to them should obviously be also transferred the present responsibilities of the churchwardens with regard to the churchyard and to the maintenance of the fabric of the church. And as responsibility implies the means of discharging it, let the present technical restrictions that make the churchwardens' office a legal farce be wholly removed. 'Our' church must imply 'our' free right of access to it. Yet as the law stands to-day, even the churchwardens themselves have no legal right of entry to the building they are supposed to keep in repair. This right of the incumbent to lock the church door from Sunday to Sunday should disappear. Then, again, the control of the council over the churchyard is also very desirable. Let us make the last resting-place of the village fathers the care of their sons and evoke the interest of ownership. Here if anywhere is land which should be the estate of our people themselves. Is it surprising that they are sceptical as to the church being for them, when, as has been done ere now, the vicar's sheep may be grazed over

Parochial Church Councils

the graves of their dead, whether they like it or not? Then, again, the church collections are a legitimate interest for the council. Formerly when the church rate met all expenses the control of the parishioners was complete. Now that the collection has happily superseded it, no corresponding control has followed. The choice of the object rests now practically with the incumbent; some will have no collections for anything outside the parish, and others adopt the opposite policy. Surely the giver is entitled to no small share in deciding such questions. Let the clergy teach boldly the rule of proportionate almsgiving, and the duty of the churchman to his diocese and to his Church, as well as to his parish, and they need not worry longer over empty alms-plates. Make the council proud of its budget, so that year by year it may cherish its growth and seek to extend its scope, casting the net ever wider and wider until there shall not be a single member of the congregation, however poor, but is supporting some work.

Lastly, as we pointed out at the beginning of this essay, these councils should be the electors of the Ruridecanal, Diocesan and Provincial Councils. The present system of indirect election practically involves the perpetual re-election of certain conspicuous names by a very few electors, while the great majority of church members have no opportunity of ever voting for any one. If all the lay representatives were chosen directly by the parochial councils, not only would much greater interest be aroused but there would be some chance of making them much more representative of the general body of church people than they now are; while the figure-head, the obstructionist, and the bore, would have short shrift. Further, the subjects to be discussed by the other councils might advantageously be previously circulated among the parish councils, whose resolutions would be an extremely valuable indication of the feeling of our people in regard to them. An informal referendum could in fact thus be inaugurated and the proceedings of the higher councils made of real interest to every member of the Church.

In conclusion, what is the first step? This—let the Diocesan Conferences throughout the country make these Parish Church Councils a subject of discussion this autumn (as they did self-government last year), and let their resolutions take the shape of the appointment of a committee to draft, in conjunction with the bishop, a 'diocesan scheme' for their establishment. Let the bishop be requested to issue this scheme and encourage his clergy to invite the co-operation of the laity in their parishes in organizing them wherever possible.

Let the keynote of every diocesan scheme be to make the office of the council real. The more work and the more responsibility they have the more chance is there of the best men coming forward to take part in their deliberations, and of all the members trying to make themselves worthy of their position.

This we know involves a self-denying ordinance of no small scope from our clergy. But it is the old question of the Sabbath once more; or we may ask, Which interests come first, those of the officers or those of the army? There is but one answer possible here, and we know the clergy of the English Church too well to doubt what theirs would be. Our task is to win them to the trial; to show them the ideal of common work, baptized members shoulder to shoulder with ordained members, as the true ideal of the Christian Church whose other name is the Brotherhood of Service. Only we must not be disappointed if this ideal be not realized all at once. Children cannot attain to man's stature in a day, and many a stumble and fall is their fate on the way. Mistakes of all kind are inevitable and failures in many places, but, rightly used, failures and mistakes are the true parents of success.

VIII

REFORM OF PATRONAGE

By Clement Y. Sturge, Barrister at Law

It seems best in an essay dealing with the reform of patronage to begin with a brief historical survey of the evils which it is desired to remedy.

The sin of simony is inveterate in the Christian Church. In its original signification, derived from the sin of Simon Magus, simony was restricted to the purchase of a spiritual gift, e.g. holy orders. This sort of spiritual depravity, now happily extinct among us, was the only form of the evil to which avarice or ambition could lead a faulty Christian in primitive times. But when the days of persecution and proscription were passed, and the Church had settled down to an undisputed empire over the souls of men, the centre of possible corruption shifted. Men began from the best of motives to endow the priesthood with lands and money in order that provision for the cure of souls in and around their own homesteads might never fail. The man of great possessions, in his pious care for his own household and the serfs who tilled his lands, made a bargain with the bishop, as the supreme pastor in whom was vested

Reform of Patronage

the cure of souls of the whole diocese, by which the bishop agreed to delegate his responsibility within a particular area to a priest whom the lord undertook to maintain at his own charges, the lord on his part stipulating for the right in perpetuity to nominate and present for the bishop's acceptance the priest whom he so maintained. Thus arose in England the system of private patronage, which has subsisted substantially in its present form for more than a thousand years. Corruption was not long in creeping in. Lingard in his *History of the Anglo-Saxon Church* [1] tells us that 'in the latter part of the Anglo-Saxon period, when the rule for ordination was less strictly observed, priests might be found elsewhere than in the episcopal monastery; and the lords of vacant churches began to negotiate with such priests for the sale of the ecclesiastical benefice, as they would for that of a secular *loen*. The abuse made rapid progress. Covenants were entered into between the lord and his nominee, by which the latter consented to purchase the benefice by the payment of a gross sum, or of a yearly rent, or by the surrender of a portion of the annual oblations, tithes, or dues, and in some cases of the whole of the church's income, in lieu of a yearly stipend.' The frequency with which after the Norman Conquest the English primates enacted canons against simony shows how deep a root the evil had struck. At the Synod of Winchester in 1070 Lanfranc framed a canon [2] 'Concerning the coming in of bishops and abbots by simoniacal heresy,' and again in 1075 at London, 'that

[1] Vol. i. p. 193.
[2] Johnson, *Ecclesiastical Laws*, ii. 1070.

no one buy or sell orders, or any ecclesiastical office wherein the cure of souls is concerned.' Anselm decrees at Westminster in 1102 'that churches or prebends be not bought,' and William of Corbeuil writes with greater vehemence in 1127 : ' By the authority of Peter the prince of the apostles, and our own, we forbid churches, benefices, or dignities to be in any wise sold or bought. If the offender be a clergyman (though a regular canon or monk), let him be degraded ; if a layman, let him be outlawed and excommunicated.' The legatine canons of Westminster passed by Alberic of Ostia at a national council holden in 1138 during a vacancy in the see of Canterbury contain the following provision: ' Let no one accept a church or benefice from the hand of a layman. When any man takes investiture from the bishop, let him swear on the Gospel that he has neither given nor promised anything for it by himself, or by any other person; else the donation shall be null, and both the giver and receiver liable to canonical punishment.' Canons of a similar tenour were enacted by Archbishop Richard in 1175, by Stephen Langton in 1222, and by Cardinal Othobon, the Papal Legate, in 1268. Simony was prohibited in 1179 at the third Council of Lateran, whose decrees were accepted as part of the law of England. It was held to be a sin of such enormity that the Pope alone could absolve those guilty of it. The mediaeval Church continued to grapple with the evil with but indifferent success; ' nor is it likely ' (says a modern writer[1]), ' whilst the sale of dispensations and indulgences openly prevailed, that

[1] Rogers, *Ecclesiastical Law*, p. 915 n.

Reform of Patronage

the laws against simony could be enforced with vigour.'
The great upheaval of the sixteenth century, by loosening the old bonds, and restraints by which the Church had held society together, shattered the weapon of spiritual terror once for all. Some other check was needed if the scant endowments which still remained as a temporal provision for the Church, when the Reformation settlement began to assume finality, were not to work the utter downfall of religion. There had been great disorder and confusion. Patrons of livings presented their huntsmen and gamekeepers to the benefices in their gift and pocketed the stipend [1]. Usurpers presented to benefices over which they had no right. It was time for the legislature to step in. Hence in 1589 was passed the statute 31 Eliz. c. 6, which is still the Church's main protection against simoniacal corruption. It struck not merely at the simoniacal clerk, but at the corrupt patron who made a traffic of his property in the benefice. For the first time the patron found himself threatened with something more tangible than a spiritual censure—a heavy fine and the loss of his patronage for that turn. 'Whether simony was an offence at Common Law before the statute of Elizabeth' (says the writer already quoted [2]) 'does not seem clear. There seems, however, to be no trace of any direct proceedings in the temporal courts. This perhaps may be accounted for on the ground that, the punishment being only *pro salute animae*, the offence was more immediately cognizable in the spiritual court. But as

---

[1] Green, *Short History of the English People*, p. 352.
[2] Rogers, *Eccl. Law*, p. 917.

in that court they could only proceed for the purpose of ecclesiastical censures or deprivation, the incumbent might hold the living till sentence of deprivation was pronounced, the presentation being only voidable; or perhaps he escaped altogether from the difficulty attending this mode of punishment.' It should be noted that section 8 of the Act expressly recognized and preserved the old jurisdiction of the ecclesiastical courts. 'One principal object of the statute was to strengthen the weakness of the ecclesiastical law, and to inflict penalties and forfeitures on corrupt patrons, who are not only made to forfeit to the Crown the presentation *pro hac vice*, but also the value of two years' profits of the church. The ecclesiastical law could only punish the corrupt incumbent; but the legislature, perceiving the serious consequences of this defect, interposed in order to punish the patron, who is generally the corrupter, and always the partaker of the incumbent's guilt[1].' 31 Eliz. c. 6, wrote Archbishop Wake long afterwards, was not *privative* of the jurisdiction of the Church, but *cumulative*. 'The object of the statute,' said Sir Robert Phillimore before the Select Committee of the House of Lords in 1874, 'was to make that illegal by the law of the land, which was sinful by the law of the Church.'

The courts of law for three hundred years have been occupied in determining whether a particular set of circumstances must be held to bring a particular presentation to a benefice within the penalties of this statute or not. The result is a curious medley. Some highly

[1] Rogers, *Eccl. Law*, p. 921.

Reform of Patronage

reprehensible practices have slipped through the meshes of the law, while other transactions which are blameless morally, and practically often desirable, are condemned as simoniacal. Thus it is not simony to purchase the advowson of a living when the incumbent to the knowledge of both contracting parties is *in articulo mortis*, so long as breath remains in his body[1]. But to covenant with a financially embarrassed clergyman, who would gladly divest himself of his cure if he could afford to do so, to resign for a lump sum down, and so set both parish and incumbent free from an alliance irksome and injurious to both, is against the law[2]. A man may purchase an advowson with a secret stipulation that the vendor shall pay him interest on the purchase-money until a vacancy occurs[3]; but the presentee may not accept the benefice under promise to pay a small annuity out of the income to the widow of his predecessor[4]. It is not simony on an exchange of benefices, arranged with the sanction of the bishop, to covenant that neither party shall exact dilapidations from the other[5]; but to pay over something in respect of the greater value of the benefice so taken in exchange would bring both incumbents within the penalty of the law[6]. 'The difference between what the law allows and what it forbids' (said Bishop Magee in the House of Lords in 1874) 'is in most cases so purely technical and

[1] *Fox* v. *Bishop of Chester*, 2 B. & C. 635.
[2] The Church Patronage Bill of 1881 proposed to legalize this.
[3] *Sweet* v. *Meredith*, 3 Giff. 610; 8 Jur. N. S. 637.
[4] Watson, *Clergyman's Law*, ed. 1701, p. 23; Cripps, *Law of Church and Clergy*, p. 471, commenting on *Baker* v. *Mounford*, Noy 142.
[5] *Wright* v. *Davies*, 1 C. P. D. 638.
[6] The Church Patronage Bills of 1875 and 1881 proposed to legalize this.

conventional, that it touches no man's conscience; and consequently evasions of a law so utterly unreasonable come to be but lightly regarded.... The law of simony has thus, as it were, slipped from off its moral basis, and been broken into shapeless fragments in its fall.' The attention of the Courts has in fact been generally directed to what may be called the niceties of the law of simony, which do not necessarily imply any moral guilt in the parties whose conduct is under investigation. But cases of a more flagrant nature have from time to time arisen which called for the exercise of the extreme rigour of the law. In 1699 Dr. Watson, bishop of St. David's, was deprived of his see by Archbishop Tenison for the offence of selling the benefices in his gift and for other simoniacal practices[1]; while so recently as 1841 Dr. William Cockburn[2], dean of York, was convicted in the Court of the metropolitan of selling the next presentations to the livings of which as dean he was patron and ordinary. He was sentenced by the archbishop to deprivation for contumacy and simony; but on appeal to the Queen's Courts he escaped on the technical ground that the charge against him ought to have been brought under the then recent Church Discipline Act, 3 and 4 Vict. c. 86, and that the archbishop had no jurisdiction to deprive at his metropolitical visitation[3]. The Dean, who had the effrontery to maintain that he was within his rights in selling his next presentations, was re-

---

[1] *Lucy* v. *Bishop of St. David's*, 1 Ld. Raym. 541; 1 Salk. 135.

[2] Afterwards Sir William Cockburn, Bart., uncle to the late Lord Chief Justice Cockburn.

[3] Dean of York's Case, 2 Q. B. 1.

Reform of Patronage

instated, and continued to hold office until his death in 1858.

In 1713 the statute 13 Anne c. 11 was passed with the view of suppressing an evil which the Parliament of Elizabeth had not foreseen. Reciting that 'some of the clergy have procured preferments for themselves by buying ecclesiastical livings, and others have been thereby discouraged,' it proceeds to enact that 'if any person . . . shall by reason of any promise, agreement &c. . . . take, procure, or accept the next avoidance of, or presentation to, any benefice with cure of souls, dignity or prebend, or living ecclesiastical, and shall be presented or collated thereupon, every such presentation &c. . . . shall be utterly void, frustrate, and of no effect in law, and such agreement shall be deemed and taken to be a simoniacal contract.' This statute did not go to the root of the evil, and so far as I am aware there is only one instance of deprivation for traffic of this nature, in a case which happened in 1869[1]. It does not seem to have entered the minds of Queen Anne's draftsmen that a clergyman was likely to buy an advowson, i.e. the perpetual right of presentation, for himself. This practice constitutes in fact by far the largest and most lucrative branch of the traffic in livings. A clergyman buys an advowson, presents himself, and sells again (with the prospect of 'early possession') as soon as he wishes to move on to a more agreeable neighbourhood. It is said that as many as six hundred benefices, where the incumbent is his own patron, have been subject in recent years to transactions of this nature. The statute of

[1] *Lee* v. *Merest*, 39 L. J., Eccl. 53.

Anne is, moreover, easily evaded. A clergyman wishing to obtain the next presentation to a living (the market price of which is less by about one-third or one-fourth than that of the advowson) deposits the purchase-money with his wife or some friend whom he can trust, who thereupon effects the purchase and presents the clerk.

There is one class of cases in which the legislature has actually legalized what was originally an evasion of its own laws. The statute of Elizabeth was felt to be irksome by many patrons, and at an early date they had recourse to a device for rendering the law more flexible by taking resignation bonds from the clerk presented, who bound himself in a heavy penalty to resign his benefice when required by the patron to do so. Such bonds were either *general*, i.e. an agreement to resign without reason assigned, or *special*, i.e. an agreement to resign in favour of a particular person, most frequently the patron's son. The practice was no new thing in the history of the Church. In 1531 the clergy in Convocation petitioned the bishops that they would not exact resignation bonds. Archbishop Warham's register contains three such bonds (to enforce residence), which he exacted of incumbents before institution. General bonds of resignation were declared to be good in law by the Court of King's Bench in two cases decided in 1610 and 1630[1], and though Bishop Stillingfleet inveighed bitterly against the practice[2], their legality was unquestioned for one hundred and fifty-years. But in 1783 in the case of *Bishop of London*

---

[1] *Jones* v. *Lawrence*, Cro. Jac. 248; *Babington* v. *Wood*, Cro. Car. 180.
[2] Stillingfleet on Bonds of Resignation, 1695.

Reform of Patronage

v. *Fytche*[1], when Bishop Lowth refused to institute a clergyman who was under bond to resign, the House of Lords held that general bonds of resignation were simoniacal and void. The case is memorable as being the last occasion when the bishops voted on a judicial issue; their votes, with the aid of that of Lord Chancellor Thurlow, just turned the scale and reversed the judgements of the Courts below. In 1827 the House of Lords went still further, and pronounced special bonds of resignation illegal[2]. A Parliament of patrons took fright, the practice of taking special bonds had very generally prevailed, and a large number of patrons and incumbents found themselves endangered by the decision. A bill was immediately introduced by the Archbishop of Canterbury (Manners Sutton) validating all such agreements in the past, and in the following year the statute Geo. IV. c. 94, which legalized and regulated bonds of resignation for the future, became law. It provided for the insertion in the bond of the names of two persons within certain degrees of affinity to the patron, in favour of whom the resignation should be lawful, compelled the bishop to accept such resignation, and imposed certain conditions as to registration and other matters. Bishop Magee warmly denounced this statute in the House of Lords in 1874, and singled out for especial censure the clause abrogating the episcopal veto in the case in which of all others it was most likely to be required. The Royal Commission on Patronage reported in 1879 in favour of repealing the Act, and recommended 'that

[1] 1 East, 486.
[2] *Fletcher* v. *Lord Sondes*, 3 Bing. 508.

the patron desiring to defer the presentation to a benefice should be required to name two future presentees as now, and that the bishop should meanwhile provide for the duties of the benefice by licensing a curate thereto, who should receive the full profits of the benefice, and be subject to all legal charges and obligations thereupon.' Most of the legislative proposals of recent years have contained a provision for abolishing resignation bonds; but such bonds are not now common, and it may be doubted whether in practice it does not work out better to put a capable man into a living under bond to resign, rather than (the inevitable alternative) to nominate a succession of aged and decrepit clergy, who can be trusted not to trouble the patron long. There is nothing in itself repugnant to a man's self-respect in accepting work in a parish for a limited number of years—the thing is done in the Wesleyan community every day—and so long as private patronage exists and men continue to regard the livings in their gift as in the nature of a provision for their families, some such legalized device for keeping livings open seems to be inevitable. It is noticeable that the clause abolishing resignation bonds finds no place in either of this year's Benefices Bills.

It will readily be conceded by every candid mind that the foregoing summary discloses a very unsatisfactory state of the law, and in fact church reformers for the last thirty years have been unremitting in their efforts to put an end to the worst of the abuses incident to the system of private patronage. Since the year 1870 no fewer than twenty-five Bills, dealing with various aspects of the problem, have been introduced into the

Reform of Patronage

House of Lords or the House of Commons, only two of which have reached the other House of Parliament. Of these the most important were the Bishop of Peterborough's Bill, which passed the House of Lords in 1875, mangled and deprived of its most valuable provisions, Mr. Stanhope's Bill, perhaps the most statesmanlike and comprehensive of the whole series, introduced into the House of Commons in 1881, the two bills of the late Archbishop of Canterbury, brought forward in 1886 and 1887, and the Benefices Bill of 1896, which, after passing the second reading by a majority of 178, and successfully running the gauntlet of the Standing Committee on Law, succumbed at the report stage to the opposition of a little knot of patronage-mongers in the House aided by some conscientious English Liberationists and the more violent of the Welsh Irreconcileables.

In 1870 Mr. (now Viscount) Cross introduced a modest little Bill into the House of Commons dealing with next presentations, sales with secret conditions, and grants of rights of patronage 'at a time when the incumbent is by reason of sickness in extreme danger of death'— to meet the case of *Fox* v. *Bishop of Chester*. This was followed in 1874 by the more ambitious scheme of Sir John Kennaway and Mr. J. G. Talbot, who proposed to establish in every diocese a body of twelve Patronage Commissioners with power to borrow money from the National Debt Commissioners, to purchase and hold advowsons, and to charge the purchase-money on the profits of the benefice. Certain of the benefices in their gift were to be assigned as the reward of long service in the Church, a private patron was required to certify to the Commissioners that the presentee had served as a curate for at least three years, and a public patron that he had so served for five years. Corrupt presentations were to be void, Her Majesty was to present to the benefice as though the presentation had lapsed to her, 'and shall continue to do so as long as the offending patron lives, who also shall be deprived of all right to sell, assign or otherwise transfer his patronage during his lifetime'—a penalty far more severe than that imposed by 31 Eliz. c. 6.

In April, 1874, Bishop Magee moved for a Select Committee of the House of Lords to inquire into the law of patronage, and in February of the following year he brought in a Bill based on the recommendations of the Committee. The Bill proposed to make it lawful for a bishop to refuse institution on the ground that the presentee had not been three years in holy orders, that he was over seventy years of age (which the Lords characteristically changed to seventy-five), or that he was 'unable from bodily infirmity adequately to perform the duties of the benefice.' It required that notice of the intended institution (or collation, where the bishop was himself the patron) should be forwarded to the 'officiating minister' and one of the churchwardens of the parish, to be published on the church doors and read in the church during the hours of divine service on two successive Sundays. It gave power to any three or more parishioners (defined as 'male persons of full age'[1]), after giving security for costs, to enter a *caveat* within fourteen days stating the grounds of objection to the proposed institu-

---

[1] No subsequent Bill contains this distinction of sex.

Reform of Patronage

tion. With the consent of all parties, the bishop with the assistance of his chancellor might hear and determine the matter, his decision to be final ; but failing such consent an appeal lay to the judge appointed under the then recent Public Worship Regulation Act, and from him to the Queen in Council. A patron or presentee aggrieved by the bishop's refusal to institute could appeal in the same manner. Both patron and clerk were required to make a declaration in terms so much more precise than the existing declaration[1] against simony by the clerk that even the laxest conscience would find it difficult to slip through the meshes, and any person making, or aiding and abetting, a false declaration, was to be ' prosecuted, deemed guilty of a misdemeanour (if convicted), and punished accordingly,' in some way not made clear by the Bill. Covenants to pay money on exchange of benefices were legalized, agreements affecting rights of presentation were to be registered in the Office of Land Registry, payment of interest on the purchase-money of an advowson until a vacancy was forbidden and donatives were abolished. The Select Committee having refused by a majority of one to condemn the sale of next presentations, Bishop Magee reluctantly refrained from dealing with them. The Bill contained, however, one very stringent provision aimed at clerical patrons who present themselves. No clerk who in his own name, or by a trustee or trustees acting on his behalf, had purchased the advowson of a benefice was to be instituted thereto until the *second avoidance* after such purchase,

[1] Under 28 & 29 Vict. c. 122. s. 5, substituted for the old oath against simony required by Canon 40 of 1603.

or until the expiration of *ten years* from the date of such purchase, whichever should first happen. The penalty for an evasion of this section was to be forfeiture of the right to present for that turn to the Crown, disqualification from ever holding that particular benefice, and payment of double the value of one year's profits to Queen Anne's Bounty. The Bill was an honest attempt to deal with the evils which the Select Committee had reported to exist; but it was clumsy and complicated, public opinion was not ripe for its more drastic provisions, and it left the House of Lords in a form which rendered it practically worthless.

The subject was allowed to slumber, so far as Parliament was concerned, for the next six years; but in the meantime the Royal Commission on the Sale, Exchange, and Resignation of Ecclesiastical Benefices, appointed in 1878, had issued its report, and with a new Parliament the matter was revived. Mr. Stanhope's Bill of 1881 made it lawful for the bishop to refuse institution to any presentee of less than twenty-five or more than seventy years of age, and empowered him 'either of his own mere motion, or at the instance of any two parishioners of full age,' to issue a commission to five persons, of whom two were to be laymen resident in the diocese, to inquire and report (1) whether the presentee was 'unable from bodily infirmity or mental incapacity to perform adequately the duties of the benefice,' (2) whether he had 'committed an offence, for which any incumbent committing the same would be liable to be deprived of his benefice, and has not since the commission of such offence sufficiently purged the same by good conduct.' If the commissioners, or any three of them, reported in the affirmative, the bishop was not to institute or collate the presentee. The bishop was required in any case a month at least before institution to issue a 'mandate' to the 'officiating minister' requiring him to give notice 'at morning service immediately before the reading of the first lesson on the next Sunday after receipt hereof' to the parishioners, any two or more of whom, if they knew any cause why the presentee by reason of immoral conduct, or bodily infirmity, or mental incapacity ought not to become rector (vicar, &c.) of the parish, were enjoined to signify the same to the bishop in writing. Payments on resignation and exchange of benefices with the approval of the bishop were legalized, sales of next presentations were forbidden, and the Clergy Resignation Bonds Act, 1829, was repealed. But the most important provision of all, anticipating a proposal put forward by the Church Reform League in our own day, was that for the establishment in every diocese of a 'Diocesan Patronage Board,' to consist of the bishop, two proctors of the clergy in convocation, and two laymen resident in the diocese who were to be nominated by the bishop and proctors. The Board was to have power to 'take, accept, and hold all gifts and assurances whatever, made by will, codicil, or otherwise, and to apply the same for the purchase of any advowson, or the improvement of benefices of which the advowsons are vested in the said Board.' In cases of lapse the Board might present to the benefice in lieu of the bishop. The Bill made little way in the Commons, and in May of the same year it was re-introduced in a shorter form and shorn of its most valuable provisions. Bills on much the same lines, but omitting the Diocesan Patronage Boards, bearing the names of Mr. Stanhope and others, were brought forward and withdrawn in 1882 and 1884. On the Radical side of the House Mr. Leatham, Mr. Rylands, Mr. H. H. Fowler, Mr. George Russell and others tried their hands at reform from another standpoint in 1882, 1883, 1884, and 1886. They proposed to restrict the sale of advowsons (1) to the lord of a manor with advowson appendant, (2) to large landowners with certain specified proprietary qualifications, (3) to public patrons, and trustees not having power of sale, (4) to the Governors of Queen Anne's Bounty, who were empowered to borrow money from the Treasury, to purchase the fee simple of an advowson from the patron at a valuation, and to charge the purchase-money on the income of the benefice, as is done in the case of loans to incumbents under existing Acts of Parliament. These proposals did not commend themselves to Churchmen, and they never saw the light again.

In 1886 the late Archbishop of Canterbury made an earnest attempt to grapple with the problem. He introduced a measure containing elaborate provisions for the constitution in every diocese of a Council of Public Patronage, to consist of an equal number of clerical and lay members, viz. the bishop, the archdeacons, one beneficed clergyman elected by his brother clergy, a representative of the cathedral chapter, one layman elected by the churchwardens of each archdeaconry, and certain other laymen nominated by the lords lieutenant or chairman of quarter sessions of counties wholly or

Reform of Patronage

partly within the diocese. This body was to have power (*a*) to purchase and hold lands, and advowsons, and any rights of presentation to benefices, (*b*) to receive and hold funds, bequests, and money for the purpose of such purchases, (*c*) in their discretion to approve or disapprove proposed purchasers of rights of patronage, (*d*) to exercise such rights of presentation and to perform such duties of inquiry into the qualifications of presentees as were conferred or imposed by the Act. Rights of patronage were to be exercised by a Special Committee of the Council, with which were to be associated (with equal rights of voting) the rural dean and the churchwardens of the parish affected. The Bill forbade sales of advowsons except (*a*) to a person described as a 'qualified parishioner,' owning property in the parish of not less than one-tenth of the total rateable value of the parish, and not less than £200 per annum, (*b*) a public patron, (*c*) a person approved by the Council of Public Patronage. Sales of next presentations, sales by auction, and the mortgaging of advowsons were prohibited; but advowsons appendant might still be sold by auction or by private contract together with the lands or hereditaments to which they were appendant. Where an advowson was appendant to lands not within the parish, or where the lands to which it was appendant amounted to less than one-sixth of the rateable value of the parish, it was to be deemed an advowson in gross and subject to the restrictions as to sale prescribed by the Act. The Council was to have a right of pre-emption except in the case of sale to a 'qualified parishioner,' and was in no case to approve as a purchaser any 'person engaged in negotiating sales or exchanges of rights of patronage or exchanges of benefices '—in other words, 'clerical agents' were excluded. Sales to the Council *during a vacancy* were to be lawful. Declarations were required from the purchaser, patron, and clerk; and the bishop (if he thought fit) could require from the presentee letters testimonial under the hands of three beneficed clergymen, countersigned by the bishop of the diocese in which each was beneficed, together with a 'declaration of all benefices, curacies, lectureships, and other appointments or employments, whether spiritual or educational, held by him since his ordination.' In addition to the grounds of refusal allowed in former Bills, the bishop might reject the presentee on the grounds 'that in the opinion of the Council of Public Patronage he is so incumbered with debt as not to be able adequately to perform the duties of the benefice, or as to give rise to scandal,' that 'such scandal or evil report exists concerning his moral conduct, behaviour, or manner of life, that he ought not to be instituted,' and that 'in the opinion of *two-thirds* of the Council he is not a fit and proper person to be instituted to the benefice in question.' Notice of presentation was in all cases to be 'published in the parish' one clear month before institution, whereupon 'any parishioner' might submit any objections in writing to the bishop, who was to refer them for inquiry to the Council. The Council reported in due course to the bishop, from whom an appeal lay to the archbishop of the province, whose decision was to be final. The Bill contained two other important provisions. (1) A benefice was to be *ipso facto* void if it 'continued for the space of one whole year under sequestration issued on the bankruptcy of the incumbent, or in aid of any writ of execution against his property,' or if the incumbent incurred 'two such sequestrations in the space of two years.' (2) Where the incumbent was a lunatic so found by inquisition, and the Commissioners in Lunacy certified that he had been 'for one whole year kept in restraint or under supervision as a lunatic, and is still of unsound mind,' the bishop might proceed to declare the benefice void, and assign to the lunatic incumbent a pension not exceeding one-third of the net annual value of the benefice. This Bill too, though a much more workmanlike production than the Bishop of Peterborough's Bill of 1875, was too ambitious in its scope, and cut too deeply into vested interests to have any chance of passing; it was denounced by Lord Grimthorpe as the most revolutionary measure affecting the Church that had been brought forward since the Long Parliament, and the dissolution of Parliament a few weeks later gave it the quietus. It was reintroduced by the Archbishop in 1887 with some important modifications. For the Council of Public Patronage and its Special Committee was substituted a Council of Presentations, chosen by a somewhat complicated system of clerical and lay election, with powers very similar to those contained in the Bill of 1886. The number of years in priest's orders requirable before institution was reduced from three to *two*, and the provision as to general unfitness for a particular benefice was omitted; but in all material respects the Bill was the same as that of the year before. Lord Salisbury moved and carried an amendment, the object of which was to get rid of the Council of Presentations, which he considered highly objectionable as introducing the elective principle into the management of church patronage and the appointment of judges, and the Bill after passing the third reading was dropped.

The energies of churchmen for the next few years were concentrated on the effort to reform and simplify legal procedure in bringing 'criminous clerks' to justice, which issued in the Clergy Discipline Act of 1892, and the question of Patronage Reform once more slumbered. But with a new Parliament it again revived, and in 1893 the Archbishop of Canterbury introduced a measure framed on the lines of previous Bills, but omitting all reference to parishioners, and throwing overboard as useless lumber the cumbrous and complicated provisions of former years as to 'Councils of Public Patronage,' 'Councils of Presentations,' &c. The limit of years in priest's orders was still further reduced to *one* year, rendering this provision almost worthless; but the Bill contained a useful definition of 'pecuniary embarrassment[1],' which might well have found a place in subsequent measures. A clerical patron was forbidden to present himself at the next avoidance after purchase —a less drastic provision than that contained in the Bishop of Peterborough's Bill of 1875. The Bill of 1893 is memorable as introducing the first attempt to deal with *incapacitated* incumbents—men past work, in plain English. It gave the bishop power on the 'representation of any three inhabitants of a parish' ('any five

[1] 'Proved by bankruptcy, declaration of insolvency, composition with creditors, sequestration, or execution upon his goods.'

Reform of Patronage

parishioners' in the Bill of 1894), 'that the incumbent of a benefice in that parish has for not less than three years last preceding been incapacitated by continuing mental or bodily infirmity from the due performance of his duties,' or 'if it otherwise becomes known to the bishop that he has been so incapacitated for that period,' to issue a commission under the Incumbents' Resignation Acts, 1871 and 1887, and to assign to the incumbent a pension of not less than one-fourth of the annual value of the benefice. This is really a matter of discipline, and, as the event has proved, is best dealt with entirely apart from all questions affecting rights of patronage.

The principal features of the Commons Bill of 1894 and the Archbishop's Bill of 1895 were the clauses aimed at sale with 'vacant possession.' The Bill of 1894 provided that no right of presentation should be exercised within *two years* of the transfer or transmission of such right, and that re-sale within two years of institution should be void. The Archbishop's Bill reduced the period to *one year*, which has been adopted in subsequent Bills. The Royal Commission of 1878 had reported in favour of prohibiting re-sale within five years after sale. In 1895 some of the more determined spirits in the House of Commons introduced a purely disciplinary Bill, in which the machinery of the Pluralities Acts of 1838 and 1885 was invoked for the purpose of dealing with negligent or disabled incumbents. If the Commissioners reported, 'having regard to the inadequate performance of the ecclesiastical duties of the benefice,' that 'the incumbent is *unable or unwilling* competently to discharge the cure of souls therein,' the bishop was to have power to inhibit the incumbent, who was to be in the same position as if he had been suspended from office, and might be required to vacate the residence-house on the appointment of a curate to do the duties of the parish. An appeal lay to the archbishop, and the Commissioners had power to adjourn the inquiry for eighteen months to give the incumbent an opportunity of performing his duties in a more satisfactory manner. The Benefices Bill of 1896 was an attempt to fuse the two measures of the year before, and its fate is within the recollection of us all. It was overloaded, and by the severity of its disciplinary provisions it roused the opposition of a large body of the clergy, who thinking themselves hardly dealt with under the Bill, joined forces with the malcontents within the House to wreck it. Two more Bills were introduced into the House of Commons in 1897. No. 1 was mainly disciplinary, and went further in this direction than any previous proposals. The bishop was to have power, if in his opinion the duties attaching to the cure were inadequately discharged, to request the incumbent to resign, and on the report of a commission that such resignation was expedient to declare the benefice void. The Bill failed, and from this time onward it was recognized that the attempt to combine patronage reform with far-reaching schemes for superannuating outworn clergy was ill-advised and hopeless. Bill No. 2 of 1897, bearing the names of Colonel Sandys, Mr. H. S. Foster and others, was little else than a bogus Bill, the object of which would seem to have been by a skilful manipulation of words to prevent any real reform from

Reform of Patronage

passing. It referred objections to institution to the bishop's Consistory Court, whose decisions were binding on the bishop, and contained the following surprising definition of 'parishioners,' viz. 'persons for the time being registered in either the local government register of electors, or the parliamentary register of electors, in respect of property or other qualification within the area of the parish.' In the same year the Archbishop of York brought in a short Bill, which was simultaneously introduced in the House of Commons, requiring the registration of transfers of rights of patronage and presentation. It was re introduced in the Commons and withdrawn early in 1898.

The repeated failure of private members in the House of Commons and of the bishops in the House of Lords to secure the passing of even the most rudimentary measure of reform—a failure extending over wellnigh thirty years—and the pressure of public opinion both in and out of Parliament have at length opened the eyes of the Government to the absolute necessity of themselves dealing with the subject. The matter has been steadily ripening for legislation ever since the repulse of the Liberals on the Disestablishment cry in 1885. Repeated discussions in the Convocations, in the Houses of Laymen, at Church Congresses, at Diocesan Conferences in London and elsewhere, have shown that Churchmen have made up their minds, and the question can no longer be shelved. The two Bills of 1898 are now before Parliament and the country, and any detailed criticism of them within the limits of this essay would be out of place. The Government Bill has the merit of being short and business-like, and if it does not go so far as many church reformers would desire, it strikes very effectively at most of the acknowledged abuses, which have figured time after time in the discussions and legislative proposals of the last thirty years. The sale of next presentations, fraudulent re-transfers, postponement of payment of the purchase money, or payment of interest thereon, until a vacancy, are forbidden. Twelve months must elapse between transfer and presentation, the grounds of refusal to institute are greatly extended, a satisfactory Court of Appeal is provided, false declarations are treated as perjury, simony is made an offence within the meaning of the Clergy Discipline Act, the provisions of the Pluralities Acts are made applicable to negligence in the discharge of duties, and donatives (that fruitful source of evil) are abolished. The Bill is open to, and will doubtless receive, improvement; but it is an honest attempt to deal with a very difficult subject in a statesmanlike way, and if it passes in anything like its original shape, churchmen may thankfully accept it as a valuable first instalment of reform.

That a case for reform of some kind has been made out few will be found to deny. It remains to consider what reforms are practicable, what are desirable in the abstract, and what is the goal which church reformers ought to keep in view. To many minds there is something inherently revolting in the fact that rights of patronage, i. e. a solemn trust affecting the spiritual interests of a number of one's fellow-men, should be bought and sold at all. What (it is said) would be

Reform of Patronage

thought of a system which permitted posts in the Government, or the Civil Service, or the Law Courts, or the Post Office, to be knocked down to the highest bidder, or bartered away by secret treaty? How much more horrible when the office thus dragged through the mire is concerned not with the temporal interests of men, but with their souls! 'Rotten Boroughs' in Parliament have gone; we have abolished purchase in the Army, and admission by interest to the Civil Service. How comes it (they say) that this most hateful traffic, which the State will no longer endure—this 'spiritual borough-mongering'—is suffered to continue in the Church of Christ? Even churchmen would shrink from a state of the law which permitted a man to purchase the Archbishopric of Canterbury for £100,000 down [1]. 'Abolish your soul-market,' said the Bishop of Ballarat at the Nottingham Church Congress in 1897; 'your system would not be tolerated for a day by the free churchmen of the colonies.' And undoubtedly there is so much that compels one's assent in criticisms of this sort, that the task of answering them is no easy one. The only answer is that the sale of advowsons is a necessary incident of private patronage. Get rid of the one and you will get rid of the other; but so long as the system of private patronage, in favour of which there is much to be said on many grounds,

[1] According to the valuation which a witness before the House of Lords' Select Committee on Patronage put upon advowsons in the market, eight and a-third years' purchase, the market value of the primacy would be £125,000. It is needless to add that the case supposed (unless a bishop were the purchaser) would involve the far more heinous offence of the purchase of *Orders*.

continues to be upheld by Parliament and by public opinion, it is idle to talk of forbidding sales. The result would simply be to stereotype existing anomalies without affording any relief. Patronage would become stagnant in the hands of its present possessors, whose descendants or representatives a few years hence might be the unworthiest of the earth. It is bad enough, as it is, that the livings in the gift of an impoverished adventurer, who succeeds by mischance to an earldom, should be in the hands of a syndicate of Jew money-lenders [1]. But the policy of retaining private patronage, and at the same time rendering rights of patronage inalienable, would land us in an *impasse* infinitely worse. Free sale in advowsons, under present conditions, is as necessary as free sale in land. We can only make the best of the system as we find it, and as practical men confine our attention to so regulating and restricting sales that corrupt transactions, which no legislation can entirely prevent, shall become as difficult as possible. This has been in fact the object of most of the Patronage Bills of the last thirty years, which have been so unjustly derided as a mere tinkering with scandals. The Bill of 1874, Mr. Leatham's Bills 1882–1886, and the Archbishop of Canterbury's Bills of 1886 and 1887, all contained proposals, more or less unworkable, for limiting the sale of advowsons. But the matter touches proprietary interests so closely that nothing short of an overpowering public demand will avail to work a change. A step in the right direction would be the establishment in every diocese of a Diocesan Trust, to which patrons

---

[1] This actually happened a year or two ago.

Reform of Patronage

weary of their responsibility might voluntarily convey their rights, and which by the aid of benefactions and bequests might gradually buy out the smaller men. It is a defect in the present law that a patron cannot transfer his right to the bishop without going to the expense of obtaining a licence in mortmain.

On the point of compensation it is worth while to quote the evidence of a witness, Mr. J. K. Aston, the Treasurer of Queen Anne's Bounty, before the House of Lords' Select Committee in 1874. He said:—

'There is no present purchasing power in the Church of England to get rid of private patronage. . . . If you deprive the patrons of the right of sale, you immediately, according to my own computations, have to deal with a property, a marketable property, worth not less than seventeen millions. . . . According to the Clergy List, I estimate the annual value of private patronage at £1,893,226; but I believe the actual fact would be nearer two millions. . . . If it were desirable to buy up the private patronage, and a charge of one per cent. per annum was put upon the benefices, I think in the course of eighty years, there would be a sufficient fund accumulated to buy every owner of an advowson out at the full marketable value.'

A suggestion is often made, which was in the minds of Archbishop Benson and others in drafting their Bills, that only advowsons appendant to a manor, or held with lands in the parish of a certain rateable value, should be permitted to be sold. It is argued that the lord of the manor, or the large land-owner in the parish, will feel a natural solicitude for the spiritual welfare of his tenants and labourers, and that when the land changes hands it is only right that the duty of nominating to the cure of souls should go with it. It is very difficult to ascertain even approximately the proportion which advowsons appendant bear to advowsons in gross: indeed it has been doubted whether, after the lapse of 600 years, advowsons appendant, in the strict sense of the term, exist at all. The late Lord Selborne expressed the opinion in 1874 that they were very rare, and when it is remembered that no new manor has been created since 1290, and that an advowson appendant, once severed or 'disappended' from a manor, cannot be 're-appended,' even though it should again come into the hands of the lord, it will be granted that this opinion fell not far short of the mark. To restrict the right of sale to the owners of advowsons appendant would, therefore, be practically to abolish sale altogether; while to insist that advowsons shall always follow the land seems unduly to narrow the field of possible patrons. It comes then to this, that private patronage and the right of sale must stand and fall together. The long procession of abortive Bills from 1870 to 1897 bear witness to the earnestness with which Churchmen have striven to guard this right from abuse.

The sale of next presentations stands on a wholly different footing. To part with a right once for all is an honest and straightforward proceeding; but here the aim is, while retaining the right, to make money out of the immediately impending responsibility. No man who really valued the right, and felt it a privilege to select a clergyman for the cure of souls, would be willing

Reform of Patronage

to part with his responsibility piecemeal in this fashion. As vacancies occur, an unconscientious patron is under a direct temptation to put in a succession of old and incompetent men that the next presentation may be sold as advantageously as possible. On the part of the purchaser the next presentation is almost always bought with a view of putting in a particular person, who is generally privy to the purchase, and the whole proceeding comes as near to buying the actual cure of souls as it is possible to go. The evil has been condemned over and over again, and there seems at last every probability of getting rid of it.

A word must be added on the subject of donatives. They stand, as it were, altogether outside law. 'These eccentric relics of papal times,' writes Mr. Chancellor Dibdin[1], 'about seventy in number of very small value, were originally chapels which, generally of royal foundation, were freed from the bishop's jurisdiction.' Some are without cure of souls. The peculiarity of a donative is that the patron collates his nominee without the intervention of the bishop, who is powerless to prevent either admission or resignation, and it can be sold during a vacancy. The incumbent is exempt from visitation, and except where expressly subjected to it by statute is not amenable to episcopal jurisdiction. The purchase of a donative with its peculiar immunities has long been recognized as a convenient instrument for effecting corrupt exchanges and forcing the hand of a bishop who refuses to accept resignation. In the diocese of Bath and Wells a good many years ago there was

[1] *Contemporary Review*, February, 1893.

a donative which was regularly used for these purposes, and changed hands about once a year. Bishop Magee said he knew of one, the selling price of which was £20, which had been sold and resold as many as five times in one year, and the writer can recall the case of a clergyman accused of a crime for which the bishop wished to proceed against him under the Clergy Discipline Act, who successfully evaded a prosecution by the simple expedient of purchasing a donative in another diocese. The bishop had refused to accept his resignation, but admission to the donative *ipso facto* vacated his benefice under the Pluralities Act, 1838, and the bishop was checkmated. Donatives also are doomed. They were condemned by the Ecclesiastical Courts Commission so long ago as 1832, and there is scarcely a Bill since 1875 which does not provide for their abolition, which cannot now be long deferred.

There remains the vexed question of the 'rights of parishioners.' What is a parishioner, and has he any rights? In law, every man, woman and child in the kingdom is a parishioner of some parish. In practice, if there are 'rights' to be exercised, there must be some limitation as to the persons entitled to them. Bishop Magee in the Bill of 1875 defined parishioner as 'a male person of full age,' Archbishop Benson did not define him at all. The Royal Commissioners in 1879 proposed to limit the parishioner's right of objection to 'resident baptized householders.' In the Bill of 1894 'parishioners' means 'parishioners of full age,' nothing being said as to sex. Bill No. 1 of 1897, as we have seen, invoked the aid of the local government and parliamentary electoral registers. Obviously if we are to have rights of interference by parishioners, we must come to some clear understanding as to who the parishioners are. Bingham in his *Origines Ecclesiasticae*[1] says, 'No man was accounted a complete layman but he that was in full communion with the Church, and had a right to participate with the faithful in all holy offices, and particularly the holy eucharist.' But the Test Act long ago made the thought of a communicant test unpopular with Englishmen, as tending to profanation and hypocrisy. A baptismal register would exclude none but Jews and Quakers, while a roll of membership or a declaration of bona fide churchmanship, though most reasonable from the point of view of Churchmen, might be objected to by others as inconsistent with the comprehensiveness of an established Church. Yet to allow every man or woman, Churchman or Dissenter, Roman Catholic or Jew, to meddle with the appointment of the parish priest could lead only to strife and confusion. A communicant roll or a declaration of bona fide churchmanship by baptized and confirmed persons are the proposals which find most favour with Churchmen, and there seems nothing unreasonable in the demand that, if Parliament consents to confer *fresh* rights on parishioners, one or other of these limiting qualifications should be recognized.

Secondly, what are the rights of a parishioner? By the Common Law of England a parishioner has the right to be baptized, married, and buried with the rites of the Church at his parish church, and to receive Holy Communion unless he be excommunicate or have been

[1] viii. 260.

warned under the rubric. The law knows nothing of any right of objection to the appointment of the parson. It is undoubtedly reasonable in theory and consonant with primitive practice that the laity of a parish should have some control over the choice of the man who is to minister to them in spirituals. But under present conditions the matter is beset with difficulties. In the American, Irish, and Colonial Churches the problem has been satisfactorily solved, because in those Churches no difficulty exists in determining who are the laity. Many plans have been suggested for conferring on the laity of England at least the right to be consulted. The Royal Commission of 1879 recommended that notice of presentation should be published in the parish church six weeks at least before the date of institution, that thereupon within fourteen days any objection signed by not less than seven resident baptized householders should be lodged with the archdeacon or rural dean, who should within ten days confer with the objectors, or if they were too numerous with a deputation not exceeding ten of them, and report to the bishop. The objections thus raised, which could only be taken on the grounds of physical infirmity or immorality, were to be tried at the suit of the parishioners by the Dean of Arches or the judge of the Chancery Court of York without appeal. This plan had many merits, but also some defects. The mind recoils from the picture of the faithful laity dependent for the appointment of a pastor on the dilatory methods of Lord Penzance!

The proposals of Bishop Magee and the late Archbishop of Canterbury for dealing with the matter by

Reform of Patronage

caveat and reference to a mixed tribunal of clergy and laity have been already described. No part of Archbishop Benson's Bills was subjected to severer criticism in the House of Lords. Lord Grimthorpe drew a lively picture of the supporters of High Church and Low Church meeting in caucus at the Bull and the Bear. No self-respecting man (it was said) would ever submit to such an ordeal, and the proposal met with such general disapprobation that in subsequent Bills it was dropped. Yet it is not easy to see what reasonable exception could be taken to giving the parishioners notice of presentation, the principle of which is already recognized in the *si quis* of the Ordination Service. The Archbishop stated in the House of Lords in 1887 that it was a daily grief to him to have made an unsuitable appointment in one instance, which he never would have made, if certain facts relating to the character of the nominee could have been brought to his notice by the persons chiefly concerned before he confirmed it. Granted that it is desirable to give the parishioners an opportunity of objecting, some such plan as that adopted by Mr. Stanhope in the Bill of 1881 (described above) seems to afford the best machinery for sifting and trying objections. The proposals of Mr. Lyttelton's Bill now before Parliament are inadequate and unsatisfactory in this respect. He provides for notice to the churchwardens, and objections by any three parishioners; but the bishop is apparently not bound to take any action thereupon, and no procedure for his guidance is laid down. The rights of parishioners, if recognized at all, must obviously be very carefully defined, the grounds of permissible objection must be specified, the bishop's duty must be clearly indicated, and a proper tribunal of reference must be established, with possibly a court of appeal. It must, however, never be forgotten that the ultimate canonical responsibility for every appointment rests with the bishop, and that the onus of admission or rejection is on him.

Reference has been made already to a matter which is much before the public mind. We hear constantly of the hardship inflicted on parishioners by the difficulty, or more often the impossibility, of getting rid of unfit clergymen, and the grievance is a very real one. Unfit clergy may be divided into three classes, the criminous, the negligent, and the incompetent. There exists now, happily, since the passing of the Clergy Discipline Act, 1892, a cheap and expeditious method of dealing with the first class. But short of drunkenness and immorality, a man may have proved himself wholly unfitted for his office by debt, laziness, quarrelsomeness, and in many other ways. Such cases present the greatest difficulty. It is very undesirable, on the one hand, to open the door to the parish spy, the parish tattler and busybody, male or female; nor would it be an easy task for any body of commissioners, however carefully selected, to determine what precise degree of impecuniousness or inability to live happily with his neighbours rendered a man unfit for his duties. On the other hand, nothing can be more disastrous to the spiritual interests of a parish than to find itself saddled for an indefinite number of years with one of these 'bad bargains of the Church.' Both the Benefices Bills of 1898 contain provisions for dealing with the *negligent*. The Government Bill leaves it to a commission under the Pluralities Acts to report to the bishop whether 'the incumbent of a benefice has been negligent in the performance of the ecclesiastical duties of the benefice,' whereupon the bishop, 'if in his opinion the adoption of such a course is expedient in the interests of the *benefice*' (? parishioners), 'may inhibit the incumbent from performing all or any of those duties' after appointing a curate to do the work of the parish. The section as originally drafted was not wholly satisfactory, as it gave the incumbent no right of appeal. Mr. Lyttelton's Bill is free from this blemish. The bishop may issue a commission (containing a stronger lay contingent) if he 'is of opinion that the incumbent of a benefice fails *through his own fault* adequately to discharge the duties attaching to the cure of souls in his benefice.' In addition to inhibition the bishop may require the incumbent to vacate the residence-house, and any patronage vested in the incumbent in right of his office is to be exercised by the patron of the living, or if the incumbent be himself the patron, by the archbishop of the province. An appeal lies to the archbishop sitting with a judge of the High Court, as in the case of refusal to institute. Questions of doctrine and ritual are of course carefully excluded. The plan seems workable, and there is no reason to suppose that a commission of clergymen and laymen of high character and standing would err on the side of severity, or be led to form harsh views of what constitutes negligence. It will be observed that the proposal goes no further than inhibition. Deprivation for negligence, striking at the 'parson's freehold,' would be a much more serious and difficult matter.

As for the third class, the *incompetent*, men incapacitated by physical or mental infirmity, whose case has been already alluded to, whatever schemes may be propounded in the future, let us deal a little tenderly with them. They have grown old in the service of the Church, and are entitled to all possible consideration. The case resolves itself into the question of an adequate pension-system for the Church. Clearly they cannot be turned adrift to end their days in the workhouse. But with falling values and diminishing tithes, livings, in the country especially, are less and less able to bear the strain of a pension charged upon the profits of the benefice. Many of them scarcely yield a living wage to the unhappy parson, as it is. A pension-system for the Church means re-endowment by the laity, and the laity will not re-endow until they are admitted to a real share in the government of the Church and the distribution of its revenues. The matter is urgent and calls for the most anxious consideration on the part of our rulers. But, as already said, these questions fall more properly under the head of discipline than of patronage reform.

One word in conclusion. It must not be hastily assumed that all who have been in any way concerned in the traffic in livings are bad men, though it is the fact that the larger proportion of scandals reflecting on the lives of the clergy, arise in connexion with men who owe their position to purchase. Witness after witness before the Select Committee and the Royal Commission

Reform of Patronage

bore testimony to the high character and blameless reputation of clergymen who had procured their positions by questionable means. Men of exemplary life and conversation, who have made admirable parish priests, have (as the phrase goes) 'bought themselves into their livings.' But an occasional blossom cannot restore life to a tree which is rotten at the core. These men were good and faithful pastors, in so far as they were such, not because of, but in spite of, the system which placed them where they were. Mr. Keble was hurt when some one in his presence once spoke disparagingly of pluralists. 'My father was a pluralist,' said Mr. Keble, meaning to convey a rebuke. But the saintliness of Mr. Keble's father did not, and could not, prevent the State from abolishing pluralism. The case is the same with the abuses that attach to private patronage now.

The wonder is that these have lasted so long. Pluralism went to the wall because only the interests of the clergy were at stake. But here the whole strength of vested interests, lay as well as clerical, has been arrayed against reform. 'English law,' said Bishop Magee in the House of Lords in 1874, 'has ever been remarkable for its almost idolatrous veneration of property.' But at last the public conscience is awakening and a better day begins to dawn. Would that Archbishop Magee and Archbishop Benson could have lived to see it! Men begin to recognize that the Church, so long-suffering, so patient under disappointment and rebuke, is at least entitled to equitable treatment at the hands of the State, whose bondwoman she has been too long. Gagged and fettered, she has been mocked and flouted by the very men who insisted most loudly on keeping her enslaved. Even in this year of grace 1898 she is refused permission by the Government of the day to reform her own representative assemblies, older than Parliament itself. We thankfully acknowledge that a better spirit prevails, and that the Whig Erastianism which came in with the House of Hanover is on the wane. But much remains to be done, and Churchmen should never rest content until the Church recovers that which is her due, and is permitted, through her self-governing synods of clergy and laity, herself to lay the axe to the root of the evils which oppress her life.

IX

PENSIONS FOR THE CLERGY

By the Very Rev. the Dean of Norwich

THE wealth of England is amongst the wonders of the world. Let her capital be represented by the poor man's labour and the rich man's treasure, and the yield is £1,500,000,000 a year. This enormous sum may be divided into two portions, expenditure and savings. The latter amount to about £240,000,000 per annum. So that about one-sixth of England's wealth, set aside annually in every country under heaven, and in every promising enterprise, enables her to amass still vaster opulence, and to strengthen her position as the El Dorado of the world.

The evidences of this wealth are numerous, varied, and widespread. They are seen in the luxurious eccentricities of society. The preparation of food is now, in some quarters, an art. A cook of French or Engadine training and experience has a larger stipend than the earnings of many a youthful physician, barrister, officer, or clergyman. Some knights of cuisine receive as much as £500 a year, with several assistants to lighten their toil. And when we contrast a wine list twenty years old with one circulated to-day, the growth of luxury is demonstrated by the numerous brands of the same wine, as compared with the few with which society was satisfied in simpler times. The same influence dominates our dress, our domestic appointments, our entertainments, our residences. All are being brought under the tyranny of extravagance. They are oppressed by the stern law which rules luxury as it rules sin. In proportion as softness loses the charm of novelty it acquires the thraldom of habit. The tendency of occasional indulgence in luxury, especially in a country where wealth can command the miscellaneous products introduced by free trade, is to make every luxury a necessity, until that which was but occasional becomes habitual, to our economical, physical, and moral detriment.

And yet, it may be doubted if ever there was a time to be compared with the present for the cultivation of thrift. True, Friendly Societies were originated in this country very soon after the first *Caisse de domestiques* was opened in Berne in 1787. Legal enactments were passed for their regulation and security, in the present century. These were consolidated during the reign of Queen Victoria. Post Office Savings Banks were established as recently as 1861, and deferred life annuities four years later. But the inculcation of thrift had then hardly touched the youth of England. It has now its rightful place in our elementary schools; and if it be claimed for the clergy of the National Church that they took the lead in educating the children of the poor in provident habits, the claim can easily be vindicated. They carried into the school the teachings they had, by

Pensions for the Clergy 239

their wives, their daughters, or their workers, given for years in innumerable mothers' meetings and Dorcas societies, as amongst the usual parochial agencies of the Church.

Thrift has come to stay. The conditions of life require it and the Church of God pleads for it. The capricious creation of new wants is symptomatic of unregulated wealth, of stony-souled selfishness, of jaded greed. Each of these is a vast moral, individual, and national peril, which has not an approach to compensation in the circulation of the substance which they scatter. And it is not a little humbling to discover that the Church to whom God has entrusted the moral and spiritual progress of the nation, and whose work He has blessed by extension, by influence, by varied acceptance, and by keen suffering, is, in this age of prodigious wealth and of eccentric luxury, now compelled, in the interests of her ever enlarging mission, at home and abroad, to consider not only how her ministry may be spared the anguish of indigence, but also how the time-worn servants of God may be relieved from work to which they are no longer equal, but which they are amongst the first to affirm must be done.

The work of the Church is the welfare of the State. The inefficiency of the one is the degeneracy of the other. If the moral life of England is in any appreciable degree affected by the systematic, continuous, and spiritual toil of the clergy, then provision must be made for the retirement of those who have borne the burden of the Lord and of their country. The presence in our parishes of senile priests will dwarf the life they are sent to develop. If this be true, then the provision of a pension for aged clergy is not without interest to the nation. Moreover, it is, economically, the next step to be taken, the laity having initiated, constructed, and consolidated the Queen Victoria Clergy Sustentation Fund. To this central organization twenty-eight dioceses are now affiliated. Liverpool and Chester appear to have 'contracted out' of the scheme. The organization of Durham is incomplete. Ely is waiting until a 'Five Years' Fund' has run out. Bangor, Oxford, and Sodor and Man are uncertain. Up to date, twenty-four dioceses have qualified for affiliation by paying one-fifth of their income. Others are coming on. The method under which the scheme works provides, in a very effective way, for rich dioceses helping poorer ones. The conscientious convictions of donors are so far respected that each can appropriate his contribution to any parish, or to any diocese. The income has increased from £11,587 in 1896 to £49,449 in 1897. Although the scheme has not 'caught on' as widely as the conditions it exists to improve, yet it can hardly be doubted that with the increased influence the laity are certain to possess in parochial affairs, and with larger and more elastic powers in operation to effect the union of small benefices, the resources of the Central Fund will rise to the height of the Church's requirements, until every beneficed clergyman, having in the conditions just referred to more work, will receive £200 per annum. But sustentation is not everything. It helps the worker. A Central Clergy Pensions Fund will also do this, and much more. It will make the work continuous, efficient, and progres-

Pensions for the Clergy

sive. It will bring repose to men who are no longer equal to their thronging duties. It will exercise energies which are now stagnant. It will give movement and flow to the tide of preferment.

The need for such a fund appears in the altered conditions of modern ministerial life; in the high scale of clerical longevity; and in some recent legislative efforts, which, while apparently hard, were really expressive of the supreme claims which efficiency has over every other consideration. There are few facts as instructive as those recited in thousands of churches every Sunday, when the vicar announces the parochial engagements for the coming week. They include classes for young men, young women, confirmands, and communicants. Thrift, temperance, purity, recreation, and religion are represented. Missions at home and abroad, prayer meetings, Sunday-school teachers' meetings, choral societies, district visiting, tract distribution, open-air services, care for those who labour in mews, in hotels, in hospitals, in ships, in canal-boats, and so forth, have their respective organizations, workers, and adequate parochial apparatus. There are, in hundreds and thousands of districts, vicars and curates who are out of their houses every evening in the week for months. Their time is tabulated as rigidly as if they were under an Egyptian lash. 'Dining out' is unknown. A 'dress coat' has not been worn since they entered the parish. All such men know of 'society' is a memory. They live from day to day in the faithful discharge of the pastoral office.

Such work demands strong men. How great is the strain appears from the fact that several of the most powerful curates in our large towns stagger under the toil ere they have passed five years in its performance. The vicars must remain. But very often it is at the cost of parochial efficiency. True, in many cases the aged clergy possess experience and the influence which accompanies lengthened residence, pastoral intercourse extending over whole lives, and sanctity of character. For these qualities, so necessary to the higher life of the Church, the Church must provide exercise in posts of spiritual influence. But can these qualities compensate for the loss of that physical strength which old age cannot retain, but which is imperatively required to cope with the ceaseless and increasing appeals which are made to it? Let it be granted that the scale of longevity is higher amongst the clergy than it is amongst the members of any other profession. Admit, unreservedly, all that Dr. Tatham has taught us as to occupational mortality and its comparative significance. That of the physician is compared with that of the lawyer in half a million deaths (in 1890-1-2) of adults, during the working period, as 966 is to 821, while that of the schoolmaster is to that of the clergyman as 604 is to 533. These figures demonstrate that the clerical profession maintains its position as the occupation showing the lowest death-rate. But this in no way invalidates the contention that vicars are generally unable, when, say, seventy years of age, to discharge such obligations 'as the modern spirit has introduced. It is unreasonable to expect them to be responsible for the increased and increasing engagements of our day. It is, alike for them and for the flock, unwise and possibly unprofitable that

Pensions for the Clergy

they should continue to undertake the multiplied and miscellaneous duties now required.

These facts—and many more might be adduced—show that whether our attention be turned to modern parochial obligations or to the longevity of those entrusted with them, there must be, in existing circumstances, a large amount of work either imperfectly done, or allowed to slide. Age very gently, very generally, and sometimes quite unconsciously, relaxes the tightness with which the hand holds the reins. Workers cease to feel the pull and the power. The laxity affects schools, classes, guilds, meetings, services, offerings, until with a speed in inverse ratio to the knowledge of the venerable rector, the parish work rapidly declines in efficiency, in extension, in vital expression. Occasion is thus opened to schismatical intrusion. Disaffection spreads in an area which was once permeated by unity, by harmony, by love. Voices are heard in favour of retirement, even by compulsion. And all this is due to the fact that a man clings to an office, the duties of which he is no longer able to discharge, but his tenure of which is perpetual.

Public attention to such cases is not likely to decline. The malignant vigilance of social jealousy, of philosophic unbelief, of sectarian iconoclasm, are certain to secure them a humiliating prominence. The splendid enthusiasm of sanctified service; the consecrated slavery of souls unworn by care and unchilled by time; the tender but fixed gaze of many upon the priceless sons of God who are being swamped in the moral morass of some huge city, or drugged to coma amid the dullness and the drowsiness of some rural parish, will combine to focus the activities of faith upon every neglected and ill-manned parish in the land. While, standing aside from both these opposing contingents, there are the thousands of the unbeneficed who are to-day excluded from independent parochial service, responsibility and opportunity; whose hopes of preferment are dimmed and dashed by the notorious longevity, irremovability, and even official tenacity of their seniors; by the fact that the Church multiplies curates three times as rapidly as she multiplies benefices; and that the excess of the former over the latter was in 1896 no less than 200. Should the disparity continue, the Church and the nation will have to face all that is represented by the fact—uniform, disheartening, but not notorious—that as curates grow old in the service to which they dedicate their lives, not only do their stipends decline and their chances of preferment diminish, but their hopes of employment decrease. The feeling upon these conditions is acute. It demands attention, sympathy, and remedial intervention. It will be effectually allayed by the promotion of that to which everything urged here is designed to lead, viz. the initiation of a Central Clergy Pensions Fund. The need for such an institution is admitted. If this be so, the next point in order is to ascertain approximately its extent as a matter of figures, and then the wisest and most workable method of meeting it. To this end the following table is submitted. It has no claim to infallibility, but it is helpful as showing the number of clergymen in thirty-four out of thirty-five dioceses, and in eighty-three out of ninety-one archdeaconries, who are about or more than seventy years of age. The figures will at least be a basis of

Pensions for the Clergy 245

discussion, without an approach to prejudice as to the debility or efficiency of those they represent:—

Diocese.	Number of Archdeaconries.	Approximate number of Incumbents about or over 70.	Total.	Remarks on Archidiaconal returns.
Canterbury	2			Canterbury, no return; Maidstone declines.
London	2	24	24	London, no return.
Winchester	3	39 + 14 + 4	57	
Bangor	2	14 + 9	23	
Bath and Wells	3	23 + 14 + 14	51	3 considerably over 70.
Bristol	1	27	27	
Chichester	2	20 + 11	31	
Ely	4	11 + 21 + 19 + 19	70	1 over 90—3 over 80.
Exeter	3	26 + 8 + 25	59	Not including Bishop & Dean.
Gloucester	2	20 + 21	41	
Hereford	2	22 + 25	47	
Lichfield	3	11 + 12 + 9	32	
Lincoln	2	43	43	Lincoln, no return.
Llandaff	2	7 + 9	16	Including Bishop and Dean.
Norwich	4	31 + 27 + 33 + 21	112	
Oxford	3	28 + 36	64	Oxford, no return.
Peterborough	3	30 + 8 + 45	83	
Rochester	3	13 + 5 + 5	23	Including Dean and 1 Canon— 1 of 80.
St. Albans	3	28 + 20 + 20	68	
St. Asaph	3	16 + 4 + 1	21	
St. David's	4	7 + 13	20	St. David's, no return; Carmarthen, no return.
Salisbury	3	27 + 16 + 12	55	Sarum, no return.
Southwell	2	19 + 16	35	
Truro	2	12 + 5	17	5 Curates over 70 in addition.*
Worcester	3	5 + 21 + 8	34	14 between 60–70 in addition.*
York	4	20 + 6 + 39 + 20	85	1 Curate over 70 in addition.*
Durham	2	22 + 12	34	Cathedral Clergy 4 additional.
Carlisle	3	11 + 17 + 8	36	
Chester	2	10 + 8	18	
Liverpool	2	5 + 6	11	3 between 64–70 in addition.*
Manchester	3	10 + 11	21	Manchester declines.
Newcastle	2	10 + 13	23	
Ripon	3	10	10	Craven, no returns; Ripon, no returns.
Sodor and Man	1	3	3	
Wakefield	2	7 + 5	12	

	1306
* Unbeneficed	23
Total	1329

This table[1] includes one bishop, two deans, and one canon, and as such dignitaries are otherwise provided for, the total may be reduced by four. But it will be observed there are twenty-three aged curates in four dioceses. These should, of course, be included; and if seventy-one be allowed for the ten archdeaconries who have made no return, then the number of septuagenarians rises to 1,400. The clergy of the archdiocese of York as well as those of Liverpool are, thanks to the munificence of the same donor, in good case. Mrs. Turner gave £20,000 to create a pension fund for each diocese, and in each as much as £200 a year may be, and sometimes is, given. As there are eighty-six clergy in the archdiocese who are over seventy years of age, there is ample room for the extension of the scheme. The diocese of Chester has funded capital for this purpose to the extent of £10,000; Manchester £11,700, and Ripon part of £16,976. These sums are inadequate for these dioceses. Hence but little deduction need be made from the total, though some might. We shall hardly be in serious error if the pensionable clergy be estimated at about 1,400.

In submitting any scheme to meet a need so great as that now under discussion, it is of importance to consider what resources are already applicable, before any proposal is made for fresh funds. This, while reasonable in any circumstances, is especially so when the subject before us is connected with an organism

[1] May I here express my gratitude to no less than eighty-one archdeacons, who, in full sympathy with their venerable brethren and at considerable toil, enabled me to compile this table?

Pensions for the Clergy

as ancient and as expansive as the Church of England. It is here we may find plastic modes, stiffened, ossified, and brittle. It is here we may discover old methods of working consigned to desuetude; and barely saved from oblivion by the witness of words which, while possessing a place in her Offices, are but little recognized by either ministry or people.

Let it be confidently submitted, that if any respect or obedience is to be given to inspired directions and to Church authority, one partial provision for the maintenance of the ministry is the sacramental offertory. There are no less than twenty sentences provided by the Church to be read at the discretion of the priest during its collection. Of these, the sixth, seventh, eighth, and tenth refer to the right of the pastorate to support from the flock. This right is urged in a series of analogies, any one of which is adequate, but the accumulation of which ought to be irresistible. The warrior has not to draw upon his personal possessions for his maintenance. The vine-dresser is entitled to the fruit he propagates. The shepherd who feeds the flock is to be nourished by the milk. The sower of spiritual seed may most reasonably expect material support. The usages of the Levitical economy, though doomed to extinction through the provisional character of the system, point to a permanent ordinance of the Lord: 'They who preach the Gospel should live of the Gospel.' The individuality of the obligation, the width of its range, the impressive admonition against ignoring it are obvious, designed, and stimulating. These 'sentences' are, moreover, used in the same connexion, and for a similar purpose, in the eucharistic offices of the Scotch, Irish, and American Churches. Yet, how seldom are they heard in the Church of England? So long as they are found where the Church has placed them, the conclusion that the offertory is intended to be applied, in part, to the succour of the ministry is established.

This contention might be supported by historic fact, even from primitive times, as well as by its occasional acceptance in our own day. Indeed, it is somewhat difficult to believe that any worshipper could or would question the authority of the principle. Its recognition includes others as well as communicants. A short time since, the sacramental offertory used to be gathered only from the latter. But the Church neither allows nor implies such a limitation. The recitation of the Scriptures is to stimulate each worshipper during the collection of 'the alms for the poor, and other devotions of the people.' The last of the post-communion rubrics (1662) speaks of 'pious' as distinct from 'charitable' uses. Whatever significance these words possess must be governed by the recognition of the rights of the clergy, enforced by the sentences read during a most solemn act of worship. With this essential principle borne in mind, the disposal of the offertory is, on the authority of the Church, 'as the minister and churchwardens shall think fit.' So far are we in the presence of a principle, its recognition, and application. We shall next see how far it will carry us.

The number of communicants was, in 1891–2, 1,437,719; in 1892–3, 1,607,930; in 1893–4, 1,701,499; in 1894–5,

Pensions for the Clergy

1,778,361; in 1895–6, 1,840,351; in 1896–7, 1,886,059. Communicants' classes increased, from 1891 to 1896, for males, from 50,662 to 76,004; and for females, from 110,566 to 165,067. Experience proves that the class multiplies the communicants. With such a series of spiritual activities operating all over England, it seems reasonable to believe that in the year 1898 the Church's communicants will have risen to 2,000,000. What is the average annual offering of each individual? This depends alike upon the amount contributed, and the number of attendances made. But even if both could be ascertained, the information would be inadequate because the Sacramental Offertory is now, with heartier and healthier recognition of obedience to the Church's ordinance, gathered from 'the people.' If the enlarged area for gathering be allowed as a set-off to irregular and infrequent attendance, the average amount contributed annually by each communicant may, without excess, be allowed to be 5s.[1] This sum represents an offertory of £500,000. It is not uninteresting to the writer to know that after these figures were arrived at, a reference to the Church's Year-book was made, which showed that under the head 'support of the poor,' the total sum given in 1896 was £541,484. The plea here urged is that one-tenth of this sum be annually applied by 'the minister

---

[1] It seemed right to test the estimate. Accordingly, information was sought from twenty-six parishes, thirteen situate in Norwich, King's Lynn, Ipswich, and Lowestoft; and thirteen in very sparsely-peopled country parishes. The result, roughly estimated, is not uninteresting. The average of each communicant in twenty-six parishes per an. is 8s. 4½d.; for thirteen town parishes for each communicant per an. is 10s. 4¼d.; and in thirteen country parishes, &c., &c. is 4s. 11d. If any value at all attaches to the investigation, the estimate in the text does not err by excess.

and churchwardens' to enable the aged and indigent ministers of Christ to live 'of the Gospel.'

This is the Church's method. It appeals, with the tender might of her voice, to those to whom she assigns the duty of appropriation. It requires no fresh legislation; no long-fought decision; no resort to conferences, to congresses, to convocations, or even to bishops. It does require a righteous reversion to type, and obedience on the part of ministers and churchwardens to the voice of God and to the laws, as lucid as they are loving, of His holy Church.

But, it may be replied, the offertory is designed for the poor. Granted. But the poor are not confined to the laity. The clergy are, all things considered, the poorest of the poor. Even were the sentences to which reference has been made absent from those designed to stimulate the generosity of the faithful, it would be difficult to deny to the clergy a share in their offerings. But the place these Scriptures occupy in the Office asserts the right which God has enjoined and which men have so long ignored. This right may still be denied. If so, these sentences ought to be removed from the Office. Include them, and the right here claimed rests upon the authority of God Himself. Once more. It may be argued that if the offertory be thus shared by the ministry, the amount will decline. The very reverse is far more likely to ensue. Let it be known, in every hamlet, village, town, city, that God's minister—aged, infirm, impoverished—is to be sustained in part by the 'devotions of the people,' and the increase will be to the advantage of those who are already aided, and to the

Pensions for the Clergy

succour of those to whom God has given a stronger title and a prior claim.

The next source of income for a Clergy Pensions Fund must be found in the clergy themselves. There is not the remotest reason to hope that any aid for this purpose will ever be afforded by the nation. England has long since cut herself off from any such practical recognition of the claims of the established Church. She makes no reckoning of it in her schools. As for her supporting the clergy, in sickness or in health, in youth or in age, she will do this when she supports her citizens with corn grown in the moon. And so long as the nation maintains this attitude, the clergy will resent any attempt on the part of the State to fix an age-limit to their work. If Parliament provided a pension, the provision would carry the right to define the date of its enjoyment, as is the case amongst the armed forces of the Queen, and the Civil Service. If the Church provided a pension, then an age-limit might be fixed. But its individual application could not be enforced without legislation. Any attempt to apply such a limit to one class of clergy and to exclude another from it would divide the Church and exasperate the Legislature. Nor, again, is there the least hope for such aid as the scheme requires in that fond imagination of the parsimonious churchman or the sectarian circle-squarer—the equalization of benefices. The few 'rich livings' in the Church are declining in number and are shrinking in value. The tithe-payers, as a rule, enter a vigorous protest against the transfer of tithe to another parish than that in which it is gathered. Even were this not so, the appropriation could not be effected without confiscation of rights which Parliament has made secure, and in the end without legislation. This given, the result would be hopelessly inadequate. Therefore the clergy, beneficed and unbeneficed, must accept the fact: a Pension Fund can only be created, sustained, and continued by individual self-help.

Nor is such a fund to be limited to either curates or vicars. The latter are now suffering as the former never have. The incomes of some incumbents have, in nearly every diocese, shrunk to starvation-point. Rates and taxes have increased. Tithe is still diminishing, while curates' stipends are as they were, or are rising. The one and the other must face conditions, to which the stern discipline of adversity enables them to bring self-sacrifice and courage. There must not be the least expectation of a 'consolation prize,' nor the least restriction to either of benefits to be earned equally by each. Moreover, in the administration of any pension scheme, there can be no place for either shareholders' profits or directors' fees. Individual members should have the full benefit of their payments and even more, and the smallest sum consistent with efficiency should be spent on working expenses. Let us now look at the possibilities of existing legislation and voluntary effort; and the age at which payments might begin and their amount. We shall then be able to estimate the pension to be paid, and the period at which it might be enjoyed.

If every benefice in the Church of England was sufficiently endowed, and if the endowment was secured against fluctuation, the provision of the Incumbents'

Pensions for the Clergy

Resignation Act, 1871, would contribute largely to the solution of the problem now before us. There would be in these circumstances three conditions, any one of which being absent vitiates the whole, viz. sufficiency of income as a working basis; security of payments to the retired vicar and to his successor; and adequate maintenance for both. Under this Act, the power of initiation is lodged in the incumbent. This power set in motion, a commission, on which he is represented, is appointed by the bishop, and it may recommend the acceptance of the resignation, and assess the amount of the pension. It 'must not exceed one-third of the annual value of the benefice, or be an amount which shall not leave a sufficient income to secure the due performance of the church services, according to the scale of stipends in the Pluralities Acts[1].'

The recent Benefices Bill, 1896, was designed to further amend the Pluralities Acts Amendment Act, 1885. The third part of the bill contained provisions as to the adequate discharge of the duties of incumbents. It was in legal touch with the second section of the Pluralities Act, 1885, and therefore it made the neglect of such 'ecclesiastical duties' as the performance of divine service twice daily an inadequate discharge of duty. The power of setting the Act in motion lay with the bishop. Should an incumbent be inhibited, consequent upon the report of commissioners, the bishop had the power to require him to vacate the parsonage, not to reside within twenty miles of the benefice, and to appoint a curate or curates, whose stipends should not be

[1] *Church Law*, Whitehead, p. 245.

less than two-thirds of the annual value of the benefice. And although it can hardly be doubted that such stern terms were designed for sadder cases than those which are represented by age or infirmity, yet the Act was described as aiming 'at facilitating the expulsion of aged clergy from their benefices without adequate provision for them in their remaining years[1].' The exclusion from its operations of archdeacons, canons residentiary, deans, and bishops—for whose retirement ample provision is secured—was regarded as unjust. It gave a powerful cry to the opponents of the bill, their indignation rising to fever height when they pointed to the fact that this treatment might be meted out to men who were aged, defenceless, and incapable of making a livelihood in any other way. This measure was slain. Reference to it here is necessary, because it enables us to see what help the clergy affected by it might hope to receive on their expulsion from active work. The Incumbents' Resignation Act, 1871, gives us definite information upon this point. But that Act is now practically inoperative, and for two reasons: first, because, with an insufficient income to deal with, what might be taken—up to one-third—is inadequate for living; secondly, because, this taken, what is left is inadequate for labour. Let this be established.

According to the latest returns, there are in England and Wales 1341 benefices, the average annual value of which is but £65; and 4566 benefices, the average annual value of which is £152. These values are in the direction of further shrinkage. With regard to the latter, it is possible that under the Incumbents' Resignation Act a

[1] *Official Year-book.*

Pensions for the Clergy

pension of £50 a year might be secured. This possibility is, however, conditioned by there being a sufficient sum left to secure the due performance of the services. This is now made improbable, because, since August 8, 1887, the pension is to vary with the tithe averages, and considering the increased taxation to which the clergy have been recently rendered liable, and which affects the commissioners' estimate of the net annual value, the probability of a pension as well as of provision for the performance of parochial duties has touched the vanishing-point. The practical issue of this is that, for 1341 benefices, averaging annually £65, and for 4566 benefices, averaging annually £152, the Incumbents' Resignation Act is inoperative. There are, accordingly, 5907 benefices whose incumbents have no hope whatever of receiving any legal pension. For them the possibilities of existing legislation present neither rest nor reward. The three final factors, necessary to any satisfactory solution of our problem, are wanting.

Let us next and now see what aid we may receive towards practical action from observing what is already in operation in, say, the Post Office schemes for deferred annuities. In the current postal guide, a man aged twenty-five, by paying in one sum £256 2s. 6d., may, on national security, purchase a deferred annuity of £100 a year, to be claimed at sixty years of age. Should he begin his payment a year earlier, twenty-four—when many deacons advance to the order of priesthood—the block sum would be about £250 for the same annuity to be enjoyed at the same time. If there are not many ordinati who could, at such a time, make any such advance, there are beyond all question some. The proportion of the clergy who possess private means is disastrously large—disastrously, because their patrimony is expected to supply the 'living' which Christ has ordained should be supplied by others, and to relieve the laity of their individual, imperative, and sacred obligation. Hence there are, no doubt, some who could pay to a Clergy Pensions Fund an amount which would secure to them £100 a year at, say, sixty. Unhappily those who could are the least likely to do so. And another idea must be reckoned with. The Post Office pension period is far too early for most clergymen to become pensioners. We are dealing with a body of men drawn from one section of the community. It is accordingly necessary to provide, with the utmost care, for such a special rate of vitality as experience directs us to look for.

It is quite an ordinary precaution for an insurance company to protect itself against the results of heavy mortality in particular trades or professions. The rates of premium vary. They are adjusted to the greater or less proved peril of the lives insured. Here we are not dealing with insurances, but with pensions, and any office that undertakes the liability, under the special requirements already indicated, must protect itself and its clients against the excessive vitality of the clergy, just as some offices protect themselves now against the excessive vitality of females. A deferred annuity of £10, payable after ten years, would, if purchased at twenty-five on a lump sum, cost a man £150, and a woman £166 9s. 2d. Indeed, it may be assumed that although the Post Office,

Pensions for the Clergy

or any insurance company, would probably grant annuities to clergymen at their ordinary rates, yet no carefully managed institution would undertake the granting of annuities to any large number of clergymen without providing, by increased premium, for their extra vitality, which is probably not over-estimated if it be placed at twenty per cent. beyond that of the average population. This excessive vitality—due probably to such causes as peace of mind, in the best sense, and to simple living—enables the clergy to continue at their work far longer than probably any other class, and if the age-limit be seventy, then the annual payments, subject if necessary to annual aid, may continue up to that period. This would give a time-extension range to their contributions; substantial security to their product and permanence; while—beginning to be made at, say, twenty-five—their burden would be light, a commencement would be made at the earliest possible time, and the habit of providence would be formed. These considerations appear to fix the period of pension payments between twenty-five and seventy. The earlier date is the average age at which deacons advance to the priesthood. The later date recognizes the notorious vitality of the clergy.

The rate of the premium as well as the amount on which it should be assessed is the next point. Both are governed by the amount of the pension to be earned, which is for all, curate and vicar alike, and speaking roundly, £100 a year, the first half-yearly payment to be made six months after the attainment of seventy years. The rate cannot be less than £3 per cent. It should be levied on £150 a year between twenty-five and thirty-five, which would be £4 10s. per annum, and on £200 a year between thirty-five and seventy, which would be £6 per annum. Such payments would produce an annuity or pension, for each contributor, of £115 per annum at seventy years of age.

Two objections at once present themselves. It will be said the amount on which the rate is levied is, in each period, and for each person paying, too high. The average stipend of curates is said to be £130, and there are 5,907 benefices under £200 a year. Let each statement stand. But at this point let aid to self-help come in. Here we avail ourselves of the tithed sacramental offertory. Let a portion of that fund be applied to aid those whose payments fall short of the £4 10s. in the one case and of the £6 in the other, care being taken that the deficit is due solely to economic causes. And it must not be forgotten that there are 10,430 benefices over £200 a year, but under £250. The holders of these would not be oppressed to the same extent as their less fortunate brethren. But if from the same causes the difficulty of payment arose, it should be met to the same extent, and from the same fund.

This paper proceeds upon the recognition of some principles which in the opinion of the writer are vital. In an ancient society like the Church of England, it is of the last moment to remember the importance of the principle of progress by least friction; the avoidance of appeals for parliamentary intervention, and the use of material—legislative, ecclesiastical, or organic—which is ready to our hand. In this last connexion it is most encouraging to be able to recognize and to commend a society which, though but eleven years old, has many of the most promising factors of success. The Clergy Pensions Society was established in 1886. With it every diocese may be connected. Already thirty-three dioceses are in practical sympathy, even though eighteen of these have, to the loss of their clergy, no diocesan committees. The principle of the Clergy Pensions Institution is mainly, though not exclusively, to aid, by substantial augmentation, deferred but fractional annuities, which the clergy purchase, at stated rates, either by annual payments or by lump sums. The importance of augmentation as well as its extent is evident when it is realized that the institution can now give, at the age of sixty-five, £42 a year, when only £15 15s. has been paid for; or to put the case in another way: If an ordinand, at the age of twenty-three or twenty-four, pays £55 7s. down, he can purchase an annuity of £15 15s. for life after sixty-five. But such is the extent of the augmenting power possessed, through revenue, by the Clergy Pensions Institution, that as much as £100 a year after sixty-five may be hoped for from the above payment, provided still larger funds are placed at its disposal, and provided the rate which investments yield does not decline.

Now although probability is the rule of life, it would be imprudent for any man to resign his benefice, though its revenue were reduced, on the basis of even a highly reasonable hope of an augmented pension. The hope must rise to realization, and the amount of the augmentation must be certain, secure, and sufficient.

In the absence of these, retirement from work will not occur. But the elements of these are operative in the Clergy Pensions Institution. Let the sacramental offertory scheme be worked into the methods of the institution, as well as into those now to be submitted, and we should have a result very little, if at all, short of certainty.

The Clergy Pensions Institution has, in eleven years, been able to invest no less a sum than £260,000. Its income is over £30,000 a year. The organization is strong in possibilities. It is in the field. It is admirably and economically administered. But its work would speedily reach to the full dimensions of present and future need if the clergy and churchwardens entrusted it with one-tenth of the sacramental offertories, and if its work was limited to this one enterprise.

Every diocese should have its Clergy Pensions Committee, allied to the central institution. It should be enabled to gather funds, on the terms already accepted in Norwich, i.e. of general contributions; one moiety should be remitted to the central institution for the purposes of general augmentation, and the other should be at the disposal of the diocesan committee, to pay, wholly or in part, the premium for a fractional pension, hereafter called an Augmented Pension; or to purchase an immediate pension, hereafter called an Elective Pension. Two important purposes would thus be served. Richer dioceses would help poorer ones, and local interest would be extended and enriched. Premiums should be made payable only to the central institution. Migration of work would thus leave the

Pensions for the Clergy

payment of the worker untouched, augmentation unaffected, while clerical labour and expense would be saved.

For the purposes of business, let us suppose that the bishops, in or out of Convocation, addressed an episcopal letter to the Church, commending to the laity the duty of sustaining aged and infirm clergy in the mode suggested by the sentences in the Office for the Administration of the Holy Communion. Let it be further supposed that at Eastertide, A.D. 1900, all 'ministers and churchwardens' agreed to tithe the sacramental offertories of, say, £500,000, thus consecrating £50,000 a year to a purpose which the Church enjoins and which her Lord approves. Let it also be understood that each deacon, on receiving a title to holy orders, is required by the bishop to join the Clergy Pensions Institution, either by advancing a lump sum or by annual payments, for the purchase of what may here be described as an Unaided Pension of, say, £115 per annum at seventy; or of an Augmented Pension of £100 at the same period. Let it be ruled that each candidate for priesthood produce and present to the Diocesan Registrar his pension-payments certificate, and let the fact be recorded. Such conditions, it is submitted, give a very practical and substantial appearance to the following scheme. It recognizes, in the ministry, those who possess private means or hold the larger livings; others, who would welcome augmentation of pension, beyond what they were enabled to pay for; and a third class who, without means and full of years, desire rest in the near future. These three classes could have pensions which might be known as UNAIDED, AUGMENTED, and ELECTIVE.

THE UNAIDED PENSION would be earned by the payment of 3 per cent. per annum, on £150, from twenty-five to thirty-five; and at the same rate, on £200, from thirty-five to seventy. The Unaided Pension would amount to £115. These figures are submitted on the high authority of Mr. J. J. W. Deuchar, Secretary and Actuary of the Norwich Life Assurance Society, to whom I am deeply indebted for help in the constructive part of this essay.

THE AUGMENTED PENSION would be enjoyed on the conditions formulated by the Clergy Pensions Institution, aided by contributions, where found necessary, from a diocesan committee, or from the Sacramental Offertory Fund, either in annual payment of premiums or in augmentation of fractional pensions, or both. Thus a clergyman aged forty-five would pay annually till sixty-five £5 13s. for a pension of £15 15s. at the latter age. The Clergy Pensions Institution can now augment this pension to £42. But if possessed of the sacramental offertory, it could be still further augmented by adding £58 per annum, or the annual payment could be reduced by aid from a diocesan committee or from the Sacramental Offertory Fund.

THE ELECTIVE PENSION would be, under the supposed conditions, £100 a year bestowed on, say, 250 clergymen of seventy years of age, to be elected, as may be arranged, from the aged clergy of the affiliated dioceses.

If 250 pensions of £42 per annum were thus augmented to £100, and if 250 Elective Pensions were bestowed, it is not unreasonable to expect both 'augmented' and 'elective' pensioners to pay to the Clergy Pensions Fund

5 per cent. on their receipts. This would realize £1,975, which with a slight addition would retire twenty more (elective) men, and these, by a similar payment, would slightly increase the number. Thus in a short time 520 clergy would be retired; almost as many benefices would be vacated; the flow of preferment would be facilitated, and the work of the Church of God be continued, advanced, and even brightened. The cost of the Augmented pensioners to the sacramental offertory would be £14,500; that of the Elective pensioners £25,000; thus leaving £10,500 to alleviate the burden of premiums, or to minister to that elasticity of executive which is required by the circumstances, and is, moreover, in accordance with the spiritual source in which the fund has its rise.

It will be observed that under this scheme the investments of the Clergy Pensions Institution (£230,000) and the annual income (£30,000 per annum) remain undiminished, except so far as they may be, and are now, diminished by the augmentation of £15 15s. (paid for) to £42. Details numerous, conflicting, and even unexpected are certain to arise. Difficulties will, of course, appear and disappear. But it is submitted that in some such outlines as are here drawn there lie the main features of a Clergy Pensions Scheme. It must be central in executive; sufficient in amount; secure against financial fluctuation; while in its administration it should recognize the presence in the ministry of those who represent diversities of substance. To this end the scheme should offer pensions which are best described as UNAIDED, AUGMENTED, and ELECTIVE.

X

THE INCREASE OF THE EPISCOPATE

By Wilfred S. de Winton

'ARCHBISHOP CRANMER and his episcopal brethren endeared themselves to posterity by a subdivision of dioceses in this country. They accomplished much in this respect, and they expressed a desire and undertook measures for further subdivision. We profess veneration for the English Reformation; let us follow the example of the Reformers and promote the principles of the Reformation.'

Thus wrote in his famous 'Letter to Viscount Dungannon' so long ago as 1860, that loyal churchman the late Bishop of Lincoln. Let us then inquire in reference to this matter what were the 'principles' that guided Henry VIII and his advisers.

When he came to the throne, Henry found in the whole of England and Wales no more than twenty-two dioceses, including Sodor and Man. Although since the Conquest the population had increased fourfold in this area, there were but two more sees than had existed when Lanfranc was archbishop. Carlisle embraced the earldom which the Red King had added to England: Ely had been carved out of the huge diocese of Lincoln.

The Increase of the Episcopate 265

Both were founded by the first Henry, and between the first and the eighth not one more had been created.

To these twenty-two dioceses the Tudor added six, viz. Bristol, Chester, Gloucester, Oxford, Peterborough, and Westminster. The names of nine others which he proposed to create we actually have in his own handwriting. Hence we know that he contemplated a total of thirty-seven dioceses. Further, an Act had previously been passed that allowed the appointment of as many as twenty-six suffragan bishops. According then to the 'principles' which guided our Reformers it was desirable to provide at least sixty-three bishops for a population of four to five million souls. Yet for a population just six times as large the Church has seemingly to content herself with thirty-five diocesan and twenty-four suffragan or assistant Bishops.

Let us again notice on what system Henry proceeded in the formation of new diocesan areas.

He found an enormous diocese of Lincoln. It stretched from the Thames to the Humber and consisted of no less than nine counties, viz. Lincoln, Leicester, Rutland, Northampton, Huntingdon, Bedford, Buckingham, Hertford, and Oxford. He took away Northamptonshire and Rutland to form the diocese of Peterborough, and Oxfordshire to form a county diocese of Oxford. He intended further that Leicestershire and Hertfordshire should each become a county diocese, and that another diocese should consist of the counties of Bedford and Buckingham. The principle was wise and intelligible, namely, to do a little at a time but to do it so well and thoroughly that no new see should be given so large an area that it would require subdivision again later on. Contrast this with the clumsy arrangements of 1836 or even of 1878. Up to 1836 Ely and Oxford were ideal county dioceses, each containing an ancient university within its territory. If the Church is to keep her hold upon the highest intellect of the age some places on the episcopal bench must be reserved for those who are conspicuous for learning rather than for administrative success or parochial experience, and no more suitable sees could have been found than Oxford and Ely; yet in 1836 it was decided to make these dioceses unmanageable by adding to Oxford Bucks from Lincoln and Berks from Salisbury, and giving to Ely Bedfordshire and Huntingdonshire from Lincoln, and half Suffolk from Norwich. Peterborough again was made unworkable by receiving Leicestershire from Lincoln, which, by way of compensation, was compelled to receive Nottinghamshire from York. In short, the redistribution of area which was made in 1836 was a huge mistake; it undid the good work done by Henry VIII and Cranmer, instead of grasping the unique opportunity which the formation of the common fund of the Ecclesiastical Commissioners afforded, for founding new sees on the true principles of the English Reformation.

In 1878 so little had we profited by seeing the result of the mischief done in 1836 that in forming the diocese of Southwell the old mistake of forty years before was repeated : to relieve the necessities of Lincoln and Lichfield a county was taken from each, not to make two model county dioceses, but to compel two areas which had previously nothing whatever in common to throw in

The Increase of the Episcopate

their lot together to make another unmanageable diocese and one more object lesson to church reformers of what to avoid.

It is easy to see why such early attention was given by our reformers to the increase of the diocesan episcopate—their object clearly was that bishops should be not, like their mediaeval predecessors, 'lords over God's heritage' but 'fathers in God' and 'ensamples to the flock.'

The danger of looking at our bishops rather as prelates than as pastors has been by no means removed. To-day they still appear to us rather as governors than as fathers. We assume in fact that their official work can be efficiently done like that of a department of the State, by secretaries or clerks, while confirmations and church openings can be suitably undertaken by peripatetic deputies, and that this is all.

But such a view loses sight of the pastoral and personal side of a bishop's work, which makes a parish-going bishop almost as necessary as a house-going parson to make a church-going people.

To quote Bishop Lightfoot :—

'The Church of England has inherited episcopacy as its form of government from the ripened and inspired wisdom of the Apostolic age. But the episcopate, to be efficient, must be adequate. The very constitution of our Church is such that no other agency can supply the defect. It is not only an office of supervision, it has also its direct personal ministrations. This twofold character it is which makes it so important to secure an adequate episcopate.'

How can a bishop exercise wisely and well the patronage in his gift, unless he knows all his clergy at first-hand from seeing them at work in their parishes? How judge of the needs of a vacant benefice, unless he has been personally in contact with the church-workers of that parish long before the vacancy has occurred? How can he hope to exercise due personal influence over the people of his diocese, if he is unknown to most of them even by face? How many of the working classes in this country know the name of their bishop, how many know even what diocese they are in?

In a small town not thirty miles from the bishop's palace the following conversation took place a few years ago, between an adult class of humble churchmen and their clergyman who was trying to interest them in an approaching confirmation which was to be held in their parish church. 'The bishop is coming next Sunday.' 'What bishop?' 'Why, *our* bishop, of course.' 'Who's our bishop?'

But there are cases to the contrary. I will mention some. It is daybreak—the place is the condemned cell of a county prison. The cell has two occupants: one is a man who will in a few hours' time pay the supreme penalty of his crime: the other, who has been his constant visitor and has brought him to a sense of his sin, is, not the prison chaplain or a Methodist local preacher, but a bishop, the successor of those proud prelates who ruled from the Thames to the Humber, should I not rather say a successor of the saintly Hugh of Lincoln?

I go now from the east of England to the westernmost

diocese in Wales. It is a Sunday afternoon. The bishop, who has more than half Wales under his care—a larger area than any of his English brethren—though he is in far from robust health, has driven four miles, after a busy confirmation in a neighbouring town, solely to administer that rite, not to the daughter of a peer or territorial magnate, but to a poor girl, a labourer's daughter, so badly crippled that she could not be carried even a few miles; whose life, though it hardly extended beyond childhood, has left a blessing behind it in this small country village.

A third instance may be given.

There is a remote, inaccessible parish on the borders of Wales containing a population of only 150 souls, which the tender mercies of a former Government had scheduled for compulsory separation from an English diocese, in order that it might enjoy the questionable advantage of being a 'corpus vile' on which to try the experiment of disestablishment and disendowment. Owing to the late bishop's death, six candidates—five labourers' children, one a mason's—would have remained unconfirmed had not the fatherly heart of the new bishop prompted him, directly his attention was called to it, to promise to undertake, at great personal inconvenience, immediately after his consecration, a visit to that parish to confirm the candidates in the morning and to preach to the people the same afternoon. The father of one of the children devoted a whole day's labour from dawn till dark to erecting an arch of welcome over the churchyard gate, and resolutely declined to be remunerated for his loss of time. To-day on this mason's cottage wall hangs a portrait of the bishop which now forms a pendant to a long solitary picture of Mr. Spurgeon!

It is such fatherly acts as these, doubly necessary as they are in these democratic days, which bind the people to their bishops and make it clear to all men that they are true to their apostolic mission in caring for the poor and in ministering to the sick, the sinful and the sorrowing. No one doubts that the bishops are one and all ready and even anxious to do these things: but how can they, except very rarely, when their dioceses are so unwieldy and claims on their time are so incessant?

The analogy of the overgrown parish is what should guide us in dealing with the overgrown diocese. In the case of the parish there are three courses open: (1) to provide the incumbent, who still retains sole charge of the entire parish, with assistant clergy; (2) to hand over a district with its church and parochial organizations to one of the assistant clergy in sole charge, the incumbent, however, still retaining the responsibility and, if need arises, control; and (3) to divide the parish. Let us consider these three courses as applied to the case of the overgrown diocese.

(1) To provide the diocesan with one or more suffragan or assistant bishops is a course with which, I am glad to say, we are now getting familiar. It is quite unnecessary to suppose there need be any antagonism between this course and subdivision. Bishop Wordsworth and Bishop Selwyn, who were the earliest and most enthusiastic promoters of the subdivision of dioceses, were equally notable, the former for being the reviver of the office of suffragan bishops, the latter for calling to his aid

several assistant bishops. But after all, this course is only a partial relief to the diocesan. It furnishes him with another pair of hands, but it does not relieve him of 'the care of all the churches,' the responsibility of government or the labour of organization. A suffragan or assistant bishop is most useful in providing greater facilities for confirmation, and such functions as consecrations and church openings, but he is only a deputy. The difference between the effect of the appointment of a suffragan and the division of a diocese was clearly put by Bishop Lightfoot at his first diocesan conference. He said:—

'The expedient of a suffragan is not new in the diocese of Durham. This solution would be easy if it were satisfactory. On this point it is well to speak frankly. If I were to consult my own convenience, I should take steps at once for the appointment of a suffragan and postpone the division of the diocese *sine die*. I should certainly get more relief in this way; for the effect of dividing the diocese will not be, I apprehend, to reduce the work of the Bishop of Durham very materially, but to enable him to do his work more thoroughly. But I do not think the expedient satisfactory. A suffragan bishop holds a very anomalous position. It is the direct personal responsibility which makes the man in himself. It is the independent personal authority which recommends him to others. The suffragan bishop has neither. He cannot feel his own strength, and he cannot make it felt by others. Thus by no fault of his own, but by the force of circumstances, he is less efficient than he should be. He may perform certain episcopal acts as well as, or better than, the diocesan: but from the mere fact that he is not the diocesan, they do not meet with the same acceptance. As a centre of corporate activity he is almost powerless.

We cannot see better how different in kind, rather than in degree, the relief given by a suffragan is to that rendered by the subdivision of a diocese, than by noticing that the Bishop of Lichfield appointed a suffragan even after the detachment of the county of Derby from his see; and that the Bishops of Exeter and Ripon have both done the same after parting with what are now the dioceses of Truro and Wakefield; and that the Bishops of Liverpool and Durham, although their dioceses are small and compact and have surely assumed their ultimate form, have both called to their aid an assistant bishop.

We may be thankful that so many suffragan and assistant bishops have been nominated—they are now twenty-four in number—but we may express the hope that the wise words of Bishop Lightfoot are borne in mind by the clergy and laity of those dioceses which have the advantage of their services.

(2) We have only seen one instance, and that a most conspicuous and successful example of this form of relief. Bishop Jackson gave the Bishop of Bedford, it is understood, sole charge of East London. Bishop Walsham How had absolute control even of the patronage within his district surrendered to him by Bishop Jackson, who gave effect to the Bishop of Bedford's appointments by attaching his signature to them when made. It is difficult for a layman to understand why so obvious an expedient, which worked so well, has not been followed. We can only suppose it is because diocesans like Bishop Jackson and suffragans like Bishop How so rarely meet. It would seem to be the common sense preliminary to the

The Increase of the Episcopate 273

creation of a new diocese, at least wherever one is formed by the subdivision of a single diocese without the accession of territory from another. Why, for instance, should not the counties of Derby and Nottingham be worked not as a single diocese, but as two dioceses at present united but soon to be divided, each county having its separate diocesan conference and other organizations quite independent of the other? Each county would thus grow accustomed to stand alone, and Derbyshire would soon feel its own strength and take steps to emancipate itself from even the nominal control of its eastern sister. In such a case an endowment fund for the new see should be at once opened, and if kept thus before the public eye it would soon receive many unlooked for benefactions. We do not realize as we should to how many people, who know and care little or nothing for ecclesiastical arrangements, county schemes and county independence would strongly appeal; nor is it sufficiently remembered how many people have a large measure of this world's goods without the faintest idea of how to bestow them, if they possess no near or at least no dear relation: a single issue of the *Standard*, some years ago, contained the announcement of a bequest of £30,000 to the poor of a small town and of £50,000 from another person towards the reduction of the National Debt.

(3) Of the relief of unmanageable dioceses by subdivision we have had, alas, but too few examples. When Bishop Wordsworth wrote the letter to Viscount Dungannon, from which I have quoted, he could do little more than restate the principles of our reformers and urge that an episcopal church without an adequate episcopate

is an anomaly. He did indeed argue from the wonderful development of the Church in our colonies since they had been provided with an adequate episcopate, that similar results would follow at home. But the only recent experience we had at that time in England was from the two sees of Ripon and Manchester, and much of the improvement there might, not without plausibility, be ascribed to the new birth of vigour and enthusiasm which naturally flowed from the Oxford movement and also from the rapid increase of population. But we are now more fortunately circumstanced. We can leave arguments from *a priori* grounds, and point to the astonishing results which the adequate subdivison of dioceses shows everywhere, whether in such populous districts as Liverpool and Durham or in thinly populated counties like Devon and Cornwall.

Of late years statistics have been carefully and elaborately kept of ordinations, confirmations, and contributions of money; and these show clearly that 'more dioceses' means more clergy, more churches, more communicants, and better work all round.

Let us look closely at the practical results of the subdivision of the dioceses of Chester, Durham, and Exeter.

I. CHESTER (out of which LIVERPOOL was formed in 1880).

1. CONFIRMATION STATISTICS.

	Year.	No. of Confirmations.	No. Confirmed.
Chester	1878	30	4,464 ⎫ 11,253
,,	1879	38	6,789 ⎭

The Increase of the Episcopate

	Year.		No. of Confirmations.		No. Confirmed.	
Chester	1884	...	27	...	2,905	} 9,501
,,	1885	...	66	...	6,596	
Liverpool	1884	...	49	...	5,858	} 12,624
,,	1885	...	61	...	6,766	

in the 2 years before subdivision ... 11,253
in the 2 years after ,, ... 22,125
Increase ... ... 10,872, or 96 per cent.

2. Ordination Statistics. Deacons Ordained.

				Chester.	Liverpool.		
Chester	1877	36	... 1885	23	+ 40	=	63
,,	1878	40	... 1886	13	+ 35	=	48
,,	1879	38	... 1887	21	+ 32	=	53
		114		57	+ 107	=	164

in the 3 years before subdivision ... 114
in the 3 years after ,, ... 164
Increase ... ... 50, or 43 per cent.

3. Financial and General Statistics.

The Bishop of Liverpool in his charge delivered in 1887, says:—

'We have 200 incumbents in the diocese; in 1880 there were 182. We have 194 stipendiary curates; in 1880 there were only 120. This is an increase of 74 curates in seven years.

'During the last seven years I have consecrated twenty entirely new churches, and opened by licence two others which only need an endowment; three others are being built, and will be completed before long. This makes twenty-five in all.

'In the seven years that I have been Bishop of Liverpool, I have ordained no less than 217 deacons; in the seven years before the see was created the number ordained for the same district was only 133. The number of young persons confirmed in the first year that I began confirming was 4,700; the annual number is now between 6,000 and 7,000, and these are supplied by only 200 congregations. During the last six years I have held 291 confirmations, and confirmed 35,458 young persons.'

Two tables are appended to the charge.

(1) The amount spent on building, enlarging, or restoring churches, on building or enlarging school-rooms, and on building mission rooms or parish rooms in the diocese of Liverpool for the three years ending October, 1884, is £145,385 10s. 3d., and for the three years ending October, 1887, £197,821 19s. 10d., making for the six years £343,207 10s. 1d.

(2) The amount raised for parochial charities, diocesan institutions, home missions, and foreign missions, in the diocese of Liverpool for the three years ending October, 1884, is £98,771 16s. 2d., and for the three years ending October, 1887, £117,508 10s. 5d., making for the six years £216,280 6s. 7d., or a grand total of £559,487 16s. 8d.; not a bad return for the expenditure of £100,000 in founding the see!

II. DURHAM (out of which NEWCASTLE was formed in 1882).

1. CONFIRMATION STATISTICS.

	Year.	No. of Confirmations.	No Confirmed.
Durham	1880	44	5,806 ⎫
,,	1881	38	5,016 ⎬ 17,130
,,	1882	46	6,308 ⎭

	Year.	No. of Confirmations.	No. Confirmed.
Durham	1883	39	5,170
,,	1884	39	5,641 } 16,372
,,	1885	40	5,561
Newcastle	1883	60	5,186
,,	1884	36	2,140 } 10,206
,,	1885	46	2,880

in the 3 years before subdivision ... 17,130
in the 3 years after ,, ... 26,578
Increase ... ... 9,448, or 55 per cent.

2. Ordination Statistics. Deacons Ordained.

					Durham.		Newcastle.		
Durham	1879	28	...	1885	36	+	15	=	51
,,	1880	41	...	1886	31	+	12	=	43
,,	1881	37	...	1887	29	+	15	=	44
		106			96	+	42	=	138

in the 3 years before subdivision ... 106
in the 3 years after ,, ... 138
Increase ... ... 32, or 30 per cent.

3. Financial and General Statistics.

In 1881, when pleading for the subdivision of his diocese, Bishop Lightfoot said:—

'I have no words but words of thankfulness, when I hear of the efforts of noble-hearted and open-handed men to supply the needs of any particular locality. They will always command my deepest sympathy and most cordial aid. But I say that if you would attack the evil in a spirit of true generalship, you will begin at once at the other end. Only plant a bishop in Newcastle, face to face with the spiritual destitution of the place, and I am much surprised if, before two or three years are passed, some comprehensive and well-considered scheme for its amendment is not devised. A centre of spiritual authority and of ecclesiastical direction is wanted, round which the zeal of churchmen, laity as well as clergy, may rally; for there is no lack of zeal in either. I appeal confidently to the experience of our Church everywhere, at home and abroad, in the colonies and among the heathen.'

Nor was he disappointed, for in his charge of November, 1886, he was able to write:—

'In nothing has the wisdom of dividing the see been more conspicuously vindicated than in its financial results. This will have appeared already in my statement respecting the Church Building Fund; but it is still more strikingly emphasized when we reckon up the expenditure from all sources on various church works in the diocese. The amounts expended since the last visitation, as given by the returns, are as follows:—

		£
I.	For sites and erection of new Churches	66,302
II.	For repairs, enlargement and decoration of existing Churches	60,682
III.	For Churchyards and other Burial Places in connexion with the Church	9,935
IV.	For Parsonages	27,416
V.	For Church Schools (Day and Sunday), sites, erection, enlargements, repair, or furnishing	39,516
VI.	For Mission Rooms, Church Institutes, and other buildings not included under the previous heads	19,874
		£223,725

'The amounts under these heads are generally larger, and, in some cases, far larger than they were for the

The Increase of the Episcopate

undivided diocese during the four previous years. If to these we add the large sums (amounting to nearly £244,000) contributed in the diocese of Newcastle during the same period, it will be plain that the money spent on the foundation of the new see has been far more than recouped to the two dioceses already.'

The present Bishop of Newcastle (Dr. Jacob) says that the clergy have increased in his diocese since 1882 from 218 to 316 in 1897, i.e. by nearly 100 in fifteen years, and that by the end of 1898 they will number 328.

III. EXETER (out of which TRURO was formed in 1877).

1. CONFIRMATION STATISTICS.

Year.		No. of Confirmations.	No. Confirmed.
Exeter 1875	... ...	124	5,401 } 11,675
,, 1876	... ...	124	6,274
Exeter 1879	... ...	106	6,348 } 12,382
,, 1880	... ...	102	6,034
Truro 1879	... ...	45	1,741 } 3,277
,, 1880	... ...	48	1,536

in the 2 years before subdivision ... 11,675
in the 2 years after ,, ... 15,659
Increase ... ... 3,984, or 34 per cent.

2. ORDINATION STATISTICS. DEACONS ORDAINED.

				Exeter.		Truro.		
Exeter 1874	25	...	1885	13	+	11	=	24
,, 1875	21	...	1886	34	+	14	=	48
,, 1876	17	...	1887	21	+	16	=	37
	63			68	+	41	=	109

in the 3 years before subdivision ... 63
in the 3 years after ,, ... 109
Increase ... ... 46, or 73 per cent.

3. Financial and General Statistics.

Archdeaconry of Cornwall, which now forms the Diocese of Truro.

	Before creation of See of Truro.			After.
	1850	1869	1876	1885
Incumbents resident	108	217	215	222
Assistant Curates	47	50	51	78
Parsonage Houses	171	190	198	210

Before 1877 the average number of churches built and restored was 3·5 per annum, since it has risen to 6·6.

It might be thought that the expenditure of £70,000 on endowing the new see, and £110,000 on building a new cathedral, and the annual sum required for the maintenance of twenty-seven additional curates, would have seriously diminished the support given to home and foreign missions; the contrary is, however, the case. Comparing the figures given in the Exeter Calendar for 1877 (the last that included Cornwall) with those in the Exeter and Truro Calendars for 1889, I find that the amounts given in a single year by the two counties of Devon and Cornwall to such objects have increased since the creation of the see of Truro as follows, Cornwall alone giving under the first head more than Devon and Cornwall gave together before 1887:—

	£
Home Missions (i.e. General Funds of A. C. S. and C. P. A. S.) have increased by	2,869
Foreign Missions (S. P. G. and C. M. S.) have increased by	1,293
Missions to Seamen have increased by	485
Total increase	£4,647

The Increase of the Episcopate

But the greatest benefits of subdivision no figures can show; they were however well stated by the present Bishop of Exeter at Wakefield in 1886:—

'I can testify that the division of overgrown dioceses is invaluable in the way of enabling the bishop to get into closer personal and individual contact with his clergy, and also with the people; it enables him to go to their homes, their schools, and their parishes, and to preach to the people.'

And by a well-known Plymouth layman, who wrote in 1888:—

'The great benefit of the division (of Exeter Diocese) has been that the bishop has been able to visit every part of the diocese more frequently, and to stay longer and show himself more among the people; and there can be no doubt that the presence of a bishop among the people does produce a very great effect. Our bishop spent ten days here last January, meeting the church-wardens, the Sunday school teachers, and other church workers, as well as the clergy, and visiting the schools, the hospitals, and the workhouse. *All this did incalculable good.*'

The evidence shown by these statistics is simply overwhelming in favour of the subdivision of dioceses. I shall not labour the point further. Let us now consider (1) the amount of subdivision we require; (2) the principle on which dioceses should be divided; (3) the minimum income of new sees and whence it should be obtained; and finally (4) what facilities are necessary for obtaining the sanction of Church and State to such subdivision.

(1) There is no safer or more experienced guide than

the late Bishop Selwyn on this point. After spending a quarter of a century as bishop of New Zealand, and some years as bishop of Lichfield, he said on this subject:—

'We (diocesan bishops) ought to be multiplied, so as to become acquainted with every parish and to spend a day or two every year in each parish. Until that is the case we shall never have the episcopal office presented to the public mind as it ought to be. . . . Why are the laity so ignorant on the subject of confirmation? Because they seldom see a confirmation. This ignorance will soon be removed if confirmations are held annually in every parish. Now with respect to another point, ordination. There is a general complaint now that examinations for holy orders are more hurried than they ought to be. I think the bishops should have more time for examination and communicating personally with the candidates; and for that purpose there must not be too many candidates at each ordination. . . . Then again, the institution of new incumbents to the cure of souls by the bishop in person is a most important element for good. . . . To know his clergy and to be known of them, is as much the duty of a bishop as it is the duty of a pastor to know his sheep and to be known of them.'

Let us remember too the rapid increase in the number of a bishop's public duties, owing to the vast development of diocesan machinery and organization; the late Bishop of St. David's said in 1894:—

'Whereas until about fourteen years ago I had ordinarily to preside at some two or three meetings of a diocesan character in the course of a year, I calculate

The Increase of the Episcopate 283

that I now spend on an average one month out of every twelve in the chair at such assemblies.'

We are forced to the conclusion that, speaking roughly and excluding Wales, the minimum we should require would be county dioceses. Not that Rutland should be compelled to have a separate bishop, or that Lancashire should be denied three or more, or even Sussex two. County dioceses were the ideal of Henry VIII and Cranmer, and with six times the population we should surely be content with no less.

(2) Very closely follows the consideration of the principle on which dioceses should be divided.

Professor Freeman seems to be worthy of attention when he says:—

'The principle that I should try to lay down is that *dioceses should follow counties.* It is the principle of old Gaul, the principle of modern Germany, the principle of England at several intermediate stages, that the ecclesiastical divisions should follow the civil. It is especially needful in England, where the civil divisions are so old, where they enter into so many points of men's thoughts, feelings and associations. A diocese made up of scraps is as bad as the last abomination in civil divisions, the pestilent 'assize county,' against which rational grand juries are protesting. Let shire and diocese be the same; let bishop and alderman sit side by side, whenever they have a chance. . . . I am sure the all but absolute identity of the shire of Somerset and the diocese of Somerset has been of the greatest practical use. The bishop and the bishopric are known everywhere as something which is a man's own as much as the shire with its sheriff and lord lieutenant. It is not so where geography is less happy. I remember the remark forty years ago when the great restoration of the church of Hereford was going on. It was said that the people of Herefordshire cared for their cathedral church; it was an essential part of their shire and city. But the people of that part of Shropshire which was in the diocese of Hereford did not care for the church of Hereford; to them it was a foreign church in a foreign city and shire.'

Again, if a county is too large an area for a diocese let civil divisions be followed in the new arrangements, e.g. in Sussex which has a distinct county council for East Sussex and for West Sussex. Or again, when the diocese of Worcester is divided, let there be three dioceses formed, one for the county of Worcester, a second for the county of Warwick, and a third for the city of Birmingham together with its numerous suburbs, thus avoiding the mistake recently perpetrated at Bristol, to which city three alien deaneries in Wiltshire were attached.

(3) The minimum income of new sees and where it is to be found. I strongly deprecate any undue denudation of the endowment of the old sees—they have historic traditions and large houses to keep up, and in my judgement £4,000 a year should be their irreducible minimum. But when we come to new sees all the conditions are changed. Where is the need for the large house of palatial dimensions? I most firmly believe that £2,000 a year and a reasonably sized house would be a sufficient minimum, in most cases, at least to start with. Let us at once consider the objections that are raised.

'It will not do to have two classes of bishops.' First,

let us consider this with relation to the House of Lords. There are at present two archbishops and three bishops who gain a seat immediately they are in possession of their see, one bishop with a seat and no vote, and twenty-nine bishops who succeed to twenty-one seats in rotation, the eight most recently appointed having to wait for succession. Surely it might be provided either that the twenty-six seats should always be attached to the original twenty-six sees, or that no new see should come on the rota for giving its occupant a seat until its endowment had reached a minimum of £3,000 or £4,000 a year, or any figure that might be desired. I cannot believe that this would constitute any very grave constitutional innovation!

But perhaps objectors mean that it will not do to have two classes of episcopal incomes. Considering that there are already no less than twelve varieties, viz. £15,000 (Canterbury), £10,000 (York), £7,000 (Durham), £6,000 (Winchester), £5,500 (Ely), £5,000 (Salisbury), £4,500 (Lincoln), £4,200 (Hereford), £3,500 (Newcastle), £3,200 (St. Alban's), £3,000 (Wakefield), £2,000 (Sodor and Man), it seems late in the day to make this objection, especially as it is not proposed to create a thirteenth variety but to follow the precedent of Sodor and Man, and that only as a temporary measure.

Then there is another precedent for a £2,000 minimum of which no one seems to have ever heard, viz. the Bishop's Resignation Act of 1869, made perpetual in 1875. By this Act, when a bishop is incapacitated by *mental* infirmity a coadjutor *cum jure successionis* can be appointed by the Crown, and draw £2,000 a year from the income of the see. He will undertake every duty, responsibility and privilege of the incapacitated bishop, except his house and his seat in Parliament. I propose that in addition to the £2,000 minimum income a house should be provided, and I feel sure that no sensible person would mind the bishop of a new see being relieved of his reversion to a seat in the House of Lords until the income had reached £3,000 or even £4,000 a year. Surely if £2,000 a year and no house was thought, by the wisdom of Parliament in 1869, sufficient for an acting bishop of London, Durham, or Winchester, it might be sanctioned in 1898 as the minimum endowment of a new county bishopric with a fair sized house thrown in, at least as a temporary expedient.

If all the old sees with the exception of Canterbury, York and London, were reduced to £4,000 a year, an annual income of £16,000 would be available for providing half the endowment of sixteen new county bishoprics, which would leave only some £30,000 or £40,000 to be raised by the churchmen of each locality.

(4) Next what sanction do we require from Church and State for the subdivision of dioceses?

We want of course a general enabling Act, giving powers analogous to those for the subdivision of parishes. One hundred years ago no parish could be divided without a special Act of Parliament. This can now be done by an order in council, when certain conditions are complied with. It is often said, and sometimes truly, that the subdivision of parishes has gone too far. I think the truth is rather that it has often been done on a wrong principle, viz. to cut off the poor part only from a rich parish, instead of making a fair division which would leave both parts with rich and poor in them. But if we have divided parishes too freely, there is no fear that we shall do the same with dioceses; because, whereas the endowment of new vicarages has come almost exclusively from old ecclesiastical sources it is not contemplated that less than half the endowment of a new see should come from public subscription. Is not the need of finding £30,000 or £40,000 from such a source a sufficient safeguard?

At present we are at a deadlock—people will not give largely till they know that parliamentary sanction is assured, and the government will not introduce a bill until the greater part of the endowment is guaranteed.

Then as to the mode of appointing to new sees. As in the analogous case of appointing to parochial benefices, the wisest plan is to make realities of the old forms we have inherited rather than to wait for the concession of any ideal method of selection—the case is too urgent; we cannot afford to wait for this. The present method of appointment to livings would work well if reasonable powers were reserved to the bishop, assisted if need be by a commission similar to that created by the Pluralities Amendment Act, to reject an obviously unsuitable presentee. So when the confirmation of bishops is made a reality there will be little reason to fear improper appointments, especially if meantime the Church has obtained for herself a thoroughly representative national assembly which can make her voice heard and her influence felt even by prime ministers and the House of Commons.

I have tried to show that nothing so vitally strengthens the Church in every department of her work as an adequate provision of diocesan bishops, and that the experience of subdivision during the last quarter of a century amply proves the wisdom and foresight of Henry's advisers at the very dawn of the Reformation.

There are wealthy people who build and endow schools, hospitals and picture galleries. Is it likely to turn out that no churchman or churchwoman will endow a bishopric? Many people will spend £10,000 on building or restoring a church in their own parish; yet surely it is a nobler ambition to have a fifth or a tenth share in giving life and energy to the Church's work in two populous counties with a million inhabitants, than to have the undivided honour of directly benefiting a few hundred souls in a single small parish. I may be told that it is absurd to suggest that any such idea will ever gain popularity; yet sixty years ago the now familiar work of building or restoring a church by voluntary subscription was thought a strange and quixotic proposal. When Bishop George Augustus Selwyn was curate of Windsor he found a debt of £3,000 owing on the security of the rates for recently rebuilding the parish church. At a meeting held to consider the advisability of imposing stiff pew rents in order to provide the interest on the loan, Mr. Selwyn startled his hearers by suggesting that the debt should be repaid by voluntary subscription, and offered his curate's stipend for two years to furnish a tenth of what was required. Within a month the congregation recovered sufficiently from their surprise at hearing so novel a suggestion to raise the required sum—the principal was repaid and the

The Increase of the Episcopate

creditor forgave the interest. Sixty years hence the endowment of new sees by public subscription, with which as yet we are scarcely familiar, may cause as little comment and surprise as building or restoring a church by such means does at the present day.

An eloquent speaker said at Manchester Church Congress in 1888:—

'We have to convince churchmen, and to convince the capitalists, that episcopacy, as a real energizing force, working as the living centre of each diocese, radiating to the very outer ring of its circumference, and sending the heart's blood of the Church to the extremities, is essential to the vitality of the body spiritual.'

I think the experience of Truro, Liverpool, and Newcastle should go far to convince them [1].

[1] On the following page statistics of the existin dioceses are given, which will afford some help in conceiving the conditions of the problem with which the Church has to deal.

STATISTICS OF
THE DIOCESES OF ENGLAND AND WALES

	ACRES. *(thousands only.)*		POPULATION, 1891. *(thousands only.)*		BENEFICES.		CLERGY AT WORK.
1. St. David's	2267	London	3245	Norwich	914	London	1417
2. Norwich	1994	Manchester	2644	Oxford	650	Norwich	1049
3. Lincoln	1775	Rochester	1938	York	629	Manchester	890
4. York	1730	York	1447	St. Alban's	627	St. Alban's	878
5. Exeter	1629	Worcester	1228	Lincoln	587	York	873
6. Carlisle	1624	Liverpool	1207	Peterborough	571	Oxford	871
7. St. Alban's	1446	Lichfield	1196	Ely	558	Winchester	857
8. Oxford	1385	Ripon	1020	Winchester	547	Rochester	789
9. Ripon	1384	Durham	1017	Exeter	508	Worcester	754
10. Ely	1357	St. Alban's	1006	London	506	Lichfield	739
11. Salisbury	1309	Winchester	976	Manchester	504	St. Alban's	724
12. Newcastle	1290	Southwell	975	Bath & Wells	491	Exeter	707
13. Winchester	1250	Llandaff	799	Salisbury	489	Ely	703
14. Peterborough	1240	Canterbury	745	Worcester	482	Southwell	687
15. Southwell	1182	Chester	730	Lichfield	469	Canterbury	674
16. Lichfield	1082	Wakefield	719	Southwell	466	Lincoln	667
17. St. Asaph	1067	Norwich	710	Hereford	426	Bath & Wells	623
18. Bath & Wells	1043	Peterborough	692	Canterbury	425	Salisbury	620
19. Worcester	1037	Exeter	629	St. David's	404	Chichester	593
20. Hereford	986	Oxford	613	Chichester	377	Ripon	562
21. Bangor	985	Chichester	549	Ripon	357	St. David's	501
22. Chichester	934	Ely	524	Gloucester	323	Durham	491
23. Canterbury	914	Newcastle	509	Rochester	308	Llandaff	460
24. Truro	869	St. David's	496	Carlisle	293	Chester	439
25. Manchester	845	Lincoln	472	Chester	258	Liverpool	428
26. Llandaff	797	Bath & Wells	429	Truro	237	Hereford	413
27. Chester	705	Carlisle	424	Durham	235	Gloucester	384
28. Gloucester	700	Salisbury	369	Llandaff	233	Carlisle	381
29. Durham	647	Bristol	366	St. Asaph	206	Truro	334
30. Rochester	316	Gloucester	329	Liverpool	196	Wakefield	312
31. Bristol	310	Truro	325	Bristol	175	Bristol	305
32. Liverpool	262	St. Asaph	270	Newcastle	171	St. Asaph	305
33. Wakefield	235	Hereford	217	Wakefield	167	Newcastle	275
34. London	181	Bangor	215	Bangor	139	Bangor	218
35. Sodor & Man	180	Sodor & Man	55	Sodor & Man	31	Sodor & Man	52

XI

CHURCH REFORM AND SOCIAL REFORM

By the Rev. T. C. Fry, D.D.

ALL allow that during the last ten years there has been a marked growth of human interest and even of enthusiasm in the solution of social problems. The cry of the workers for better conditions of life, for a juster share in the fruits of labour, has been heard by the conscience of men who are not themselves wage-earners. It is at last widely recognized that there is a large social question, and that we are all concerned in its solution, not merely because we are affected by its issue, but because we are each of us more or less responsible for its existence.

The broad and popular division of men—a division often condemned as by implication hostile to wealth—into the classes and the masses is in the main sufficiently true. Capital and labour are, as a matter of fact, being slowly ranged into two great camps, however much each camp may contain various grades within itself. Neither profit-sharing voluntarily granted from above, nor labour co-partnership organized from below, has as yet made any appreciable difference to our main social division.

On the whole, therefore, the classes represent capital;

the masses represent labour. The capital of the capitalist is by no means always the just reward of his own wits. The classes have been largely created by our laws of inheritance, and by the inherent power of money, under present economic conditions, to gather to itself more money. In part owing to the power of money, in part to the advantages of inheritance, the classes have most culture. They have larger opportunities of education; money gives them more leisure, leisure gives them more culture. By virtue of their capital, individual or associated, they constitute the employing class; they thus largely dictate the conditions of labour. They supply, for the most part, out of their own ranks the captains of industry. They form the majority of both legislative and administrative bodies. Through a Cabinet of politicians they promote or impede new laws. They possess, to put it briefly, in largest measure the best chances of common life.

On the other hand the working masses live by a weekly wage. Even the more successful of them have but a small chance of becoming capitalists: the industrial revolution has steepened the gradient. The best they can hope for is regular work. Some of the more highly organized can by combination provide against sickness in manhood and the workhouse in old age. But to the majority work is neither regular nor highly paid. Improvement in their condition can only be obtained by the pressure that combination can enforce or by a desolating industrial war. Through isolation, suspicion, or ignorance the majority do not combine at all: but whether combined or no, there are indeed few who are free from fear of the outlook when they stay to reflect on the industrial accidents of life.

Upon the marginal edge of either class is a fringe that belongs to neither the capitalist nor the wage-earner. There is a border, so to speak, to either fringe where men shade off into common economic and social conditions, wherein perhaps only inherited sympathies or antipathies serve to keep them apart. The tradesman class includes the larger and the smaller tradesman; the clerk may be the son of an officer who is thought to have sunk, or the son of an artisan who is thought to have risen; the farmer may hunt twice a week or may drive his own plough; even the professional man is differently classified according to the sum total of his fees or the social rank of his *clientèle*.

For the men in these fringes the struggle for life is often more severe than for highly skilled artisans in regular work. Yet on the whole the sympathies of these men are definitely on one side or another of the line of social cleavage. Their cause is the cause of the classes or the cause of the masses.

Roughly speaking then it is reasonably accurate to say that the questions at issue between capital and labour make up the social problem. On the one side stands the class of men who either possess capital of their own, or have easy access through credit to capital. To this class belong the millionaire, the moderately wealthy, the *entrepreneur*, and the larger distributor. Just below these are the professional classes and the tradesmen who contribute to joint-stock companies, most of whom may be regarded in relation to capital as 'within the margin of sympathy' with it. On the other side stands the worker proper. He has now discovered that mere political enfranchisement is not economic freedom. Conscious of inequality of opportunity, he is in an attitude of attack. The capitalist is in an attitude of defence. The position is one of estrangement.

All attempts to paint in broad colours will, we allow, seem to exaggerate, to fail in accuracy of detail and so, of course, in suggestiveness. Little, for instance, has yet been said of distinction between town and country. In the country the details of the problem are indeed different. The often loud voices of the town contrast strangely with the silence and even suspicion of the villager. But in essence the problem is the same. It is in part one of distribution, in part one of production. Both problems are complicated by the conditions introduced by the world market. The American corn rings can affect a Suffolk wage. Corn is low; rents are low; the squire has no money; the farmer has little money and less enterprise. He is not yet won to co-operate. The labourer finds less work; and what he finds is less well paid. His cottage is leaky, and is not his own. He may get an allotment, with which he may eke out his wage; but if his children grow up unsuccessful, how is he to escape the workhouse? The labourer is reticent: he tells his neighbour little and his parson less. If he has ambitions, they connect themselves vaguely with the land; or else he refuses to stay, migrates to towns, and while maintaining the vigour increases the difficulties of the workers there. So the fight for existence grows fiercer: rents rise: the belt of town lands grows more

Church Reform and Social Reform

valuable. The owners of the ground grow wealthy. Dukes are enriched by 'lodging houses in Bloomsbury.' The country contributes out of its very stagnation to intensify the contrast between mansion and slum.

Of course it is not contended that there are not compensations and growing elements of hope. In many respects there has been an improvement in the condition of the poor. Organized labour has obtained, after severe struggles, better conditions than existed at the beginning of the century. Unorganized labour, at least in towns, has to some extent followed suit, though rent and rates often devour the improvement in wage. Where abuses exist they cannot be entirely neglected. The workers have votes: voters may be deceived and misled, but they cannot be ignored; and, however slow the process, there is hope wherever a problem is seen, stated, and acknowledged. Further, as has been said above, the conscience of many in the comfortable classes has been touched. The remarkable spread of the Christian Social Union is one effective proof of this. Ten years ago it did not exist: yet the committee of the Lambeth Conference on Industrial Questions recognized every one of its principles and expressly repudiated some of their contraries. The University and College settlements witness to a new sense of a social duty to the dwellers in the 'cities of the poor.' Lay men and women have gone down into streets of workers, whose employers have often abandoned them for the suburbs; and they have gone there to pay a social rather than an individual debt. They have brought their art, their experiences, their brains, their faith in fellowship, to the service of their fellows; they have received as much as they have given, and their unselfish work is serving to bridge the chasm that a growing plutocracy has not scrupled to create.

But the chasm is not yet bridged. These devoted men and women would be the first to confess that the result of their work, hopeful as it has been, is but as a drop in the ocean of social need. The division remains still, the classes on one side, the masses on the other. But it was exactly this division of privilege *versus* struggle that the Church was created, if not all at once to obliterate, at least to modify, alleviate, and gradually remove. The very conditions of the Incarnation necessitate it. From Bethlehem to Calvary the very meaning of it all is peace for men through self-surrender. The words of life, 'Sell all thou hast,' were but the individual rendering of a gospel which in principle is addressed to us all. This gospel is found, even before our Master's birth, plainly expressed in the Magnificat. It is applied by St. James to condemn such a petty detail (so it would seem to many) as the 'partial' seating of worshippers in church. This mere detail the Apostle calls respect of persons: and respect of persons, he adds with equal plainness, is nothing else than sin. There is in fact a common plane of spiritual equality to which, even in details and of course in principles, the wealthy man should be brought down and the poor man raised up. It is the Church's mission to proclaim this gospel. That mission is not fulfilled, so long as the rich remain unpersuaded that, to save their very souls, they cannot be indifferent to the environment in which the character of their poorer brethren is being degraded. Equality of opportunity

Church Reform and Social Reform

for the formation of Christian character in all men is part and parcel of the gospel. The rich and the powerful themselves need saving: and they are being lost, in every higher sense, by the luxury, the selfishness, the oblivion of spiritual equality, brought about not by wealth used as a trust, but by wealth used as a possession. This ideal of the necessary spiritual equality of men was manifestly the ideal of the early Church. The voluntary communism at Jerusalem was prompted by it. When she was planting herself in the busy cities of Greek life, she at once found a similar division between rich and poor to that we ourselves know of. Yet St. Paul did not hesitate to declare that the separatist spirit of the Corinthian agape, as well as its drunkenness, annulled, so to speak, the eucharist that followed. No one can read the New Testament and not see that the principle of spiritual equality and of equality of opportunity is inherent in Christian principles.

Nor in later and less pure days, even after the ambitions of secular supremacy had entered into her life, did the mediaeval Church forget that she was specially the advocate of the struggling, the defender of their liberty and of their progressive status. The great leaders of the English Church were true friends of the people. Both Theodore and Dunstan promoted an education that was popular rather than aristocratic. Lanfranc was the friend of the slave: under him the Church produced real leaders of men. Anselm fought for general liberty as much as for his own. It was a happy thing for the English people that the Norman kings could crush the baronage but could not crush the

Church. The tyranny of the Crown was alone prevented by the courage of great churchmen. Nothing else can explain the extraordinary popularity of Becket. The instinct of the people was a true one. They saw only the man who dared to support a merciful code against officials; it is easy to forgive them for not foreseeing that the development of their own freedom would altogether modify the self-will they dreaded. It was Becket's courage, rather than his cause, that made it possible for Stephen Langton to lead resistance to John. A far greater contribution to human liberty was that oath exacted by the Archbishop at St. Paul's than the oath taken in the Versailles tennis court nearly six hundred years later by the early French revolutionists.

But why, we may well ask, labour the point further? In her best and purest days the Church of Christ witnessed faithfully to her mission: and she is equally bound to-day to be the ally of all just progress. She should know no worldly distinction in her proclamation of the truth; peer and peasant, master and workman, are to her only souls to be redeemed. That one should have more than he needs for a humanized life and another less, should be to her as intolerable as the selfishness of Corinth once was to St. Paul. The very purpose of wealth is to supply need. Bad cottages, bad drainage, bad water, sickness anywhere untended, poverty unaided and unguided, labour insufficiently rewarded, injustice, hardness, division, all this she must struggle as earnestly to see altered as once she strove to free the serf or ransom the slave. To supply that which lacketh in life or in love, this is her mission to all.

Does she do this now? That is the question. Does she speak on social matters in the trumpet tones of St. James? Is she fully trusted by the people to stand between warring classes, with a special mission to care for and represent the poor while capable of perfect justice to all?

The answer must, we think, be in large part 'No.' But why not? It is simply because at present her own condition protests, so to speak, against the power within her of these social principles. The social situation is as a whole reflected by the present condition of the Church. The clergy, mainly drawn from a class, too often share in the prejudices of their class. In the newspaper correspondence that quite lately followed on the publication of Mr. Arch's life we have a very recent example of a spirit that we should have scarcely ventured to assert as still so strong. Even where individuals amongst the clergy have misgivings, their social *entourage* makes it often difficult for them to speak out. This alliance with the comfortable classes is typified to the workmen by the presence of our leaders in the House of Lords. We may readily grant that nowadays the bishops are entirely indifferent to any such position: indeed, if they were not, their position there is rather an indication than a cause of any peril; the truth is that the general social environment creates the danger for all, bishops and clergy alike: it makes men timid at a crisis: and there are crises in front of us, when nothing but the most outspoken courage will avail to save our reputation for justice with the best men of both sides.

To the difficulty created by the present social situation is to be added another. It is said that the Government have refused to consent to a bishopric at Sheffield unless £100,000 is raised. We are in urgent need of more bishops: yet, if such a sum as this be demanded, we can only obtain them on the condition of putting the Church under excessive obligation to rich men, a step that will not contribute to her social independence.

A further severance is in our opinion created by the difficulty that men of lower social rank meet with, when they desire, for themselves or their children, the opportunity of being entrusted with the ministerial office. This is more specially the case with the Anglican Church than with any other branch of the Catholic Church. It is said that we must have an educated ministry. This is quite true: but is the answer quite sincere? If education means, in part at least, theological experience, the thing we need is not now being secured either by our tests of candidates or our organized opportunities for continued study. If it means *savoir faire*, or to put it plainly, good manners, the training of a French priest might supply a reasonable solution even for this. But the point is that no solution is attempted. It is said, and often—though not always justly—that such a ministry would be least acceptable to working-men themselves. Yet it was thought to be an effective point in the Archbishop's speech at Shrewsbury that he declared himself as above all a working-man, having (to his honour) borne no less privation and labour. The truth is that every priest, be his social origin what it may, should be educated in an age of general education; and it may be granted that certain elements of character greatly need strengthening in working-men; but this should only stimulate us to some solution of the problem. Has the Church then vigorously developed any system of bursaries by which really able and earnest youths, who may chance to be poor, are reasonably sure to secure in school and college those opportunities of education which would fit them for the priesthood? Most certainly not. Hence it is that her ministry, devoted as it is, remains so largely a class ministry: and this is one reason why a majority of her clergy, though—we gladly recognize—a yearly decreasing majority, however kind to the poor as individuals, are not impartial in their social sympathies.

The prevailing influence of social sympathies is, further, no mean factor in the process that has created the burning questions of the neglected curate and the unemployed clergy. In every residuum, if we may use the word without intention of offence, there are of course incapable men. But it is not always incapacity that leaves a man a curate at fifty. There are known to many hardworking clergy who would, one is reasonably sure, long before have secured promotion had they had influential connexions. Yet the influence of social relationships in the matter of ordinary promotion is not felt to be unchristian: the disgrace of it must be generally recognized before patrons—public and private— know no distinction save that of duty nobly done. As long as patronage is free from any control, direct or indirect, as long as without control patronage and property are united, so long will social standing have the power to turn the scale against merit, ability, and service.

That which social authority thus begins, allied political prejudice often completes. The vested interests of social life have created a general tendency to regard any one who is willing to modify them as an untrustworthy person. Except in the big towns, few priests who are in favour of wide reforms can afford to speak out. If they do, they certainly secure their positions as no more than curates. Partly in consequence of this, the reformers generally go to the big poor town parishes; the rest of the clergy are for the most part frankly conservative. In many cases vicars are survivals of the fittest; and, in the eyes of too many patrons, sometimes *caeteris paribus*, sometimes *caeteris imparibus*, the fittest is a conservative. There is a steady, if half-conscious, social pressure in this direction.

But influence, promotion, and patronage are not the worst forms in which social authority manifests itself so one sidedly. There is the power of the purse amongst the laity. Many an earnest priest, whom other reasons (shortly to be set forth) makes a silent voter on the conservative side, is in sympathy wholly one with progress and with the poor. In his eyes Apollyon is plutocracy; the enslavement of everything to wealth; the supremacy of riches. The historic noble is mostly poor; the squire has had to let and go; it is the plutocrat who has to be borne with as patron and subscriber. Sometimes, of course, he is really a generous and faithful son of the Church, even though our economic system—which men misname providence—forbids him the possibility of much self-denial in his generosity, so long as he remains a plutocrat. But very often he is a plutocrat and nothing more. And then his influence upon society about him and upon Church matters, if he profess an interest (or no interest) in them, is wholly bad. The influence of the old noble, if he be worthy, has about it something of the romantic dignity of history; the squire's may be built upon the solid ground of a well-sustained and faithfully supported tradition. The plutocrat has no history often but that of wealth, made by speculation, or monopoly, or sweating, and used, as often, for personal display. He acknowledges his responsibility of patronage by the new school wing; his sense of the claims of the poor by his subscription to the clubs; and his belief in his own importance by the withdrawal of all help from the vicar who opposes his theology or his politics. That is in many English parishes the position of the plutocrat: he is enthroned on the suppressed rights of the rest of the laity.

The decisive social cleavage has been said above to be made between classes and masses. The Church is mostly administered and officered by the classes; her influential laity belong almost wholly to the classes; she is doing a great and growing work amongst the masses; but the deep sympathies of her clergy with the poor as such are largely obscured to the eyes of the masses by the fact that social rank and social position secured by wealth and tradition still count for so much in her service, both amongst clergy and laity. The masses do not realize her mission; she scarcely fully realizes it herself. They do not realize how she is daily changing; how the Christ-spirit as regards this social cleavage is spreading in her children; and so they still feel of her that she is not wholly the friend of their aspirations.

The friend of their aspirations! Yes, if they once trust her as their friend, they will listen to her criticism of their faults. Nothing here written is meant to minimize the shortcomings of the workers. No one who has moved much amongst them can fail to know that there are moral elements of character wanting that, alas! are only too often the cause of their failures. No one is more deeply conscious of this, no one indeed suffers more from it, than the best of the workers themselves: and, what is more, no class is less unwilling to listen in patience to criticism and even to reproof when it is felt to come from a friend. But, be their faults what they may, it must not be forgotten that the Church herself is in part to blame: the gospel that has been often in the past, if not often now, proclaimed in her pulpits has not been an impartial gospel: it has not seemed to have at heart, or at least to have in mind, those aspects of the social question that the poor long felt so deeply, yet once said so little about. And it is in part because the workers found their voice on these matters, before the Church found hers, that many of them still hesitate to believe in the growth of her new sympathies.

Are they right? It is not surprising that many of them should think so. For three parties, who say they ought to know, tell them so: and these three are often one. There is the official Liberal party, the Radical press, and the political Puritan.

In the first place the official Liberal party has to

Church Reform and Social Reform

bethink itself of the 'sinews of war.' Elections cannot be fought and cannot be won without money. If elections are not won, office is not to be had. Now the men who have found the money for the official Liberal party, since the defection of some and the impoverishment of others amongst the old traditional Liberal nobility,—the Whigs in fact,—have been the Nonconformist manufacturers.

Now it is certain that the Nonconformist manufacturers, as a whole, have been more willing to attack the Church than to attack the economic abuses of manufacturing. In this policy of attack upon the Church they are at one with the less wealthy or even poor Puritan in smaller towns and counties. They have also, all of them, inherited the policy from the older but now extinct Manchester individualism. The officials of the Liberal party, therefore, speaking with the voice of the men who still supply most of the sinews of war, and many of whom doubtless are quite sincere in so saying, declare the Church as a Church to be against the policy of progress. The official Radical press very naturally support them. The men on the staff of a great daily who are not Churchmen but Nonconformist or Roman are not likely to modify the outcry, even though the editor himself is striving to be impartial and just. To the aid of these two against the mighty comes the old-fashioned political Puritan.

He at all events is in genuine and deadly earnest, and is still the iconoclast of old. To him every Churchman is a 'sacerdotalist'; Church doctrine is 'Romanism'; sacramental teaching the basest superstition. To destroy is still his mission; to plant the Bible (by which he means his own interpretation of the Bible) upon the ruins of the creed of the Church his one hope and aim.

Thus is the position intensified and exaggerated. Is there anywhere any relief? Most decidedly yes. It has been already pointed out that a slow leaven is everywhere at work in the Church. A no less effectual leaven is at work in the nation. Quite apart from existing political divisions, churchmen are learning the deeper social meaning of the Incarnation. A new light has thus been cast upon the kindred movement for social reform. In this light the new plutocracy has its dangers and baseness revealed. The star of Bethlehem, the star once 'seen in the East,' is rising again over our social wilderness. The magi with their gifts are following to the stable and the manger, where the shepherds too are coming to kneel. The infallible theologians and the social Sadducees who despise Galilee are losing their hold. Not long hence the Church shall have grasped her mission to the poor, as she once grasped it to the slave—a mission not merely other-worldly but for to-day. All churchmen will enter on an equal inheritance.

Meanwhile the awakened workmen in the big towns have made a discovery. They are finding out that economic views have nothing to do with sectarian divisions; that a Nonconformist employer is quite as ready to use force to put down a strike, if he does not like it, as is an employer who is a churchman; that some at least of the clergy of the Church, that has been so bitterly and, alas! at times so justly censured, are, after all, much more democratic in their sympathies and

Church Reform and Social Reform 307

view than the largest subscribers to the local Liberal caucuses. Labour has begun to find a welcome in the Church and the parish room that it has not always had at the political council board. Further it has, in these cases, appeared to them that to weaken a great institution rather than to promote its reform is not a very obvious advantage; and that to disendow the one independent man in their midst might just possibly put the truth somewhat more under the heel of the plutocrat. Further than that, the worker's own desire for social reforms has become overpowering; it has blotted out the traditional programme in England; and it has altogether altered the area and the strength of political pressure. It would seem as if *pari passu* with the spread of deeper and more unselfish views of the Church's social obligations a new opportunity for effective mission were opened out, an audience were gathered eager to hear if she still has the great message of Christ to give to the weary and heavy laden.

At the same time and everywhere there has been a new spirit of fraternization amongst men of differing views. Outside the irreconcilable circle of the fanatics, earnest men of all religious parties are learning that God has something better for us to do than to attack each other in the interests of the wolves round about us. It may yet be possible to stay the foolish and futile conflict of allies, to cultivate a real toleration, to abandon the bitterness of our ancient enmities, and the theological jealousies more worthy of the Dervish than the Christian; and in one common social movement compel the submission of the evils that grow strong upon our Christian divisions. If this be not possible, we may well despair both of our professional Christianity and of the future of England.

For the truth is now clear to all men that the social reforms called for at this time are a test of parties never yet applied. The housing of the poor will demand a large readjustment of the taxation of the rich; the settlement of industrial disputes cannot be effected except by a willingness to submit strong wills to impartial judgements; equality of opportunity in education, in chances of progress, in command as well as in service, can only be effectually granted by a Christian surrender of privilege; a determination to solve such evils as, e.g., are found to accompany the uncontrolled power of the liquor interest will demand from the best men of both parties the preference of national good to party advantage. On all these questions, in fact on every question except the question of religion, there is a much closer affinity between the needs and even the aspirations of less well-endowed citizens of all classes than they themselves suppose. Eliminate the strife over the Church, and social politics would rapidly divide men, not by traditional programmes but by an unselfish sympathy in righteousness and justice. This is even now taking place. The social cleavage of the future will be between the kingdom of Christ and the kingdom of mammon.

But assuredly in this great conflict the Church cannot, as she might, fulfil her mission as things at present are. The Church reflects too much of that in the social situation which will have to be changed. Church reform is a necessary complement to social reform. This reform

Church Reform and Social Reform

is essential for the social authority of the Church. It is impossible that the masses should feel that the Church is theirs, if they find no place in her active life. The working-man may trust some individual priest whose zeal he is witness of and whose sympathy he has tested: but he has had no voice, however indirect, in his coming; and will have none either in his successor's coming, when his own friend goes. Many of the well-to-do classes have become hardened by custom to the sale of livings: some are themselves guilty of the traffic. But the thoughtful working-men are alienated by it; whenever it is presented to them, it appears to unchristianize the Church. Pew rents are another obstacle to popular influence wherever they exist; scarcely less so are seats appropriated on any ground save that of equality between all parishioners. It may appear right enough to secure the claims of parishioners against strangers: but then the parishioners whose claims are thus secured are not often the poor but the well-to-do. If the workers had a place upon parochial Church councils, as they may now have on civil councils; if their presence and voice were as much welcomed as the gentleman's or the big tradesman's—as in fact it is in places where gentlemen and big tradesmen do not live;—they would be won back in thousands where to-day they are but won back in scores. Dissent is often narrow in theology and bare and unattractive in ritual. When it attracts, it is because it is a more democratic system; it finds more for the poor layman to do. Whenever the Catholic Church is frankly democratic as regards persons, catholicity triumphs. The representation of all classes of the laity on Church councils will be a revival of lay churchmanship. Nor is it merely in relation to the workers that this reform would take effect. The Church and the Church house would be as is some conciliation chamber in our industrial life. There would meet there as coequal Christians in the service of a common Master men often in part estranged elsewhere. The silence of strife would issue in a kindlier expression. The peace that grows out of common action might be sealed before the altar. There at least the secular distinctions, marked by exclusive patronage, preference for office, appropriated pews, would best be seen to be inconsistent with a common divine need and a common divine call. The wealthy would learn as much, if not more, than the poor. There are places and churches in England where this is true now. It has but to be made true everywhere. But at present the one most striking fact in the position of the Church is the powerlessness of her laity. The parish priest is comparatively unassailable even by his bishop. Not only his rights but often his wrongs are protected. He may shoot, or hunt, or neglect the sick, or preach twaddle, or limit privilege by denying frequent communion; but so long as he gives just the statutory services no one can say an effective word. A parish cannot say nay to the least desired appointment; it cannot promote the withdrawal of the least successful and least suitable incumbent; it cannot, without scandal and conflict, prevent the arbitrary alteration of a perfectly legal ritual; it cannot suggest new forms of activity to any one who is not enamoured of hard work: it can do nothing except by stopping its sub-

Church Reform and Social Reform 311

scriptions, which is a mean action, or by open opposition, which is a schismatical action. Be the parish priest who he may, do he what he may, the ordinary layman must just endure it. There are those who say that the first step in church reform will be to promote a rebellion against this state of things among the laity.

It is true that the English clergy are setting a brilliant example of work and devotion. It is also true that an Englishman always respects a hard worker, even when he disagrees with him. But it is no less true that this is not a universal rule of clerical work; and that some of those who are working hardest have scarcely the necessary means of life at their command. Is it not very possible that a franker and fuller recognition of lay rights would bring home to laymen, through the knowledge born of responsible action, the need of a wider generosity? The clergy, it is allowed, largely support the Church's needs out of their own pockets; is it not in part because the laity have no recognized position in church administration?

But no mere parochial representation will meet the case. The Houses of Laymen must be quickened. The present election is a thoroughly respectable farce. A few belated members of a diocesan conference stay behind and choose for their representative whoever does not positively refuse to go. If he goes, he goes without authority to join in an irresponsible discussion. Few know that he has been chosen, and fewer still care. Until the Houses of Laymen are really elected by the direct votes of the churchmen of every parish, be the area of representation what it may, no one will ever care more; and no one of real importance will go with a purpose of real importance till some recognized authority attaches to laymen's acts.

The reform of Convocations, the establishment of Houses of Laymen with recognized authority, the definition of their respective spheres, and the grant of freedom of legislation subject, if we remain established, to parliamentary control, are essential, if effective reform is to be carried out. If she is to fulfil her true mission to all classes, the Church must have her utterance and action free. The things that need reform, many of which have been already enumerated, good churchmen disapprove of even more than their critics; churchmen see all the pity of it and deplore the loss. But what are they to do? Are they to spend fruitless years in a struggle with parliamentary committees? Are they to suffer obstruction by men who are, many of them, in favour of 'a free Church in a free state,' but not so violently in favour of organized labour within an organized state? Are they to be alone forbidden the controlled autonomy that belongs to every urban board?

To those who demand disestablishment and disendowment, our answer is fair and simple: it is this. By all means, if you desire to do so, if you think that it will benefit the nation or your party, make it a direct issue. But at all events be fair. Until you do so, or when, having done so, the nation negatives your proposal, help to treat a great institution with common justice. Give it, or help to give it, the power to reform itself, suffer it to give free expression to its true voice. And if it had this freedom and refused to use it, or misused it, you at least would have no reason to regret it. The arguments you had used would be thereby established, 'Cut it down: why cumbereth it the ground?'

But in other ways social reform and church life, once free, will act and react on one another. For what is it that the social reformer needs to assure his way? It is a steady pursuit of reforms for the sake of principles. And it is the principles of Christianity that can alone energize and guide the course of social reform.

Yet the principles, the energies, the wisdom, of a Christian policy can only dominate society when they dominate the Church herself: and this they cannot fully do, while all that expresses the living voice and convictions of the Church at large is cabined, cribbed, confined within the walls of the two Convocations. It is a proof that the will of the Church as a whole does not dominate her policy that such a scandal as the sale of livings still continues. As a whole, the Church is in hearty favour of the abolition of this and kindred scandals. But the Convocations are timid and slow because they are not in full touch with the constituent clergy; and behind the Houses of Laymen there is but the force of the coteries who elect them. Quicken both with life, power, and opportunity, and principles would assert themselves.

But church life offers more than principles to the reformer: it affords a common ground of unity on a plane above all class divisions. It needs must be that men who meet in a common activity in the service of the Church would understand each other better, would be more patient, more forbearing, more just towards one another in social life. There is no force so binding as common service in religion. You cannot expect the active and thoughtful layman to be helpful, if he is expected just to keep quiet and teach a class in a Sunday school. He must have a voice in counsel in all things lawful to a layman. The working-man is, after all, of much the same fibre as his employer. Elect both, use both, unite both; and you are carrying into daily life a unity that will soften more than religious animosities.

Thus only can be made alive certain principles which lie at the root of the Church's practical life. These principles cannot be called by any name but democratic. The term has been indeed woefully misused even by those who lay special claim to be democrats. Still, there they are plain enough in the New Testament, and in any successful active policy built upon the New Testament. We may perhaps best range them under four heads.

Firstly, there is the principle of religious equality. At present, as has been said, religious equality does not obtain in the Church. Our system of patronage largely obstructs it. Thereby property dictates to the rest who shall look after their souls. If patronage were in the hands of the acknowledgedly wise or experienced, something might be said for our present arrangements. But such a contention would be ludicrous. It is ultimately money alone that sits enthroned. Just for one moment put aside special pleading, and imagine St. James' view of this! Yet it could not be difficult to give, under due safeguards, some form of control over patronage, in which the poor man should be equal in suffrage to the wealthy. But inequality rests on more than our system of patronage; it is maintained by appropriation of seats, by the bar in front of the ministry, by the overwhelming power of social position, except in the cities of the poor, in places like Southwark and Bethnal Green.

Secondly, religious equality rests upon the personal dignity of redeemed men; indeed, as seen by the light of the Incarnation, of men as such. A member of Christ, St. Paul has argued, is more than on a level, if one may say so, with another member. The least honourable are the most honourable limbs of the body: so is it with the body of Christ. The motto of a pope —*servus servorum Dei*—is a witness to the greatness of God's highest call. To minister is to reign. The exaltation of the humble is the true Christian Magnificat. Our present social system reflected in our church system has inverted the divine order. The Christ Himself became the son of a carpenter's wife. The humblest in the body of Christ shares thus in the glory of his Lord's self-emptying. If this is only the sentiment of the pulpit, then farewell to all Christian sincerity.

Thirdly, any other system will render all religious co-operation impossible. Build upon anything less divine than the unity of the one body and the absolute equality of all men in the sphere of religion, and you build upon the sand. Yet, in the days before us, it is hourly more manifest, co-operation is the only principle, the only method, that can stand. Any other way lies the anarchy of human society. Any other way the chaos of our competition must end in hate and strife. And when men co-operate in the less, they will deny the name of greater to all in which they do not co-operate. Co-operation, even in religion, is built upon the equality of men. Equals must they be, not indeed in wisdom, in experience, in faith, in sainthood, but so far as all secular and spiritual opportunity can go. Men are not thus equal yet under our existing arrangements.

Lastly, upon religious equality is built our one hope for the Church of an immaterial ideal of life. How are the great mass of our people to learn the worthlessness in God's sight of wealth and rank, of 'pomp and vanity,' when wealth and rank, and not character and worth alone, are allowed a place in patronage, and lay church life and representation denied so often to that which in God's sight is alone of value? If within the House of God we break St. James' clear and emphatic rules, how are we to preach with effect to the poor that they, in their lack of pomps and vanities, are really nearer the kingdom of heaven? Our policy contradicts us: they see, plainly enough, for all our eloquence, that 'the quality' really have the best of it. And so they do not believe us when we exalt the immaterial ideal: we are too plainly ourselves seeking the material. And yet what a strength, what an inspiration, in that other! When the 'gentleman,' as men call him, 'has learnt the lesson of the eucharist, and laying aside his secular distinctions, through and in his Christianity takes his place unostentatiously yet manifestly on a level with the humblest fellow-churchman, what a reaction sets in! How the leaven slowly permeates the perhaps hostile opinion about him, and rough and even cantankerous critics among the masses learn the much-needed lesson of humility for themselves! Years ago a visitor to Madresfield might have seen its 'noble' patron in the

Church Reform and Social Reform 317

almshouse chapel showing strangers at times in simple courtesy to their seats and then himself worshipping, quiet and unnoticed, far back amongst his poor. Contrast the late Lord Beauchamp's estimate of lay equality before the altar with some screened pew beside the sanctuary, where power or wealth displays its contempt for or its ignorance of the meaning of the Gospel.

But, of course, there are dangers even in the recovery of freedom. There is, some say, the danger of revolution. Sudden freedom disconcerts the contented prisoner, and the fanatic seizes the occasion, as the Jacobin once in France. There might be men who were determined by their freedom to force violent and rapid changes on the Church. We believe the danger to be almost entirely imaginary. Freedom to legislate, subject to the veto of Parliament, will not be a rapid process. It is not supported as a rapid process, but as a hopeful one. It is the right way, and the right way always has a thoroughfare. The idea of the church laity in England using their freedom to promote a social and religious revolution is too ludicrous to be discussed.

But there are two other dangers in quite the opposite direction. If the principle of equality be not recognized, and some control on appointments allowed to the laity, greater freedom might only mean enslavement to the power of money. This danger is real enough in America, both in educational and church matters. It is impossible to guard too strictly against it. As matters now stand, disestablishment accompanied by disendowment would bring it on us in full force. Those who would prefer the policy of disestablishment in the interests of the mass of the laity may well halt before they compel the work of the Church to depend wholly upon the money of the classes to-day. There would not be, in many churches where it is most needed, much enforcement of a social Gospel.

The other danger is lest we should be organized on a class basis. This would turn not merely on the manner of election but even on such a detail as the hours of meeting of parochial church councils, and on the resolution shown by our leaders to secure equal opportunities of representation to all. A church parliament, consisting of and voting by orders, must include clergy and laity : but no section of clergy and no class of laity must be left unrepresented. And, though no precaution should be neglected to secure men of the highest character and the sincerest churchmanship, mere wealth and social position *per se* should be absolutely disregarded.

There are a growing number to whom the social outlook, grave as it is, is full of hope ; but, God be thanked, they cannot dissociate their divine optimism from their equally divine ambition for Christ and His Church. The social reform they work for is inseparable from church reform. To set free the Church, without wounding her, to loose rather than rend the bonds that bind her, to induce the State to hear the free expression of the Church's voice, to unite on the only enduring basis— the basis of unity in Christ—men divided by social jealousies, this is their passionate desire. Thus only will the true voice of the Church be heard ; not merely the voice of bishops or archdeacons or ecclesiastical proctors, but of all men who love and serve her. Thus only can she really be Christ's instrument for inspiring and softening those great social changes that lie before us, changes slow perhaps and not always noticeable in the making, but surely developing even now. Thus only can Christ's Church be fully set forth amongst us as a commonwealth of its own, of which all, from richest to poorest, are citizens, and to which the religious liberty and the social fate of all is equally a trust from God.

XII

THE POSITION OF THE LAITY IN THE AMERICAN (PROTESTANT EPISCOPAL) CHURCH

By the Bishop of Vermont

The purpose of the following essay is to state the polity of the American Church, with special reference to the position given to the laity by our canonical legislation and in actual practice, without formal discussion of the questions which may be raised as to precedent or authority for that position.

The general principle of our constitution is to give to lay members of the Church an equal share with the clergy in all matters of legislation and government, reserving only to the clergy the actual ministry of the word and sacraments. The question here at once arises as to the limitation or extension of this term. Does 'the ministry of the word and sacraments' cover only the actual administration of the sacraments, and the public preaching of the word with private exhortation out of the same? Or does it not also include the enactment of such disciplinary canons as govern in some sense both ministries, laying down who may be admitted

The Laity in the American Church

to the sacraments and on what terms, and insisting on certain truths and doctrines, the acceptance of which, whether for faith or for life, shall be necessary for the Church's communion?

Such legislation would seem to belong to the commission to bind and loose, which, if not an exclusive prerogative of the ministry, was intended to be exercised by the Church primarily through the organ of the ordained priesthood or, perhaps more strictly, the episcopate.

The General Convention, which is the supreme legislative body of the Church in the United States, meeting every third year, consists of two Houses, the House of Bishops and the House of Deputies. Each diocese is entitled to representation in the lower House by both clerical and lay deputies, four of each order, elected by the Diocesan Convention. The lay deputies must be communicants and residents in the diocese which they represent. Clerical and lay deputies have perfectly equal rights and powers. The House votes by orders whenever this is called for by the clerical or lay representation from any diocese. In this case the clerical and the lay deputation from every diocese have each one vote[1]; and a concurrence of both orders is required to carry any motion. All measures require the concurrence of both Houses, i.e. of a majority of bishops, clergy, and laity.

Thus, while of course the laity can enact nothing without the concurrent action of the bishops and the

[1] If the clerical or lay deputies from a diocese are *equally* divided on any point, the vote of that diocese is declared to be 'divided.'

clergy, it is in their power practically (though not in form) to veto what is agreed on by bishops and clergy. This arrangement can only be defended, in theory, as a concession on the part of the spiritual authority, agreeing that no canons shall be enacted without the consent, thus expressed, of the laity. It will be observed that any special legislative authority of the episcopate is altogether lost, so far as the general Church is concerned.

It may be noted that in practice the laity are commonly found to be the most conservative element, both for good and for evil, being often reluctant to accept changes which the bishops as spiritual leaders may desire to make.

The above provisions extend, we must remember, to *all* matters of doctrine, discipline, and worship. Special safeguards against hasty action are provided with regard to the Prayer Book, in which no alteration can be made unless carried by two successive General Conventions, with notification of the proposed change to each Diocesan Convention in the meantime, so as to secure opportunity for each diocese to express its mind on the subject. The same safeguard is provided with reference to alterations in the 'constitution' or more fundamental canons of the Church.

Diocesan Conventions, like General Convention, are composed of clergymen and laymen with equal rights of voice and vote. The bishop of course is president, but only in a few dioceses does he possess a veto on legislation. The qualifications for membership, both clerical and lay, in a Diocesan Convention vary in

American (Protestant Episcopal) Church 323

different dioceses[1]. In some, all clergymen canonically connected with the diocese[2] have full rights; in others, there are what may be called 'fancy franchises,' a vote, or even a seat, depending on the clergyman being regularly connected with some parish or cure, unless indeed he has retired from regular work on account of disability after a certain length of service. The lay members are elected by the different parishes, generally through the vestry: either a prescribed number for each parish, or in a few cases a number proportionate to the number of communicants. One chief difficulty in carrying out this scheme of 'proportional representation' is the absence of any canonical definition of a 'communicant[3],' and the loose way in which communicant rolls are kept.

In Diocesan Conventions voting by orders is generally required for questions of importance; and in most cases, where proportional representation does not obtain, the lay vote is taken by parishes—as in General Convention by dioceses—and not by individuals.

It is coming to be generally recognized that lay representatives in Diocesan Convention ought to be communicants. But this restriction is by no means always laid down in diocesan canons. In the recollection of the writer an unbaptized man was a prominent

---

[1] With over sixty dioceses, each having its own body of canons, liable to revision each year, it is impossible to be exact as to matters of diocesan arrangement. The statements in the text are sufficient to make clear the principles and the general rules followed.

[2] See p. 329.

[3] Under what conditions, short of formal exclusion from the Holy Table, does a person once admitted as a communicant forfeit the privileges which belong to this position?

member of the convention of one of our oldest dioceses, and as such contended against the imposition of baptism as a necessary qualification.

In some dioceses all officers, parochial and diocesan, are required to be communicants. But this requirement, alas! is not general. There is often a real difficulty in country places in finding male communicants competent to serve as vestry men or delegates to convention. It would seem better in such cases to refrain from definite organization for a while[1], rather than to commit the interests of the Church to those who are not ready to commit themselves to her discipline. The evil effects of the contrary practice are manifold. In a few dioceses or missionary districts the experiment has been tried of admitting women to office.

While the Church in the United States is entirely free from all connexion with the State, and from all civil control save such as the State must always exercise over all corporations, yet in many cases the civil law under which religious societies are incorporated does seriously affect the interests of the Church. For instance, at any rate until quite recently, in the State of New York no qualification of being a baptized person or a communicant was contained in the statute regulating religious societies, and none could therefore legally be imposed in our parishes. In Massachusetts, where the general laws concerning religious corporations were originally drawn up under Congregational influence, the

---

[1] The difficulty is felt not only in new places, but also in decayed parishes organized several years ago in places from which the population has subsequently shifted.

rector is not a member, much less the president, of the parochial vestry. These are exceptional instances, but they illustrate the need of securing civil legislation which will allow the Church to organize herself in accordance with her own constitution, and to impose qualifications which unmistakably belong to her proper discipline.

Vestries have not only the control of the temporal concerns of the parish, but they (or in some cases the parish in general meeting) elect the pastor, ordinarily giving him a 'call' to become rector of the parish at a specified stipend. In most cases the bishop has no direct or official voice in the selection, and is bound to accept the clergyman elected by the parish if he is in good and regular standing. In some dioceses the bishop must be consulted before a call is given. To the charge of missions, i. e. congregations not formally organized as parishes, the bishop ordinarily appoints.

Provision is made by canon that a pastoral connexion once regularly established shall not be terminated without the consent of the rector, or, on appeal, the decision of the bishop; but where there are no endowments, and the stipend is raised by voluntary contributions, nothing can compel a vestry to continue the clergyman's support. Even where a formal contract has been made, if there is no money in the parochial treasury, individual members of the vestry or parish cannot be assessed for the amount due or promised. So that those who hold the purse strings really have the power of dismissal.

One remedy for this evil would be the creation of central diocesan funds for the support of the clergy to which all local contributions for this purpose would be sent, and out of which the stipends would be paid, thus relieving the clergyman from direct dependence upon the congregation. Under such an arrangement the amount of the stipend, while never falling below a fixed *minimum*, would not necessarily be in proportion to the amount raised in each particular place, but as the bishop, acting along with a board elected by the Diocesan Convention, judged expedient in consideration of the needs of the locality. In this way it would be possible to place clergymen of experience and ability in new and difficult cures, which under the present system are commonly served by the least capable or the most crude. The difficulties in the way of establishing such a system (which works very well in the Canadian diocese of Quebec) would be many. Old-established parishes would be exceedingly reluctant to surrender any of their independence. But at least where cures receive diocesan aid the plan could be carried out. Some such scheme seems necessary if the Church is really to fulfil her mission to the people of the land, and not to be content to minister only to select groups of people who for one reason or another prefer her worship to that of other religious bodies. With no real territorial jurisdiction (only provision to prevent direct rivalry and clashing of interests) the Congregational system, which, most markedly in large cities, is the real basis of our parishes, is apt to become intolerably exclusive and selfish.

American (Protestant Episcopal) Church 327

In each diocese there is a standing committee elected by the Diocesan Convention, which acts as a council of advice to the bishop, much as cathedral chapters were intended to do[1]. Its recommendation to the bishop is required by any one desiring to be admitted as a candidate for holy orders, and again before his ordination. The bishop, of course, has the absolute right to refuse to ordain any candidate, but he may not ordain any without the recommendation and consent of the committee. During the vacancy of a see the standing committee acts as the ecclesiastical authority of the diocese, calling in a bishop for the performance of any distinctively episcopal ministration.

This committee ordinarily consists of both clergy and laity (four or three members of each order), though in two dioceses (Connecticut and Maryland) it is composed wholly of clergymen. In any case the clerical members alone are to act for certain purposes, e.g. during the vacancy of a see in the discipline of the clergy, or in the superintendence of deacons and of candidates for holy orders.

In the election of a bishop there are three stages.

1. He is elected by the clergy and laity of the diocese in convention; (1) in most cases by a majority of both orders, in a few dioceses a two-thirds majority of each order being required; (2) in most cases by a simultaneous ballot of clergy and laity, while in some the clergy vote first, their choice requiring the assent of the lay representatives.

2. This election by the diocese has to be confirmed by

[1] See Abp. Benson's *Essays on Cathedrals*.

a majority of the standing committees of the different dioceses throughout the Church. If the General Convention is to meet within three months, the confirmation goes to the House of Deputies instead of to the several standing committees.

3. Consent to the consecration of the person thus elected is required from a majority of the bishops in the United States.

This arrangement, which was devised when the Church was comparatively small, needs certain modifications now. It is open to two practical objections. (1) Standing committees at a distance, perhaps across the continent, can in many cases know little of the qualifications of the person elected, save through newspaper reports. (2) No opportunity is given for objections to be formally made by responsible persons, nor for the person accused, it may be, of grave faults to clear himself. A provincial court, at which neighbouring dioceses would be represented by their bishops and standing committees, and before which all necessary documents could be laid, would seem to be the most reasonable plan for guarding the interests both of the Church and of the bishop elect[1].

Whether the laity or clergy of other dioceses, as distinct from the comprovincial bishops, ought by right to have the power of vetoing the election of a bishop by the clergy and laity over whom he is to rule, is a further question.

The election of missionary bishops for districts not yet organized as independent dioceses is by nomination of

[1] Such a court is provided for in the canons of the Church in South Africa.

American (Protestant Episcopal) Church

the House of Bishops, confirmed by the House of Deputies or by a majority of the standing committees.

No suffragan bishops are allowed, and only one coadjutor in a diocese, who always has the right of succession. Coadjutor bishops have equal rights with diocesans as members of the House of Bishops. Consent to the election of a coadjutor bishop must first be obtained from the bishops and the standing committees, such consent being of course distinct from the subsequent confirmation of the election of any particular person to the office.

The translation of bishops is not provided for, except in the case of missionary bishops who may be elected to diocesan sees.

One feature of our discipline which is unlike that of the English Church, and which it seems difficult for English Churchmen to understand, is with reference to the clergy. A clergyman from the day of his ordination (indeed, from his reception as a candidate for holy orders) can never be unattached. He belongs to the diocese in which he is ordained until he is formally transferred to another diocese. This canonical connexion with a diocese and allegiance to its bishop does not depend upon the clergyman being actively engaged in the exercise of his ministry, or licensed to a particular cure.

In ordinary cases a term of three years' candidacy is required before ordination, during which time candidates are under the direction of their bishop, both as regards their daily life and their theological studies. Testimonials are required from responsible laymen as well as from clergymen before a man can be admitted as a candidate for the ministry, and again before he can be ordained.

A general canon prescribes the duties of lay-readers, with distinct limitation of their functions. They must be licensed each year by the bishop.

In canonical provisions for the exercise of discipline the laity are hardly touched. Elaborate provisions are made for the trial of a bishop, so elaborate as to be almost unworkable. He must be tried by his peers. And this principle is generally recognized with regard to presbyters, though the mode of their trial is left to diocesan arrangement. A bishop alone has the authority to pronounce sentence, and in most cases he has the right to modify the sentence agreed upon by the court, though not to inflict a severer punishment than that recommended.

The great fault of our judicial system is the absence of any provision for appeals. A diocesan court might, in deciding the case of an individual clergyman, not only do him serious injustice, but also commit the Church (so far as an unreversed local decision could do so) to a most unfortunate position with regard to some question of doctrine. If for no other reason, to remedy this anomaly some sort of provincial organization is imperatively needed.

It will be clear from this statement that the American Church freely and fully recognizes the laity as a constituent part of the high-priestly body, and accords to them all the privileges of co-operative citizenship therein. This probably tends to the creation generally of a more intelligent and interested churchmanship than is common in

England. On the other hand, it is open to question whether distinctive prerogatives of spiritual rule have not been unwarrantably abandoned by the ministry, and more especially by the episcopate. It will certainly be granted that this is the case where provision is not made that the laymen admitted to a share in these powers of government should be perfectly initiated and loyal members of the Church.

XIII

RELATION OF THE LAITY TO CHURCH GOVERNMENT IN THE PROVINCE OF SOUTH AFRICA

By the Rev. J. Watkin Williams

From the first the Church of South Africa has been credited with a desire to become 'ecclesiastical'; it has been supposed to aim at clerical rule. As a matter of fact, no doubt, Bishop Gray, on arriving in Cape Colony in 1847, found an irregular state of things prevailing with which he had to cope. The amount of authority which he himself asserted was exactly the amount which he would hand on to the Church which he was organizing; and while he resisted the illegitimate pressure of the civil power, he demanded the co-operation of the laity. The twofold characteristics of his position were the repudiation of the intrusion of the State, and an assertion—a vigorous assertion—of the rights and office of the laity, properly so called, in the Church herself.

When Bishop Gray arrived he found an irregular state of things prevailing. He found the governor inheriting the position of ordinary from the previous Dutch Government; and to the style of ordinary he added the functions of an English ecclesiastical ordinary, and he

Laity in the South African Church

had under him a number of chaplains. It was presumed that these would do what their superior told them, and he had no small idea of his functions. On one occasion he carried a claim to dispense from the marriage law so far as to order the marriage of an uncle and niece. In fact he governed by no law, and there were no limits to his claim.

In this chaos it was that Bishop Gray found the Church.

His life, no doubt, was one long protest against the illegitimate claims of a State which was not necessarily Christian at all, and against claims which were not asserted on any Christian basis. That was the protest; and in every department the Church of South Africa bears evidence of it. It was a protest that was made equally strongly by the Church in America; and in Bishop Gray's great struggle in regard to the Natal litigation his position was appreciated alike by Scottish presbyterians and by the American Church, although, unhappily, many of the leaders of the English Church failed to appreciate his aim.

On the other hand, given the laymen in any true ecclesiastical sense, there was something more than a willingness to recognize their position. For something like ten years Bishop Gray possessed his soul in autocracy, and then he freed himself. In 1857 he called his first diocesan synod, and he had something to give it. He had the power which had accrued to his office because of his clear insight into the principles of ecclesiastical organization. He knew exactly that the Church consists of laity as well as clergy. The English conscience had forgotten both the office and the fact of the laity; it had accepted an attractive ideal of a Christian nation whose Parliament, along with Convocations, represented the laity and the clergy. That might have been possible in England once. At the Cape the ground was possessed by a presbyterian community, not English speaking, and by multitudes of heathen. These clearly were not 'laity.' The English Government had assisted the former by sending Scottish presbyterian ministers; the English Church had neglected the colonists, and the Wesleyans, if any one, had done the proper work of the Church.

Clearly then some new conception of a layman must be found. Perhaps the actual definition arrived at was not wholly satisfactory; but from the very beginning laymen defined by some test appeared in synod. And here Bishop Gray had to contend with two opposing parties. The admission of laymen to the synod was definitely opposed. They do not therefore appear there *per incuriam*, and Bishop Gray defends their admission in his primary charge—he defends it and insists upon it. It is worth while to remark who his opponents are. There is a certain section who declare that never in church history have laymen occupied such a position in synods. That position is intelligible, and in theory much may be said for it. Bishop Gray could and did say much against it. Experience has proved him right from a practical point of view.

But on the other hand there was a very different opposition, led by persons who did not desire to be reconciled, and who were clearly bent on opposing any synodical action whatever. They did it on the familiar ground that they belonged to the Church of England; they were Puritans, and they fancied that they found in their claim the only hope of supporting their Puritanism. The Church of England, they said, has her synods, the convocations; and the convocations know nothing of laymen in their assemblies; therefore, since we belong to the Church of England here, we cannot have laymen in our synods. Bishop Gray replies, fully admitting the difficulty of the situation; and it is worth while to try and realize how great that difficulty was in an isolated country, when history was not studied as it has been since, when there were no experts at hand to consult, and when a man really desirous of knowing the right course hardly knew where to turn.

He says—

'What the precise position of the laity was in these councils of the Church has never yet, so far as I know, been fully discussed or strictly defined. It is clear, I think, they had a right to be present at them. They certainly had nothing to do with the framing of the Creeds or defining articles of faith; but, with the exception of this, they appear to have had a share in all that passed in the councils of the Church[1].'

Again,

'If it be unlawful for them to be present it must be either because there is some law against it, or because their being so is an innovation upon the constitution of the Church. All admit that they were present in the apostolic age, and at later councils, and in Anglo-Saxon

[1] Charge of Bishop Gray at first visitation, 1857.

assemblies. If it, as I affirm, be no innovation, if it be in strict accordance with the Church's law and constitution and not in violation of any civil law, we need no other authority than that of the chief pastor of the Church to render their presence in the synod of their diocese perfectly lawful[1].'

When we recollect the attacks made on Bishop Gray for his alleged arbitrary ecclesiasticism, there is something pathetic in listening to the strong claim he makes that the voice of the laity shall be heard and given its due place in the councils of the Church. At any rate, in the constitution and acts of the first synod of the diocese of Cape-town the section on the constitution of synod opens thus:—'The bishop, clergy, and laity of the diocese of Cape-town shall hold periodical meetings in synod for the regulation of church matters within the diocese.'

That still remains the definition of the constitution of the synod. The constitution varies in detail perhaps in the various dioceses, particularly in the mode of the election of the lay representatives from the diocesan synod to the provincial synod. The provincial synod meets every seven years on the summons of the archbishop; the diocesan synods meet, some every three years, some annually. Due notice is given to all the parishes which have a licensed clergyman, and they are summoned to elect a duly qualified lay representative to represent the parish in the forthcoming synod. Such representative must be a

'man of the full age of twenty-one years, who shall not be under church censure according to the second and

[1] Address by the Bishop of Cape-town at the first synod, 1857.

third rubricks before the communion service, or according to any rules of discipline accepted by this diocese (of Cape-town), who shall have been a communicant for the twelve months preceding his election, i. e. he shall have received Holy Communion at least three times during the preceding year at the hands of some clergyman either of the Church of this province or of some other Church in communion with same.'

Such a representative holds office until the summoning of the next synod, when his office determines and a new election is held.

The constituency which elects such a representative is no doubt open to criticism. It is thus defined in the Cape-town acts.

'Every male parishioner being of the full age of twenty-one years, not being under church censure, who is on the list of communicants, or who being baptized and not being a member of any other religious body, is an habitual worshipper in the church or chapel of the parish or district in respect of which he claims to vote, shall be entitled to vote for a lay representative for the parish or district to which he belongs.'

At the meeting summoned for the election the clergyman has no rights, unless he is elected as chairman; in that case he may speak, but only to points of order.

No doubt it is difficult to defend the enfranchising of non-communicant parishioners as defined above. Probably most South African churchmen would agree that their admission would be impossible if there were any large number of them who would claim the vote. But practically it may be defended on the analogy of a conscience clause. Like the conscience clause it serves to remove the sense of grievance, or injustice; and like it it is seldom or never brought into use.

The admission of non-communicant parishioners appears to have been accepted without hesitation, even without discussion, and certainly it can be said that no difficulty has resulted. The present writer knows of no instance where such a person has claimed a vote, far less where any number have influenced an election. The provision reminds us of the ill-instructed condition of large numbers of excellent people whom the Church of England had sent out to South Africa. Nominally members of the Church of England, they did not realize the privileges of their position; and some such provision may have been necessary to meet their case. Practically it is a dead letter. For electing a bishop a different constituency is provided. Whatever may have been necessary in the case of the synod, none but communicants are allowed to vote for the election of a lay representative to the 'elective assembly,' which elects the bishop.

In the conduct of the business of the synods, both provincial and diocesan, the synod habitually sits, speaks and votes as one house. It does, however, really consist of three houses.

In the provincial synod, if at any time the clergy and laity desire to deliberate apart from each other, they can do so whenever the majority of either order desires it. When the house of bishops desires to deliberate alone, the prolocutor becomes the president of the joint assembly of clergy and laity; and, if a vote by orders be claimed, no measure can be passed unless it has a majority in all of the three houses; thus, neither clergy nor laity can force any measure upon an unwilling episcopate. Similarly in the diocesan synod, to take the case of Cape-town, the bishop constitutes a House by himself if he please; that is, he can veto any measure, and no resolutions become acts of synod until he has himself at the closing service confirmed them solemnly at the altar.

During the synod either laity or clergy may claim a separate vote of orders, and no resolution is then adopted by the synod unless carried by a majority of each order and assented to by the bishop.

In the case of the elective assembly, every parish or congregation with a separate minister is summoned to elect a lay representative. Such representative must of course be a communicant himself, but the electors in this case must also be communicants. There can be no election of a bishop unless one half of the clergy and one half of the laity are present in the assembly. A bishop may be elected either by direct election; or the assembly may choose one or more persons to whom they commit the charge of selecting the bishop for the diocese.

The provincial canons define that the bishop of any diocese shall be elected by the clergy of the diocese with the assent thereto of representatives of the laity, if the number of priests in such a diocese be not less than six. The laity cannot take the initiative, but their assent is necessary to any election. In the case of Cape-town, when the house of the clergy shall have made a choice they are to send down their decision to the laity for their assent or dissent. If no election be made nor power be given to others to elect, the choice lapses to the bishops of the province.

In case of the direct election of a bishop two-thirds is required as a majority of the clergy; and the person so chosen is deemed to be elected, unless two-thirds of the laity negative the election.

With regard to the appointment of the parochial clergy, the right of presentation may according to canon be vested —by law or by contract sanctioned by the bishop—in patrons of various kinds. Thus the diocese of Cape-town at its first synod passed a resolution stating that it was strongly of opinion that the appointment of clergymen to the cure of souls in the diocese should rest entirely with the bishop for the time being, adding in the synod of 1861 that it was also of opinion that no clergyman resident within the diocese should be elected to the charge of a parish against the expressed wishes of a majority of the communicants in the parish. In practice, though not in theory, the parishioners have a considerable moral weight in the choice of their minister, and it is difficult to conceive of a case in which a clergyman would be thrust upon an unwilling laity. Only it must be remembered clearly that the Church has discovered what she means by a layman.

There is, of course, some danger of the laity bringing pecuniary pressure to bear. In South Africa very few parishes have any endowment. This is guarded against by the practice, very largely though not universally adopted, of the parochial contributions being paid through the Diocesan Finance Board. Parishes which receive no assistance from the central funds usually pay their clergy through their churchwardens. But in neither case is it ordinarily considered decent to bring pecuniary pressure to bear on a parish priest if he be unacceptable to his parish.

In the administration of a parish the clergy are assisted by churchwardens and sidesmen. Every adult *male* parishioner is entitled to vote for the election of these and in all other parish matters. All landed church property, being alienable, is under the management of the minister and churchwardens of the respective parishes, subject to a certain control by the Diocesan Trust Board; and the churchwardens, as representing the parish, look after the parsonage and the lands attached thereto, the parishioners bearing the expense of dilapidations and insurance.

The power of the laity then in the Church is very considerable. It is not nominal or complimentary. They do not merely constitute honorary committees, or committees of advice and consultation; but they sit in synods which are absolutely the governing bodies of the Church; they form a constituent part of them, and any one who knows anything of the working of the Church in South Africa will not hesitate to say that their presence in synod has been of immeasurable strength to the Church. Work has been done which, from the nature of the case, could scarcely have been attempted without the encouragement of the laity. It would be more true to say that the laity have at times not merely encouraged, but made the work possible and carried it through. To take one instance, the question of lay discipline is a question which is sometimes spoken of with bated breath. What could a purely clerical synod hope to effect in a matter of this sort? The provincial synod had demanded the opinion of the diocesan synods on the subject. It is a question which presses in a country where a large proportion of the Church consists of heathen who are being brought into the fold of Christ. For such congregations no one questions the necessity of discipline. Probably no one would question it in the case of any other congregation had they not learned to do without it; but that is not the point. The question of discipline could not be dealt with on behalf of the coloured laity alone; and, when the report of the committee was presented, considerable feeling was aroused. It seemed not unlikely that the question might be shelved, when, after a prolonged debate, a legal member of the house of laymen proposed and finally carried, on a vote by separate orders, a very satisfactory statement including a mode of legal procedure which covered the ground. The moral weight which thus accrued to the report as finally adopted would have been impossible without such a lay house.

We believe then, we in South Africa, that we have indeed been forced to seek the co-operation of our laymen. We have been forced, under God's providence, through the wisdom of our first bishop; but the success and the power which their co-operation gives us would of course have been only possible on the condition that our laity are recognized to be occupying a clear and definite office in the Church of Christ.

XIV

FUNCTIONS OF THE LAITY
IN THE SCOTTISH (EPISCOPAL) CHURCH

By R. T. N. Speir

UNTIL the year 1863, the laity of the Scottish Church had no legally defined rights. The condition of the Church for long after her disestablishment, resulting from her sufferings and persecution, was not conducive to the consideration of internal reform. When however the penal laws against her were repealed at the end of last century, she was able to turn her attention to the improving and strengthening of her internal economy; but it was not until the first quarter of the present century had passed, that the question of the rights of the laity became a subject of consideration. The growth of the young Church of America, attributed in a large measure to the active co-operation of the laity in the management of her affairs, was then strongly pressed as an argument that the mother Church in Scotland should follow her daughter's example, but without effect; and the agitation seems to have slumbered until revived into new life by Mr. Gladstone, in his celebrated pamphlet on this subject, addressed to the Primus, in the year 1852. In it he suggested, that the synod should consist of three chambers, bishops, clergy, and laymen; that the latter should be communicants, and elected by communicants; that the representation should be through the diocesan synods to the general synod; and that the initiation of all legislation should rest with the bishops' chamber alone. The interest of the Church was keenly excited by Mr. Gladstone's letter, and the episcopal synod met to consider the proposal, and passed a resolution to the effect, that the admission of the laity to speak and vote in the synods, on certain subjects and in certain conditions, was not contrary to God's word nor the constitution of the Church.

The question was also discussed in the diocesan synods, but the resolutions come to were conflicting, and the subject was again dropped, and nothing further was done until the year 1863. In that year the general synod, which had been assembled the year previous, passed a canon entitling each congregation to elect a lay representative, whose duty it was to vote on the election of a bishop, in the lay chamber; a majority of votes being made necessary to a valid election, both in that and the clerical chamber; although the right of nomination was reserved for the clergy alone. Laymen were also, if communicants, permitted to be present at diocesan synods, and, with the bishop's approval, to address the meeting. At the same synod the order of lay readers was also sanctioned.

This was a considerable gain, but the position of the laity was still far from satisfactory. Their presence at synods was only on sufferance; they could neither bring forward a motion, nor vote on a division; and in consequence their interest in the Church's corporate life was languid, and their attendance at her councils very scanty; few of them extending their care for the well-being of the Church beyond the limits of their own congregations.

The subject of the rights of laymen continued from time to time to engage the attention of the Church, but it was not pressed to any definite issue until the year 1870, when the episcopal synod again took up the question. The bishops appointed committees to consider the matter, and finally summoned a conference of the whole Church, which meeting in 1875 and 1876, drew up the constitution of the Representative Church Council as it now exists. This constitution was accepted by the general synod in 1876; and by Canon XLV the Church Council was accepted, and recognized as the organ of the Church in all financial and temporal affairs; doctrine, worship, and discipline, being the only matters specially excepted from its control. This Representative Church Council consists of the bishops, the clergy, certain diocesan lay-officials, and the lay-representatives, one of the latter, who must be communicants, being elected annually by the communicants of each congregation, and three in addition, by each diocese.

There is, in connexion with the central council, and subsidiary to it, in each diocese a diocesan council, which manages the affairs of the diocese. This council is composed of the lay-representatives of the central council belonging to the diocese, with a few extra members, and manages all diocesan business.

There is likewise in each congregation a 'Central Fund Committee,' which collects contributions for the various schemes of the council, and furnishes information to it; the secretary of this committee being the ordinary medium of communication between the congregation and the council.

The Church Council meets annually in one of the chief towns of Scotland. Its meetings are usually preceded by a day's conference, which is of much the same nature as the English Church Congress, but this is not connected with the business of the Church Council proper. Between the times of its meetings the work of the council is carried on by various committees and boards. First of these is the Executive Committee, composed of forty-seven members, viz. the bishops, the chairmen of the boards, one priest and three laymen from each diocese, and seven extra members, chosen by the council; and it appoints a 'Sub-Committee on Business,' of its own members, to which the investment of funds is entrusted.

The four boards of the council are, the Clergy Sustentation Fund, the Home Mission, the Foreign Mission, and the Education Boards. The bishops are ex-officio members of these boards, to which each diocese sends one clerical and one lay-representative, and the council adds certain members of its own appointing. The proportion of clergy and laity on these boards is about equal, but on the Executive Committee the laymen out-number the bishops and other clergy by about two to one. The chairman is also a layman, and at the present time this is the case

in the Scottish (Episcopal) Church 347

with all the boards, with the exception of the Education Board. This will show how completely the lay element takes its place in the corporate work of the Church, and what is the case in the central council is, in this respect, equally so in the diocesan councils, and their committees and boards. At the sitting of the Church Council all the money grants for the year are passed, the various committees and boards are appointed, and their reports for the past year are received and considered; and all the other business connected with the corporate work of the Church for the year is finally adjusted. The Church Council has the custody of the central funds of the Church, it also acts as trustee for such congregational funds as are committed to it, and arranges for their investment. It safeguards the interests of the Church generally, in looking after the title-deeds and security of church property, and collects and distributes money for the various general purposes of the Church. Chief among these is the Clergy Sustentation Fund, which is collected by means of subscriptions, given monthly, quarterly, or annually, through the congregational committees. Every member of the Church, above the line of pauperism, is expected to contribute something to it, and the whole amount received, after deduction of a certain portion for grants to the poorer charges, is divided into equal shares, three of which are given to each bishop, and one to each incumbent as an addition to his local stipend.

The Clergy Fund of the Scottish Church is not placed upon so sound a footing as the 'Sustentation Fund' of the 'Free Church of Scotland'; in the latter the bulk of the stipends of the ministers comes from the central fund, and is supplemented by local contributions, while in the former this is reversed; but the fund has great advantages, as, with the special grants to poorer charges, it lessens the disparity between the richer and poorer livings, the wealthy congregations contributing many times the amount they receive back in the shape of the 'Equal Dividend,' while the poorer can only send up a fraction of that amount. It also has some effect in checking congregationalism, and takes the place of endowment, giving the priest at least part of his stipend independent of his people.

The Clergy Fund Board also administers the Aged and Infirm Clergy Fund, out of which all priests, who have reached the age of seventy, or are certified as incapacitated for duty by infirmity, and have served for twenty years in the Scottish Church, are entitled to a pension of £80 a year; while smaller annuities are given to those of less than twenty years' service. Bishops on their retirement receive three times the amount of the annuity given to the priests. This fund is raised by interest on capital, by a grant from a charitable bequest, and by a one per cent. tax on the stipends of the clergy, paid by their congregations.

The fund next in importance, administered by the Church Council, is the Home Mission Fund. It promotes the extension of the Church, by assisting in starting and maintaining mission stations, in the poorer parts of the large towns, and in outlying districts, many of which develop in time into settled incumbencies. The Home Mission Board also looks after the fishermen and curing hands at the various stations during the fishing season. It maintains a Probationary Home for fallen women, gives grants to 'rescue and preventive work,' and collects, and administers, an Additional Curates' Aid Fund.

The foreign mission work of the Church is also in the hands of the Council, which collects and transmits money for various objects, and decides, through the Foreign Mission Board, upon the scope and policy of the Church's action in the mission fields with which she is specially connected.

The Education Board assists all church schools with an annual grant out of the Education Fund, and with emergency grants for building, &c., in special cases. It gives advice when consulted by school managers, distributes prizes for Sunday schools, and issues a syllabus of religious teaching. The Church Training College for Teachers, at Edinburgh, is the property of the Council. It also owns and maintains the Church's Theological College, though it does not interfere with the teaching staff, which is entirely in the hands of the bishops.

All expenses connected with the legal business of the Church, and with the meetings of the episcopal and general synods, are defrayed by the Council.

It will be seen from the foregoing statement of the work done by the Council, that through it the Church does herself much, if not all, that the sister Church of England does, by means of such societies as the Additional Curates' Society, the Society for the Propagation of the Gospel, the National Society, &c.

It might seem likely, that so large a portion of the Church's work being carried on by the Council, there would be a danger of its clashing with the synods. No doubt it is difficult to draw the line where the Council's province should end in some matters; but it can be confidently asserted that, during the twenty years of the Council's existence, there has never been a difficulty of this kind. One reason for this perhaps is, that like the House of Commons, the Council has the power of the purse, and if anything proposed to be done has to be paid for by the Council, it is only natural that it should be consulted, as to the propriety of the measure, and the manner in which it is to be carried out.

Another reason no doubt is, that owing to the large number of clerical representatives on the Council, no discussion would probably be permitted of any matter really belonging to the province of the synods, while the fact of their having such weight in the Council, prevents the clergy being unduly sensitive of their synodical rights.

The chief reason, however, lies, I believe, in the desire of the clergy, and specially of the bishops, to trust the laity and to make full use of them, and in the loyalty of the laity towards their bishops.

The twenty years' work of the Church Council has had a marked effect upon the life of the Church, which has grown out of all proportion to the increase of population, or to that of the surrounding Christian denominations. During this time the number of the clergy has been increased by nearly a half, the members of the Church have been more than doubled, and the communicants nearly so; and we have now about five times as many mission stations as at the beginning of the period. But above all, the scattered congregations, which after their disestablishment had wellnigh been stamped out by the persecution of the 'Penal Laws,' and had almost lost touch with each other, are now banded together in a living whole of common interest and mutual support; and though congregationalism is not yet dead, it is much diminished, and church feeling is in consequence much stronger.

To sum up, the position of the layman in the Scottish Church is this. As a communicant he has the right to vote in the appointment of a vestry to manage the affairs of his own congregation, and in most cases with the vestry rests the patronage of the living. He has also a vote in the appointing of a lay-elector, who, when a vacancy in the see occurs, votes in the appointing of the new bishop. He also elects a lay-representative for his congregation to the Church Council, who represents it at the Diocesan Council as well. Nor are his powers for usefulness confined to financial and secular work only, for as a licensed lay-reader he is permitted to read the Litany and Morning and Evening Prayer, and to preach in consecrated buildings. It is indeed a common practice to send a layman well versed in the work of the Church Council, with a special licence from the bishop for that particular occasion, to address a congregation in church on the duty of almsgiving, to plead with his fellow laymen for the general schemes of the Church, and to explain their objects. In small mission stations the services are sometimes conducted entirely by lay-readers, under the charge of a neighbouring priest, who visits them occasionally to celebrate Holy Communion; and laymen are utilized to a considerable extent, notably the St. Andrew's Brotherhood, in breaking ground in mission work in the large towns.

It may be said however, that having only the right to be present at synods, and to take part in the discussion with the permission of the bishop, but neither the power to bring forward motions nor to vote, the layman is still only partly enfranchised. To this I would answer, that the practical life and work of the Church is carried on in the Church Council and in the Diocesan Councils, and there the layman finds a full field for his energies. In the synod the bishop meets his clergy, and matters of doctrine and discipline are discussed; but it is not there that the real work of carrying on and extending the Church is done. I think it is not too much to say that the laity are now quite satisfied with their position and powers, and the best proof of this is, that during the twenty years that have elapsed since the formation of the Church Council, nothing more has been heard of the once much vexed question of the 'lay-claims.'

XV

THE CONSTITUTION OF THE CHURCH OF IRELAND

By the Rev. R. Travers Smith, D.D.

The Church of Ireland claims to belong by its apostolic constitution and doctrine to the body of the Catholic Church. The great majority of its members are strong Protestants, but its unimpeached succession and lineal connexion with the primitive church of the land are highly valued and jealously maintained.

It was until thirty years ago an established Church as the English is now. Some of the conditions of state acknowledgement under which Englishmen have chafed were not severely felt in Ireland. The Privy Council decisions troubled but a few. But the Irish Church had been exploited by the government for political ends to a degree never known in England. That any vital religion survived in her after the eighteenth century was not the fault of the English government. This condition of things had passed off before disestablishment, but many effects of it remained. The education controversy, which at a later date had caused great separation between some of the episcopate and the majority of the clergy, was also nearly at an end. The Church met the stroke of disestablishment in a very united spirit, whether we think the principles of its union the most catholic possible or not. There was only one bishop on the bench who favoured disestablishment: the very bishop who perhaps succeeded best in the long run in attaining popularity and advancement in the Church.

But there was no one either among the bishops or their advisers provided with a scheme for the constitution of the disestablished body. Many had ideas and many were at search. But it was surely very excusable that a great contrast was for the time presented between the bill which Mr. Gladstone conceived, elaborated, explained, defended, and carried through in its completeness, and the attempts at defence and reconstruction with which his measure was received by those whom he assailed. He had but to fell and cut up a visible and measurable 'Upas tree.' Our leaders had to make an enforced expedition into a pathless wood. But at this distance of time one may say that the bill was not framed in a spirit of indifference to the future of the Church, but expressed a clear presumption that she was still to live, with suggestions of no slight value for the continuance of her life, which were duly adopted and used, though with very few compliments to their author.

The Church of Ireland is too small a body to be able to dispense with the help of all its members, much less to view with indifference any secession from her ranks. The great question for her responsible advisers was how to retain and interest the laity. The position which the laity hold in the church system was not the result

The Constitution of the Church of Ireland

of a process of contention on their part. There was indeed, at the time of disestablishment, some muttering of a storm upon the vote of the bishops in the new legislature of the Church. But there was no general disposition on the side of either clergy or laity to provoke a contest. The position of the laity in the new constitution arose naturally and irresistibly out of the position which they held in the Church itself.

The Irish Convocation, indeed, was still in nominal existence. But it had not been called together since 1711, and the cessation, without reason given, of the practice of summoning it showed that nobody cared about it. The Irish bishops had plainly proved in Archbishop Whately's time that they did not desire it. Meanwhile the lay power, if it had not determined the Church's doctrine, had determined often very fatally who should be her teachers. The question of disestablishment with all its spiritual results was being decided by a lay parliament, and the laity of the Church were her most effective defenders. The laity at large could hardly be expected to see their position in the Church's assemblies ruled by precedents taken from times when lay education had not spread, and when representative government in the State had not suggested its use in the Church.

The continuity between the new constitution and the old was indeed carefully preserved. Pressure was put upon the government to permit the ancient synods of the Church of Ireland to assemble. The injustice of proposing to parliament such a change as disestablishment, while forbidding the threatened body to call together its assembly, was so patent that the boon could not be refused. Accordingly the synods of Armagh and Dublin met, first separately and then as a united national synod, in the month of September, 1869. But the meeting took place only for the purpose of authorizing the assemblage of a general synod upon a new basis of clerical representation and in which the laity should take part. The proposal to include the laity would appear to have originated in the lower house. An amendment reserving questions of doctrine and discipline for the clergy alone was rejected by the lower house, and no such proposal seems to have been received in the upper.

Already in the April preceding the meeting of Convocation a conference of representatives of the clergy and laity in equal proportions from every diocese in Ireland had taken place. It was called for the purpose of protesting against the disestablishing bill, which was at that time passing through Parliament. And care was taken to avoid any appearance of establishing a permanent assemblage, lest the Church should be taunted with consenting to the bill and setting up a church body such as it prescribed. Nevertheless this conference in which the two orders met and deliberated together pointed naturally to similar assemblies when the inevitable Act had passed.

An important lay conference was held upon a formal system of representation in the month which succeeded the assembly of Convocation. A meeting of the church parishioners was held in every parish, at which parochial delegates were elected. These delegates elected representatives to the lay Conference, which was thus com-

The Constitution of the Church of Ireland 357

posed of 417 members. It included all that the Church of Ireland could boast of rank and ability, and it was so far from being held in any spirit of opposition to the clergy that the Archbishop of Armagh was chairman on the first day of its meeting. And it must be remembered that in assuming the fact that a general synod was to be created in which the laity were to be represented, the lay Conference was proceeding upon the resolution of Convocation.

Upon resolutions of the lay Conference, accepted by the Archbishops Beresford and Trench, the structure of the General Convention of 1870 was founded. The Convention was the body which passed the constitution and preceded the General Synod, differing from it in name only because the disestablishing Act had not come into operation in the year when it sat. The lay Conference resolved that it was expedient that the number of lay representatives in the Convention should be to the clerical in the proportion of two to one. The reason of this provision lay in the expectation, which has proved to have been well grounded, that the clergy would attend more regularly than the laity. It was acceptable to the clergy as inevitably drawing with it the vote by orders. And the Convention was summoned accordingly.

In addition to this suggestion the lay Conference recommended the appointment of a committee of organization to prepare a draft constitution for discussion in the general convention. The committee of organization consisted of the bishops, together with a body of clergy and laity in equal numbers. It worked with great ability and assiduity, and presented to the Convention a draft which in its main features passed into law. The plan was not wholly original. The constitutions of various colonial Churches were opportunely reprinted for the Church's use by Rev. William Sherlock, and were used, though in an independent fashion.

The draft proposed the admission of the laity to a share of the government of the parish in secular matters by the creation of a select vestry having twelve elected lay members, together with the churchwardens; and a similar lay participation in the secular affairs of the diocese through the Diocesan Synod, in which the laity should double the numbers of the clergy, and the Diocesan Council, elected by the synod for constant work, and in which the same proportion should prevail. The election of bishops was entrusted to the synod of the vacant diocese if it gave to any name a majority of two-thirds in each order; failing this, it should send up to the bishops for selection the names which should obtain largest support. Appointments to cures should be made by a board of patronage, consisting of the bishop with three diocesan and three parochial nominators elected triennially by the diocesan synod and by the parish respectively. Thus the laity were to share in most parts of the work of the Church. But where the work partook of a spiritual character, as in the case of the membership of the general synod and the office of nominator, parochial or diocesan, none but communicants should act; a man's own declaration being accepted as sufficient proof that he met that description. All these proposals were carried.

Setting aside the question of the wisdom of this draft, its form and completeness were admirably fitted to set the new legislature to work in businesslike fashion and furnish it with useful practical work from day to day. The Convention in its two sessions of 1870 sat in ample numbers for fifty-six days. And the interest taken by the members from all parts of Ireland in their work may be judged from the fact that the General Synod mustered similar numbers and sat for a somewhat similar time in all the years of the revision debates. The rules and method of debate were those of the House of Commons, many members and ex-members of which sat in the convention; while all were proud to follow the example of freedom and order which that great assembly sets to representative bodies.

The example of parliament rather than that of ecclesiastical assemblies prevailed. The leading men were more intent upon keeping the Church united and at peace than upon reproducing ancient precedents. Nothing, therefore, was said in the draft constitution or inserted in it by the Convention about keeping doctrine and discipline for the cognizance of the bishops and clergy. There were a very few who upon this ground refused to recognize the new constitution, or drew back from it when they conceived that the forbidden subjects were touched. No one acquainted with church history will doubt the weight of their objections. But it is impossible to think without sorrow of the loss which the Church suffered by their defection from her councils, and of the absence of any benefit to their successors from their withdrawal. Meanwhile they left behind them among the managers of affairs men who, from their own point of view, were not at all indifferent to the dangers of lay tyranny, or blind to the anomaly of subjecting the teachers to the taught. The provisions for giving the clergy their independent voice were so efficient, and have proved so easy to use, that Irish priests in general consider that in few ecclesiastical assemblies has their order been better able to stand out for itself than in the Irish: while the safeguards against hasty changes in the laws and formularies of the Church are so strict that some have wondered how any changes came to be made at all. A vote by orders may be demanded by ten of either order upon any question whatever. But changes in the formularies or laws must of necessity be put to the orders separately, and cannot be carried except by majorities of two-thirds of both orders in two successive years. The house of bishops can vote separately upon any question, and a majority of them can stop a measure, save that when it has been repeatedly carried by both clergy and laity and has finally received a two-thirds majority of both these orders a two-thirds majority of the bishops is required to hinder it from passing. These rules form part of the constitution, and were used in the Convention and handed on to the General Synod, in which they still prevail.

The Convention had not held its second session in 1870 when a strife began which put its provisions to the severest practical test. A vehement agitation for the revision of the Prayer Book arose in the Church. Regrettable as such an incident was, it was in no wise wonderful. Doctrines and expressions which many of us recognize as the very signs of the fundamental catholicity of the Prayer Book were honestly believed by Irish

The Constitution of the Church of Ireland 361

Protestants to be scraps of obsolete dogma left behind by some chance when the house was cleared out at the Reformation. They live in a Roman Catholic country; and St. Paul's rule of becoming as a Jew in trying to convert Jews is generally reversed by modern Christians in their relations to faiths differing from their own. Their Protestant ancestors had won the best part of the country at the point of the sword; and in such cases the war spirit lasts long both in vanquished and in victors. The most numerous and masterful of them were the descendants of Puritans, and many of them had Scotch blood in their veins. All the vital religion they knew came from the evangelical work of the last and present centuries. The revival of 1859 showed how disposed they were to a subjective religion. And though interesting remains of the Anglicanism of times long past lingered about the country, it was not obtrusive, and was rather to be relied on as a help in the long-run to resist change, if the contest could be protracted, than as a defence against sudden assault. It must also be remembered that at the time referred to the lay mind in England was extensively roused by the suspicion of Romanizing tendencies in high churchmen. It was not yet recognized what high churchmen have to give the people in worship and work. And if in England at that time a select vestry of twelve laymen had been returned by the votes of all professing members of the Church in each parish, with a similar lay representation in synods diocesan and national, churchmen might have fared ill at their hands; all this was the case in Ireland. It is true that the law of the Church does not entrust the select vestries or diocesan synods with any cognizance of doctrine or ritual. But if these bodies do not even at the present always remember the limits of their jurisdiction, it was hardly to be expected that they would remember them in the first blush of their new found authority. A small spark sufficed to kindle so much inflammable matter. A tract so innocent that now it would scarcely produce excitement in any Irish parish was given by a clergyman to a maid-servant. Her master, an Englishman, found in it a suspicion of the confessional, and called attention to this evidence of a Roman conspiracy. Oceans of resolutions flowed in from the select vestries. And a motion was made and carried in the second session of the Convention of 1870 to appoint a committee for the revision of the Prayer Book. The originator of this committee was a man of the highest and most Christian character, but of narrow views. He succeeded, however, in inducing many members to serve who merely desired to render the revision, since it was to take place, as good as might be. And when in the first session of the General Synod the personnel of the committee was altered its character did not essentially change.

This vanished controversy is recalled only that the reader may understand how formidable was the trial to which the constitution of the Church of Ireland was subjected before the ink with which it was written was well dry. A system of church government which can face such a storm through seven long years without either fatal injury to the Prayer Book or disruption in the Church must have some elements of strength. The present writer does not believe that the revision was a

The Constitution of the Church of Ireland 363

success. The book is far better without it. Nobody will find in the revised passages any incentive to the improvement of worship or the better performance of duty. Revision was of a negative character, aiming at the discouragement by very irritating, vexatious, and ineffectual restrictions, of Romanism and ritualism. But few proposals were made which had in view the devotional bettering of our Church handbook, and fewer still were carried. It is indeed a good thing that the Church of Ireland should have a law of ritual : her English sister would be the better for having one too. But it is most harmful to the Church of Ireland in her sisterly competition with England for the services of her best divinity students that many observances and appendages of worship, which in England have passed wholly beyond the sphere of controversy, should in Ireland be still the subject of prohibition. But after all, no critic of any authority, however disposed to judge severely of the Irish Church, has ventured to assert that anything she has done suffices to render doubtful her communion with the Anglican body.

No one acquainted with the history will doubt that the agency which hindered radical change was the clerical minority working through the vote by orders, and very often availing itself of the provision that one-third of either order can prevent a change. The majority bore with great patience to see its wishes baulked by a handful : no attempt was ever made to alter the constitution and deprive the minority of its rights.

The general synod in session presents no doubt in its mixed confusion of orders a great contrast to clerical assemblies. Nor do its debates resemble greatly those of such bodies. The laity do not generally argue in the tone of technical divinity; and when they do adopt that tone, they are not usually successful. And though they are patient listeners to those who have anything to say, yet it is naturally found that arguments which are too theological do not win their assent. There were many questions in the revision debates which needed far stricter theological discussion than they received; more especially since it has proved that the privilege of private and separate debate and vote which the bishops possess is almost unused. Even in the open debates of the synod the bishops had much more power than they were aware of. There were some of them, a few words from whom would have hindered many an objectionable change. Nor if they had exercised their right of separate voting, is there the smallest reason for supposing that it would have failed in securing cheerful submission.

Anger and occasional disorder have doubtless occurred in the synod, as is the case in other assemblies. But in truth a better-humoured body never met. No private enmities ever arose from its differences. And great though the defects of the discussions were, it is generally agreed that they have led to a wonderful diffusion of information and softening of party spirit. One advantage at all events has undeniably resulted from the popular character of the Irish synods, in the general disuse of public meetings outside the machinery of the Church as a means of influencing church opinion. The men who would naturally call such meetings and address them are, if they are persons of any popularity, members of the synods,

The Constitution of the Church of Ireland 365

and free to speak their views there. And it is much more satisfactory to listen to violent and one-sided speeches, where the privilege of reply exists, than to read them in the papers without the answers. The thought of the revision agitation fought out by a series of public meetings on the one side, and a clerical convocation on the other, is appalling even to imagine. The laity who make themselves disagreeable in select vestries and synods have their counterparts in churches where no such institutions exist. And any trouble that has been caused in parishes or dioceses by the admission of the laity to the share which they possess in the administration of the church's affairs is outweighed a thousandfold by the benefits which result from it. It is not merely that the best intellect which the community possessed has been ungrudgingly and with conspicuous success devoted without fee or reward to the management of the church's finances; nor that the best lawyers of the country sit to assist the bishops upon her tribunals. Lay help of this sort would have been enlisted under any constitution. There has been a great deal of lay activity of a much rougher kind than this, and which has not always seemed helpful. But if you want not merely the lay element of the refined and selected character which shall serve best to do the church's work, but the lay element in that form and extent which shall give the whole community the sense of being represented and having a share in the government, you must be prepared to find that you cannot always 'bind him with his band in the furrow.' If it is anywhere found in Ireland that the abundance of mixed assemblies tends to secularize clerical life and work, that is not the fault of the constitution, which leaves the bishop and his clergy absolutely free to stir up the gift that is in them by their intercourse in the sacred bonds which Christ instituted and maintains, and to minister the word and sacraments as the servants, not of synod or vestry, but of Him.

The maintenance of the clergy is provided for by diocesan schemes which, husbanding the sums which were handed over under the Act to provide for the annuities of the existing clergy, and adding to these the sums which from the first began to be paid into the sustentation fund, are able to give back to each parish for the income of its ministers a much larger sum than that which it pays in. The subscriptions and gifts to the sustentation fund have been, if not ideally generous, yet liberal to a degree which it would be very hard to induce a people unaccustomed to the idea of paying their clergy to imitate. The bishops are not so richly paid as in England, nor the poor incumbents so poorly. And the diocesan schemes are so admirably managed and so safe that we may assert with confidence that the finance of the Church of Ireland could not have been better done. But whether the same can be said of the arrangements for filling vacant cures, is a matter on which it is more difficult to pronounce. There is no doubt that they have on the whole worked well in cities. In Dublin the cure of souls was in a very unhealthy condition while the Church was established. The appointments to parishes in half the city were in the hands of a chapter, and were made on a system of rotation with little care for fitness. In this region the parish churches were attended by a few sober citizens, while the enthusiastic flocked to the pew-rented churches, where the popular preachers of the day poured forth their eloquence. In this quarter of the city a revolution has been worked partly no doubt by the declining importance of the pulpit, but also by the popular system of nomination; the parish churches are full and the pew-rented empty. But in the country parishes the new system has not always proved so satisfactory. Parochial nominators have insisted on obtaining the appointment of the parish favourite. And as the parish can back its choice by the refusal to pay its assessment, the diocesan nominators and the bishop have sometimes yielded even when the parish choice was made with insufficient information and poor powers of judging.

The system of nomination, however, is closely connected with that of the rearrangement of parishes, in which though much is done much still remains. So many small parishes in country parts have determined to preserve their separate existence, that there are dioceses in which there are almost no curates, and the younger clergy have no opportunity of learning their trade except by the experience of their own mistakes. A very small parish, however, is better off when united to a neighbouring parish provided with an experienced vicar than it is under a novice of its own who can be easily tempted to leave it. But the most promising plan of all would be that of grouping several parishes under a priest of experience, provided with a staff of curates. The regular hours of divine service would have to be varied in the outlying churches, but the work would be better done.

It has been often objected to the Irish arrangements

that they afford no rewards for men of learning. There is no doubt that learning in the Irish Church requires encouragement. But whether easy posts richly endowed would give such encouragement is doubtful: happily so, as no posts of the kind are likely to be established. The literary output of Scotland, where no such posts exist, may well put not only Ireland, but England, to the blush. And Ireland possesses in considerable numbers cures of the sort in which genuine literary work has usually been done, namely, such as afford a sufficient maintenance to an unmarried scholar, without engrossing parochial duties.

Posts of importance, in which learning may be made useful to the Church, exist in the Irish bishoprics, which are not like the English, overwhelmed with work. We could have Dr. Creighton as an Irish prelate without submitting to see the History of the Papacy a fragment. A bishop fit to lead the mind of his diocese is an immense blessing, especially in Ireland, where intellectual life is not active; and it would be unfair to say that the claims of learning are disregarded in choosing Irish bishops. But so many other qualifications, positive and negative, are taken into account, that it is to be feared the Irish bench will never be overweighted with learning; the less so if a tendency which has for some years manifested itself among the clergy of certain dioceses should prevail, of determining to choose the bishop from among themselves.

The Church of Ireland has many dangers and difficulties before it. It has within its small sphere to face the problem in some places of too much work to do and in others of too little; and, outside, the anomaly of seeing the

The Constitution of the Church of Ireland 369

mass of Christian people in the country members of another church. She has need of great humility, considering the greatness of her task and her many defects. But it does not appear that any of her difficulties are due to the constitution, which was framed at a critical time in an earnest spirit of unity and good faith, and has borne most formidable trials without disaster. If only the Irish Church is filled with that power which no earthly constitution can provide, she can do her work without any essential change in the laws which she has made for herself.

APPENDED NOTES

Note A.

ON ECCLESIASTICAL TRIBUNALS. BY THE HON. MR. JUSTICE PHILLIMORE.

THE religious tribunals of any established Church, or indeed of any Church tolerated though not established, cannot of themselves constrain persons or affect property.

They will require the assistance of the State, which can make its own terms before lending help, can inquire, and then assist or refuse, assent or forbid.

Chief Justice Hale says : 'I conceive that when Christianity was first introduced into this land, it came not without some form of external ecclesiastical discipline or coercion, though at first it entered into the world without it ; but that external discipline could not bind any man to submit to it, but either by force of the supreme civil power, when the governors received it, or by the voluntary submission of the particular persons that did receive it ; if the former, then it was the civil power of the kingdom which gave that form of ecclesiastical discipline its life ; if the latter, it was but a voluntary pact or submission which could not give it power longer than the party submitting pleased ; and then the king allowed, connived at, and not prohibited it[1].' . . . .

This is the language of an English lawyer ; but it would be

[1] MS. quoted by Lord Hardwicke in *Middleton* v. *Crofts*, 2 Atkyns (3rd ed.), p. 668. See Phillimore, *Ecclesiastical Law* (2nd ed.), p. 16.

easy to find parallel expressions among the lawyers and statesmen of France and of other countries in Western Europe.

The maxim of the French lawyers before the Revolution, 'toute justice émane du roi [1],' is the same as that conveyed by our longer and more sonorous expression, ' over all causes and over all persons as well ecclesiastical as temporal within her dominions supreme.'

Thus far there is no difficulty. But the actual drawing of the boundary line defining the legitimate interference of the State with the tribunals of the Church has been found in practice most difficult; and the debateable ground is very large.

Certain points however are assured. The church courts have substantially three heads of jurisdiction. (1) The spiritual discipline of their members, lay and clerical, *pro salute animae*, and for the avoidance of scandal to the rest of the congregation. (2) The discipline of their office-bearers, lay and clerical, their suspension from office, removal or restoration, whether by itself, or coupled with the spiritual discipline of head (1). (3) The decision of disputes in church matters between members, either on questions of individual privilege, such as claims to seat in church, or sepulchre in churchyard, or private chapel, or between parties in a congregation differing as to the ornaments of their church or the mode of ritual; causes which may be called by analogy with temporal justice 'civil suits'; while those under heads (1) and (2) may by like analogy be called ' criminal.'

It is obvious that in causes coming under heads (2) and (3) the Church could not enforce her decrees without the assistance of the State. Her courts could *declare* only, they could not *compel*.

In causes coming under head (1) it might be different; the declaration might be the sentence, and act automatically. But even here, if the effect of the declaration were to fit or unfit

---

[1] Dupin, *Requisitoires, Plaidoyers et Discoures de Rentrée*, vol. i. p. 7.

Note A

a person for relief in causes coming under heads (2) and (3), the State might claim a voice.

Moreover, even for a decision under head (1), temporal machinery might be required to compel the attendance of a witness or to administer an oath.

(*a*) The State which has an established Church may insist that the office-bearers of this church should be competent, diligent, and pure. It may require for these purposes that the church courts administer strict discipline, that the Judges give ear to complaints, and proceed with due expedition against offending ministers, lay and clerical. When it was attempted to compel the late Bishop of Oxford to institute proceedings against Canon Carter, the late Lord Bowen as the bishop's advocate urged that in English history and law it had been hitherto unknown that the ecclesiastical tribunal should be 'spirited on.' But in theory the spiriting is admissible. To use the language of English law, the writ of *mandamus* as well as the writ of *prohibition* may issue to the court Christian.

This is a permissible system of relations between church and state courts.

(*b*) Another system, and a more common one, is for the authorities of the State to say to the dignitaries and officers of the Church, 'We have confidence in you. You know your work better than we do. Divine grace will be with you. We will execute your decrees on matters within your ken as you render them, in full trust and without inquiry.'

(*c*) A third system, and a commoner still, is for the State to trace out for the Church, or to satisfy itself that the Church has traced out for itself, certain broad outlines, to leave the rest to be filled up by the administrators of the Church, and to interfere only on certain defined grounds and in gross cases.

This was the practice in England, at least from Edward I to William III; in France, and under the German Emperor, at least in the seventeenth and eighteenth centuries.

Within the wide limits covered by these three systems of relation between church and state courts, anything seems permissible in theory, and the particular arrangement seems to be a mere question of expediency and discretion.

Outside these limits it is otherwise. No self-respecting or independent civil government can admit the claim, put forward by some Popes and some Presbyterian bodies, that the State should inflict temporal punishment, even capital, blindfold and at the demand of the church court.

On the other hand, no Church can, without forfeiting its claim to be a religious body, admit the right of the secular court to inflict merely spiritual sentences, or to compel the bestowal of sacraments (either directly or through the medium of an enslaved church court) upon those whom the Church has pronounced unfit to partake of her spiritual blessings.

Note B.

ON THE GOVERNMENT OF THE ANGLICAN CHURCHES IN
CANADA, NEW ZEALAND, AND AUSTRALIA. BY THE EDITOR.

THE above essays xii-xv give a sufficient account of the position of the laity in church government in the Anglican Churches of the United States, South Africa, Scotland, and Ireland. It must suffice to say here that also in Canada, Australia, and New Zealand, the laity share in church government, parochial, provincial and diocesan; that the suffrage is allowed to all [male] persons who declare themselves 'church members,' without further definition, but that those elected to serve on church councils must be male communicants of full age. The constitution of the American Church served as a guide to these churches, and the defects in that constitution which it was generally sought to remedy were—

(1) that the bishop has no veto in the diocesan council. (The principle generally arrived at in later constitutions has been that the concurrent assent of the three orders of bishops, clergy and laity—if necessary, voting separately—should be necessary to the validity of all acts of synod. This is also the recommendation of the Lambeth Committee of 1867, of which Bishop Selwyn, then Bishop of New Zealand, was chairman.)

(2) that the power of the congregation or vestry, in the patronage of livings and the payment of the clergy, has been unduly developed at the expense of the clergy.

(3) that the management of church affairs has been committed to church members who need not be communicants.

The requirement for communion has not however been made upon lay *electors* in Canada, Australia, or New Zealand.

The Rev. Dr. Langtry, who kindly supplied information about the Church in Canada, concludes his remarks with an expression of opinion which appears to be shared in most parts of the world as to the conservatism of the lay element in church councils :—

'The dangers which Englishmen fear from the presence of laymen in the councils of the Church have not been encountered by us. From the nature of the case they are less *en rapport* with the movements of the time than the clergy are, and so they act as a decidedly conservative element. It would be impossible with our safeguards to carry any proposed change into law till the mind of the whole Church was saturated with it and prepared to receive it. And such a safeguard, often irritating to ardent spirits, is needed in these transition times, and is salutary in its operation.'

THE END

www.ingramcontent.com/pod-product-compliance
Lightning Source LLC
Chambersburg PA
CBHW072130220426
43664CB00013B/2197